Women and Socialism

Women and Socialism
Class, Race, and Capital

Fully revised and updated edition

Sharon Smith

HAYMARKET BOOKS
CHICAGO, ILLINOIS

Haymarket Books
P.O. Box 180165
Chicago, IL 60618
773-583-7884
www.haymarketbooks.org

ISBN 978-1-60846-180-6

Trade distribution:
In the US, Consortium Book Sales and Distribution, www.cbsd.com
In Canada, Publishers Group Canada, www.pgcbooks.ca
In the UK, Turnaround Publisher Services, www.turnaround-uk.com
All other countries, Publishers Group Worldwide, www.pgw.com

This book has been published with the generous support
of Lannan Foundation and the Wallace Action Fund.

Cover design by Julie Fain. Cover image of a Black Lives Matter protest
in Oakland, California, by Annette Bernhardt.

Library of Congress Cataloging-in-Publication Data
is available.

Printed in Canada by union labor.

2 4 6 8 10 9 7 5 3 1

Contents

Preface

I was a bit too young to participate in the social upheavals of the late 1960s but old enough to have become radicalized by them. Growing up in a low-income, blue-collar family in Providence, Rhode Island, where Dad missed no opportunity to assert his status as "king of the castle," I supported the goals of the women's liberation movement instinctively. My sister and I refused to do any housework (and urged our mom to do the same) on August 26, 1970—the date of the "Women's Strike for Equality" called by the National Organization for Women (NOW). We had heard about it on the radio that blared every morning in our kitchen.

I considered myself a committed feminist when I entered college in the mid-1970s. That college was Brown University, and I was there on a full scholarship. I had looked forward to attending my first meeting of the campus feminist group but was immediately disappointed. They were snobs, it turned out. Shortly into the meeting, some began complaining bitterly that college-educated women earned less than "some stupid janitor." At that time, both my parents' jobs involved cleaning toilets at a private school. I was keenly aware that their earnings fell far below those of typical college graduates. The fact that my mom was also a woman contradicted the Brown feminists' assumption that all janitors were men. I left the meeting, without voicing my outrage at their ignorance.

After this experience (and others like it), I found myself alienated by the feminist movement, at least in the way it was expressed in its upper-middle-class form at an upper-middle-class university. While I maintained my commitment to the fight for women's equality, I turned instead to local labor organizing—focusing in particular on the costume jewelry industry, Rhode Island's main manufacturing employer at that time.[1] Like the garment industry, jewelry manufacturing has historically relied on a majority-female workforce, low wages, and sweatshop working conditions.

This included a large cottage industry in Rhode Island, in which entire working-class families labored in their homes for subcontractors to large factories. My own family took in jewelry "homework" when I was a child, and my mom worked in numerous sweatshops over the years, never earning more than the minimum wage. She also never earned a single day's paid vacation. I found it personally gratifying to help support union organizing efforts among jewelry workers and efforts to improve their working conditions through the Rhode Island Committee on Occupational Safety and Health (RICOSH) while in college.

During that time, I also became a Marxist through my involvement in the movement against South African apartheid on campus. I went on to find a political home among Marxists, joining the International Socialist Organization as a college student. I remain a member to this day, and continue to believe that Marxism provides not only a strong foundation but also, perhaps more importantly, a *method* for fighting for the liberation of women of all social classes—while placing particular emphasis on the plight of working-class women.

My political training as a socialist involved reading classical Marxist texts from the nineteenth and early twentieth centuries, including those of Karl Marx, Frederick Engels, V. I. Lenin, Rosa Luxemburg, Clara Zetkin, Leon Trotsky, and Alexandra Kollontai. These Marxists, while staunch theorists and fighters for women's liberation, also strongly opposed the feminist movements of their time—composed largely of upper-class women interested primarily in winning rights for the women of their own social class, often at the expense of the working class.

For example, the early-twentieth-century German women's suffrage movement did not challenge the property requirements that denied working-class men the right to vote—knowing that such requirements would also deny voting rights to working-class women. Maintaining such property requirements could only strengthen the political weight of the middle and upper classes, while the working class would remain politically voiceless. Zetkin refused to support this approach, calling instead for universal voting rights for the entire population, male and female, as a socialist demand.

Likewise, in the United States most white suffragists in the early twentieth century chose to struggle for voting rights for women without also championing those denied to Black people in the Jim Crow South. When women were granted the right to vote in 1920, the racist status quo remained intact—denying suffrage rights to Black women and Black men, thereby strengthening the system of white supremacy.

Hostility to the feminist movements described above was entirely justified. But just as the Marxist movement contains within it many different and often opposing political strands, so too does feminism. Because of my personal experience with the Ivy League feminist club, I accepted the all-too-common blanket rejection of all feminists as liberal, white, and middle class—still customary in some (so-called) Marxist circles. It proved to be an enormous mistake, as I have since learned.

The self-identified women's liberation movement of the 1960s and 1970s was composed not only of liberal, predominantly white feminist organizations but also of socialist feminists and Marxist feminists, as well as Black feminists and other feminists of color. These movements raised demands and won victories that not only improved the lives of women but also raised the expectations of women on a mass scale. All of these movements warrant examination, despite the near-invisibility of anything other than liberal feminism in the political mainstream. I will examine their contributions in the chapters ahead.

This book was initially intended to be a simple "update" of *Women and Socialism: Essays on Women's Liberation* for its second edition. But my thinking on feminism has evolved significantly since it was first published in 2004. While I still think much of the book remains useful, its main treatment of "feminism" focused almost exclusively on critiquing its white, middle-class wing. I felt a strong need to correct that error, which would necessarily involve a serious study of the feminist movements described above, so often neglected.

In a stroke of luck, Canadian Marxist David McNally generously shared a copy of the new introduction he and Susan Ferguson had written for the Historical Materialism edition of Lise Vogel's *Marxism and the Oppression of Women: Toward a Unitary Theory*.[2] Their excellent introduction not only inspired me to learn more but also led me to a starting point for my research: social reproduction theory. From that point forward, one area of research led to the next. What had started as a month-long project stretched into two years of reading and writing—and to this completely revamped second edition of *Women and Socialism*. This revised edition is an effort to examine the fight for women's liberation both theoretically and historically. It relies heavily on the insights of the many theorists and activists, past and present, whose aim has been to help develop a strategy that can best advance the project of ending women's oppression.

While classical Marxism provides a solid theoretical foundation for understanding the root of women's oppression, no foundation can or should be viewed as a finished product; it must be built upon to realize its potential. Theory must be further developed and adjusted as necessary to reflect changes in material circumstances, while also correcting past errors that become clearer with hindsight.

More than 150 years have passed since Karl Marx and Frederick Engels published the *Communist Manifesto* in 1848. The world has changed significantly since then. Although they were often able to anticipate future sites of struggle, they were also constrained in other respects by the historical limits of the social relations of their time. Marx and Engels's articulations of women's oppression often contain contradictory components—in some respects fundamentally challenging the gender status quo while in other respects merely reflecting it. Their most significant limitation was that they believed, along with their contemporaries, both that humans are innately heterosexual[3] and that women are biologically suited for a nurturing and childrearing role in the family.[4]

Indeed, despite the enormous achievements of the 1917 Russian Revolution—including the legalization of abortion and divorce, the right of women to vote and run for political office, and an end to laws criminalizing both prostitution and gay sexuality—it did not produce a theory that challenged either heterosexual norms or the primacy of women's maternal destinies. As Marxist historian John Riddell describes, "Communist women in that period viewed childbearing as a social responsibility and sought to assist 'poor women who would like to experience motherhood as the highest joy.'"[5] Yet, recognizing these historical limitations does not diminish the enormous contributions of the early Marxists who helped forge the revolutionary socialist strategy for women's liberation, and their accomplishments will also be examined at length in this volume.

◆ ◆ ◆

It is also important to recognize that the politics of the 1960s women's liberation movement did not arise out of the blue but were the product of twenty years of prior history. The 1940s saw the large-scale entry of women into the manufacturing workforce to fulfill the needs of war production during World War II—only to see those women be forced out of their industrial jobs immediately afterward to make way for returning veterans. The postwar years witnessed an ideological onslaught glorifying marriage and motherhood while women's participation rate in the labor force and higher education plummeted. By the 1960s, however, women began enrolling in higher education and entering the labor force in larger numbers.

But the women's liberation movement that arose in the late 1960s also bears the political imprint of important debates and struggles that took place among organized Marxists during the 1940s and 1950s. During the immediate post–World War II period, women in the Communist and Trotskyist movements initiated debates seeking to further define the role of women's domestic labor in capitalism, while also beginning to address the interlocking oppressions of gender, race, and class. In addition, Black women's struggles against their systematic rape (often at the hands of white supremacists) involving civil rights activists as well as Communists in the 1940s and 1950s, helped to lay the groundwork for approaching the issue of rape in the context not only of gender but also of race and class. Likewise, the Daughters of Bilitis, formed in 1955 as the first national lesbian organization in the United States, began the process that paved the way for the rise of the gay liberation movement.

The 1960s-era struggle for women's liberation contained different political wings, sometimes acting in unison but also often in sharp disagreement. In the process, they opened the floodgates of debate, exploration, and ultimately political advancement. Two political advances stand out in particular: Black feminists' concept of intersectionality and Marxist feminists' social reproduction theory. Below I outline the main contours of each.

Black Feminists' Concept of Intersectionality

Black feminists, Latinas, and other women of color were strongly critical during the 1960s and 1970s of both the predominantly white feminist movement for its racism *and* of nationalist and other antiracist movements for their sexism. They rightly asserted the racial and class differences among women because white feminists largely ignored these differences, rendering Black women and other women of color invisible in theory and in practice.

Since the time of slavery, Black feminists had been developing a distinct political tradition based upon a systematic analysis of the intertwining oppressions of race, gender, and class. Since the 1970s, Black feminists and other feminists of color in the United States have built upon this analysis and developed an approach that can provide a strategy for combating all forms of oppression within a common struggle—which has since become known as *intersectionality*.

This approach to fighting oppression does not merely complement but in fact strengthens key elements of Marxist theory and practice—which seeks to unite not only all those who are exploited but also all those who are oppressed by capitalism into a single movement that fights for the liberation of all humanity.

Social Reproduction Theory

One of the most important theoretical achievements of socialist feminists and Marxist feminists in the 1960s and 1970s involved a debate over the role of domestic labor, which resulted for some in what has become known as *social reproduction theory*—situating women's domestic labor as a crucial aspect of the social reproduction of the capitalist system as Marx conceived it.

Those involved in what became known as the "domestic-labor debates" attempted to locate the economic root of women's oppression in capitalism. Marx had implied a theoretical framework for this understanding but did not pursue it himself. Domestic-labor debates electrified many socialist and Marxist feminists and a small number of organized Marxists during the 1970s, yet their significance receded for the majority of both feminists and Marxists in the 1980s.

Marxist feminist Lise Vogel, who has played a key role in developing social reproduction theory, recalls the marginalization of the domestic-labor debates: "Most feminists eventually rejected the domestic labor literature as a misguided effort to apply inappropriate Marxist categories. Most Marxists simply disregarded the debate, neither following nor participating in it. Neither potential audience fully grasped the ways that socialist feminists were suggesting, implicitly or explicitly, that Marxist theory had to be revised."[6]

Marxist theory did need some revision and also further development. For those Marxists who believe that this project represents an "abandonment" of Marxism, I hope to demonstrate in this volume that Marxism remains as important as ever to winning women's liberation. But Marxist theory can only benefit by incorporating the numerous aspects of feminism that strengthen our common project. Increasing our understanding of oppression does not detract from the revolutionary agency of the working class, but should only enhance it.

Chapter One

Women's Liberation: The Marxist Tradition

If women's liberation is unthinkable without communism, then communism is unthinkable without women's liberation.

—Russian revolutionary Inessa Armand[1]

The classical Marxists of the nineteenth and early twentieth centuries—among them Karl Marx, Frederick Engels, Clara Zetkin, Rosa Luxemburg, V. I. Lenin, Alexandra Kollontai, and Leon Trotsky—developed a theoretical framework tying the fight for women's liberation to the struggle for socialism. While their theory has required updating,[2] their enormous theoretical, historical, and political contributions have too often been dismissed or ignored outside the Marxist left.

Indeed, Lenin argued in 1902 that "working-class consciousness cannot be genuine political consciousness unless the workers are trained to respond to *all* cases of tyranny, oppression, violence, and abuse, no matter *what class* is affected—unless they are trained, moreover, to respond from a Social-Democratic point of view and no other."[3] This brief passage tied the fate of the working-class movement to the ongoing fight against all forms of oppression, establishing a political framework central to the Marxist tradition since that time. Moreover, the history of those who carried on the Marxist tradition in relation to women's oppression during the mid-twentieth century has frequently been rendered invisible—yet these activists and theorists provided an indispensable thread that continued between the victory of women's suffrage in the 1920s (often referred to as US feminism's "first wave") and the rise of the 1960s women's liberation movement (known as its "second wave").

Marx and Engels located the root of women's oppression in women's role within the family in class societies. They understood that women's role as biological "reproducers" results in their subordinate status inside the family and, consequently, throughout society. In capitalist societies, women in property-holding families reproduce heirs; women in working-class families reproduce generations of workers for the system.

The capitalist class has become dependent on this method of "privatized reproduction" within the working-class family because it lessens capitalists' own financial responsibility for the reproduction of labor power, which is instead largely supplied by unpaid domestic labor performed primarily by women. The precondition for women's liberation thus requires an end to their unpaid labor inside the family. This, in turn, necessitates a socialist transformation of society, which cannot be achieved gradually but only through a process of social revolution, in a decisive battle between classes.

Marx and Engels early on identified the revolutionary agency of the working class, or proletariat, as the only class capable of leading the transformation to a socialist society. In the *Communist Manifesto*, they state, "What the bourgeoisie therefore produces, above all, are its own grave-diggers. Its fall and the victory of the proletariat are equally inevitable."[4]

As Hal Draper notes,

> The classic formulation of the self-emancipation principle by Marx was written down in 1864 as the first premise of the *Rules* of the First International—in fact, as its first clause:
> "CONSIDERING, That the emancipation of the working classes must be conquered by the working classes themselves."[5]

Marxist theorists of the late nineteenth and early twentieth centuries did not downplay the importance of combating women's oppression. As Leon Trotsky argued, "In order to change the conditions of life, we must learn to see them through the eyes of women."[6]

Like Marx and Engels before them, later generations of Marxists recognized the revolutionary agency of the entire working class—and regarded working-class women as a key component in achieving its revolutionary potential. They emphasized the plight of working-class women and attempted to organize explicitly working-class women's movements.

European Marxists from Germany to Russia were often at the forefront of the fight for women's liberation, while advancing Marxist theory on what was then called "the woman question." They did so not only in an era of growing interimperialist conflict leading to World War I but also in the context of rising revolutionary socialist movements. The outbreak of world war brought about a whirlwind of patriotism in all the belligerent countries and became the dividing question within the socialist movement itself, as entire socialist parties of the Second International threw themselves into the war efforts of their "own" ruling classes.

The chasm between revolutionary socialists and those they called "bourgeois feminists" was not due to minor tactical or strategic differences but to crucial political principles. In the case of tsarist Russia, for example, ruling-class women joined the war effort as a tradeoff in return for voting rights. The League for Women's Equality called on Russian women to "devote all our energy, intellect, and knowledge to our country. This is our obligation to our fatherland, and this will give us the right to participate as the equals of men in the new life of a victorious Russia."[7]

As socialists Hal Draper and Anne G. Lipow describe, revolutionary socialists "gave strong support to all the democratic demands for women's equal rights. But this movement differed from the bourgeois feminists not only in the programmatic context in which it put these 'democratic demands,' but also—and consequently—in its choice of immediate demands to emphasize. It viewed itself, in Marxist terms, as a class movement, and this translates into *working-women's movement*."[8]

The Self-Organization of Socialist Women

Engels encouraged German socialist August Bebel, who had authored *Woman and Socialism* in 1878, to assist with the founding of a socialist working women's movement within the Social Democratic Party of Germany (SPD). The result was the formation of a women-led party bureau in 1891, with Clara Zetkin—a leading member of the SPD—at its political and organizational center. At the time of the founding of the SPD women's bureau in 1891, women in Prussia were legally barred from attending political meetings or joining political parties. Finally in 1902, as Bebel notes, "The Prussian secretary of state condescended to give women permission to attend the meetings of political clubs, but under the condition that they had to take their seats in a part of the hall specially set aside for them."[9]

The achievements of the women's bureau, viewed in this context, were substantial. Its publication, *Gleichheit* ("Equality"), reached a circulation of 23,000 by 1905 and 112,000 by 1913. Meanwhile, female membership in the party grew from roughly 4,000 in 1905 to 141,000 by 1913.[10]

The German working-women's movement soon became the epicenter of an international movement of socialist women under the rubric of the Second International, with organizing women workers into trade unions its priority. In 1907, Zetkin organized the first international conference of socialist women in Stuttgart, held in the days leading up to the Second International's full congress. At that congress, the Second International voted for universal suffrage for all women and men.

The issue of whether to fight for "universal" or "partial" women's suffrage was a strong point of controversy. Some women's suffrage organizations demanded (and in some European countries, won) partial suffrage for women—with voting rights based upon property holding and the payment of taxes (that is, restricting voting rights to those women of financial means). But in many of these same societies, male suffrage was also partial, denying working-class men the right to vote. Thus, partial suffrage merely increased the voting power of the upper classes.

Leading women of the Second International, including Clara Zetkin, Rosa Luxemburg, Alexandra Kollontai, and Eleanor Marx, clearly distinguished the socialist demand for women's suffrage from that of "middle-class women." They championed universal suffrage in the context of the class struggle. In a position paper in preparation for the 1907 Stuttgart women's conference, Zetkin argues for the right to vote for all women, regardless of class:

> But when we demand Woman Suffrage, we can only do so on the ground, not that it should be a right attached to the possession of a certain amount of property, but that it should be inherent in the woman herself. . . .
>
> From this point of view of history, we demand the political equality of women and the right to vote as a recognition of the political rights due to our sex. This is a question which applies to the whole of women without exception. All women, whatever be their position, should demand political equality as a means of a freer life, and one calculated to yield rich blessings to society. Besides, in the women's world, as well as in the men's world, there exists the class law and the class struggle, and it appears as fully established that sometimes between the Socialist working women and those belonging to the middle class there may be antagonisms. . . . This middle class should agitate for the Suffrage, not only in their own interests, in order to weaken the power of the male sex, but they should also labour in the cause of the whole of social reform, and give what help they can in that matter. But while we are ready as Socialists to use all our political might to bring about this change, yet we are bound to notice the difference between us and them.[11]

Zetkin led this work on behalf of the Second International—until it split over the SPD's support for the First World War. She left to join a small number of other antiwar revolutionaries—including the Russian revolutionaries Lenin, Trotsky, and Kollontai, who went on to lead the Russian Revolution of 1917—to found a principled international socialist movement against the interimperialist war. Zetkin helped to organize an international socialist women's antiwar conference in Berlin in 1915 and then cofounded the revolutionary Spartacus League in Germany in 1916, along with Karl Liebknecht and Rosa Luxemburg.

Social Class and Women's Oppression

In 1909, Russian revolutionary Alexandra Kollontai wrote what proved to be a defining contribution to the Marxist analysis of women's oppression, "The Social Basis of the Woman Question," in which she argued,

> The women's world is divided, just as is the world of men, into two camps: the interests and aspirations of one group bring it close to the bourgeois class, while the other group has close connections to the proletariat, and its claims for liberation encompass a full solution to the woman question. Thus, although both camps follow the general slogan of the "liberation of women," their aims and interests are different. Each of the groups unconsciously takes its starting point from the interests and aspirations of its own class, which gives a specific class coloring to the targets and tasks it sets for itself . . . however apparently radical the demands of the feminists, one must not lose sight of the fact that the feminists cannot, on account of their class position, fight for that fundamental transformation of society, without which the liberation of women cannot be complete.[12]

But the other side of Kollontai's approach involved an effort to convince working-class men of the need to support the demands of women workers. The Bolshevik Party, which led the 1917 Russian Revolution, intervened in strikes and struggles involving a majority of male workers, arguing that working men's class interests lay in fighting for demands such as maternity protection and equal pay for women.

In preparation for the First All-Russian Congress of Trade Unions in 1917, Kollontai called upon working-class men to support equal pay for women workers, arguing, "The class-conscious worker must understand that the value of male labor is dependent on the value of female labor, and that by threatening to replace male workers with cheaper female labor, the capitalist can put pressure on men's wages, lowering them to the level of women's wages. Therefore, only a lack of understanding could lead one to see the question of equal pay for equal work as purely a 'woman's issue.'"[13]

At the same time, it would be inaccurate to assume that these Marxists disregarded the plight of middle-class or even bourgeois women. On the contrary, Clara Zetkin expressed clear empathy with all women subjugated within the nuclear family. As she argued in 1896, family law dictates to upper-class wives that their husbands are their superiors: "She is still dependent upon her husband. The guardianship of the weaker sex has survived in the family law which still states: And he shall be your master."[14] She also argues,

> The bourgeois woman not only demands her own bread but she also requests spiritual nourishment and wants to develop her individuality. It is exactly among these strata that we find these tragic, yet psychologically interesting Nora* figures, women who are tired of living like dolls in dollhouses and who want to share in the development of modern culture. *The economic as well as the intellectual and moral endeavors of bourgeois women's rights advocates are completely justified.*[15] (Emphasis added.)

In the same contribution, Zetkin also argues that middle-class women

> are not equal to men in the form of possessors of private property as they are in the upper circles. The women of these circles have yet to achieve their economic equality with men and they can only do so by making two demands: The demand for equal professional training and the demand for equal job opportunities for both sexes. This battle of competition pushes the women of these social strata toward demanding their political rights so that they may, by fighting politically, tear down all barriers which have been created against their economic activity.[16]

There is an important distinction, noted by Zetkin above, between ruling-class and middle-class women. Middle-class women, like all members of the middle class, experience wide-ranging financial, employment, and life circumstances. The upper-middle class approaches the lifestyle of the ruling class, while the lower-middle class faces conditions barely discernible from workers. Thus, middle-class women can be pulled in different political directions—some gravitating toward the bourgeoisie and others identifying with the interests of workers. Indeed, Zetkin, writing in 1896 with tremendous foresight, remarks on the increasing tendency toward the proletarianization of "mental labor" affecting academics and other professions—a factor that is far more relevant today than in Zetkin's time:

---

* Nora is the Norwegian wife and mother in Henrik Ibsen's classic play, *A Doll's House*, who realizes that her life has been an empty pretense.

Within the bourgeois intelligentsia, another circumstance leads to the worsening of the living conditions: capitalism needs the intelligent and scientifically trained work force. It therefore favored an overproduction of mental-work proletarians and contributed to the phenomenon that the formerly respected and profitable societal positions of members of the professional class are more and more eroding.[17]

The Early US Movement for Women's Liberation

The early-twentieth-century movement for women's suffrage in the United States differed somewhat from its European counterparts, but its class dynamics were similar. While the US government had granted "universal suffrage" to men, it did not block Southern states from imposing Jim Crow poll taxes and other restrictions intended to deny the vote specifically to Black men.

Thus, Jim Crow segregation effectively imposed partial suffrage on men, denying the right to vote to Black men within former Confederate states. Sidestepping this vital issue, US suffragists called for "universal suffrage" for women (even though Black women would also be denied the right to vote in Jim Crow states). The white-led National American Woman Suffrage Association (NAWSA) allowed Southern affiliates to practice racial segregation and to call for votes for white women only.

Overt racism was not limited to Southern chapters, however, as demonstrated in a letter to a local congressman from suffrage leader Carrie Chapman Catt in 1918: "The women of New York are now the political equals of the men of New York, but the white women of the south are the political inferiors of the negroes."[18]

African American women, including Mary Church Terrell and Ida B. Wells-Barnett, organized for women's suffrage in conjunction with the NAWSA, but primarily through the National Association of Colored Women and the Alpha Suffrage Club. Wells-Barnett played a key role in integrating the 1913 women's suffrage parade, yet she was asked to walk at the end of the march. She responded in anger, "If the Illinois women do not take a stand now in this great democratic parade, then the colored women are lost."[19]

US socialists and radicals could have joined their European counterparts in fighting for full suffrage for both men and women, regardless of their class or race. Unfortunately, they did not. In the United States in the early twentieth century, socialists and other radicals held frequently overlapping membership in both the revolutionary syndicalist Industrial Workers of the World (IWW) and the Socialist Party

(SP), which was a member party of the Second International. Both the IWW and the SP were committed to the emancipation of working-class women and closely linked the class struggle with winning women's right to birth control, although they disagreed on the value of winning women's suffrage.

While the IWW was unapologetically antiracist, it refused to involve itself in electoral activity and flatly opposed the suffrage movement, which they labeled "rich faddists for woman suffrage."[20] The IWW's fiery organizer Elizabeth Gurley Flynn stated plainly, "To us society moves in grooves of class, not sex."[21] At the same time, IWW organizers were outspoken in fighting for working women's equality. The IWW made a point of encouraging women to take on leadership roles in strikes and other struggles, with tremendous success in the 1912 Lawrence textile strike. Flynn argued, "The IWW has been accused of putting the women in the front. The truth is the IWW does not keep them at the back, and they go to the front."[22]

Lucy Parsons, widow of Haymarket martyr Albert Parsons and a leading radical in her own right, emphasized the power of women workers in her speech to the IWW's founding conference in 1905:

> We, the women of this country, have no ballot even if we wished to use it, and the only way that we can be represented is to take a man to represent us. You men have made such a mess of it in representing us that we have not much confidence in asking you, and I for one feel very backward in asking the men to represent me . . .
> [Women] are the slaves of slaves. We are exploited more ruthlessly than men. Whenever wages are to be reduced the capitalist class use women to reduce them, and if there is anything that you men should do in the future it is to organize the women.[23]

The Socialist Party

In contrast to the IWW's boycott of the suffrage movement, the SP worked alongside suffragists—but without a policy to systematically challenge their adherence to the segregationist status quo. Indeed, the SP was divided between its left and right wings on the crucial issue of racial segregation. On its left wing, Eugene Debs, the SP's most inspirational orator, was an unabashed revolutionary who opposed racial segregation and refused to speak in front of segregated audiences. On the right, Victor Berger argued that socialism in the United States and

Canada would only be possible if they remain "white man's" countries. Berger also warned that if the tide of immigration into the United States was not stopped, "This country is absolutely sure to become a black-and-yellow country within a few generations."[24]

But the division on racial segregation was not solely between the SP's left and right wings. Some of those associated with the SP's "left wing" also supported racial segregation. Kate Richards O'Hare, one of the party's most popular agitators, penned the pamphlet "Nigger Equality," in which she argues,

> But you ask what is the solution of the race question?
>   There can be but one. Segregation. If you ask me what I am going to work and speak and write and vote for on the race question, when it is to be settle [*sic*] under a Socialist form of government, I can tell you very quickly. Let us give the blacks one section in the country where every condition is best fitted for them. Free them from capitalist exploitation; give them access to the soil, the ownership of their machines and let them work out their own salvation. If the negro rises to such an opportunity, and develops his own civilization, well and good; if not, and he prefers to hunt and fish and live idly, no one will be injured but him and that will be his business.[25]

The issue of racial segregation went unresolved for a number of years after the SP's formation. While many on the party's left wing, including Debs, tended to shun internal SP debates, Berger and the party's right wing dominated the party's organizational apparatus, thereby exercising considerable influence over policy. The right wing of the SP placed a premium on winning electoral office and increasingly regarded this as the path to winning a socialist society.

After some internal debate, the SP voted to establish a National Woman's Commission in 1908—charged not only with overseeing work among women, including suffrage, but also "for organizing the attack upon male superiority among Socialists."[26] As historian Ira Kipnis remarked, however, "women socialists seem to have carried on the fight for equal rights with little aid from the male members of the party."[27]

The Right to Birth Control

Nevertheless, women from the SP played a crucial role in organizing among working-class and immigrant women in the early decades of the twentieth century. They joined other women radicals, including the much-admired anarchist Emma Goldman, in building the first reproductiverights movement in the United States. Much of this work centered around educating and aiding working-class women in accessing reliable birth control, as a way to limit family size and repeated pregnancies in conditions of pervasive poverty. Historians have focused much attention on the pioneering role in the early birth-control movement of then-socialist Margaret Sanger, who later converted to a racist eugenics viewpoint.

But many other women radicals in the IWW and SP received far less acclaim yet maintained a lifetime commitment to fighting for the right of women to control their own reproductive lives. At a time when even dispensing information about contraception was illegal, these activists faced police raids and arrest as they continued their work among women.

Antoinette Konikow, a Russian revolutionary who migrated to the United States in 1893, dedicated herself to this project while remaining central to the US revolutionary socialist movement until her death in 1946. Konikow explicitly tied women's right to control their fertility to the fight for women's equality. As she put it in her 1923 pamphlet *Voluntary Motherhood*, "Women can never obtain real independence unless her functions of procreation are under her own control."[28] Konikow never veered from this approach, presaging themes that emerged in women's liberation movements of the 1960s.

Konikow's offices were raided regularly, so she kept her medical files in code to prevent police from prosecuting her patients. As socialist feminist Diane Feeley comments, "Although the overwhelming majority of her patients were poor immigrant women, whenever Dr. Konikow was arrested, she found that bond was quickly posted by some wealthy woman, who, given Massachusetts' repressive laws, may have had to turn to this revolutionary for help."[29]

As a medical doctor, Konikow describes how university training left doctors ignorant of birth-control methods and therefore unable to help their women patients urgently seeking to control their fertility. In response, she authored *The Physician's Manual of Birth Control* in 1931, which included not only a detailed discussion of the female anatomy but also information on what she considered the most reliable method of birth control at the time—the diaphragm with spermicidal jelly.[30]

The First "Women's Day"

The SP also devoted itself to supporting striking women workers and encouraging their union organization to join the American Federation of Labor (AFL), even though the labor federation did not welcome women, Blacks, or immigrants into its fold. In this project, women SP members collaborated with suffragists and other middle-class reformers, although substantial friction sometimes existed between these reformers and women workers.[31]

The New York City garment workers' strike of 1909–10, often referred to by labor historians as "the uprising of the twenty thousand," involved a largely immigrant and teenage female workforce that fought its way to the bitter end, with most—though not all—shops winning union recognition with Local 25 of the International Ladies' Garment Workers Union. When the strike began, the strikers received strong support not only from the SP but also from suffragists and the middle-class Women's Trade Union League (WTUL), known as "allies" of the strikers. The SP maintained its commitment to the strike throughout, although the interest of the middle-class allies waned as the strike dragged on and the strikers voted down a contract proposal from the employers. One angry member of the WTUL made a proposal to "start a campaign against socialism," because "socialism is a menace. . . . It just makes those ignorant foreigners discontented, sets them against the government, makes them want to tear down [sic]."[32]

But the inspiration of the garment workers was profound. When the Socialist Party organized "Women's Day" marches in 1910, their march through the streets of New York City was a massive display of solidarity and class consciousness among women workers, including sizeable contingents of garment workers, putting forward demands for higher wages and better working conditions, along with the demand for the right to vote.

The heroism of the New York City garment workers inspired German revolutionary Clara Zetkin to move a resolution at the 1910 Second International Conference of Working Women to declare International Women's Day an annual socialist holiday, a tradition that continues to this day.

In February 1917, women textile workers in Petrograd organized a demonstration for International Women's Day under the theme "Opposition to the war, high prices, and the situation of the woman worker," resulting in a massive strike movement which, in turn, overthrew the tsar. This day became, effectively, the first day of the Russian Revolution.

Revolutionary Russia and the Challenges to Realizing Women's Liberation

The leaders of the Russian Revolution of 1917 had from the beginning made combating women's oppression a central aspect of their revolutionary project. During its brief existence, this revolutionary government offered a glimpse of what a genuinely socialist society could offer in creating the material conditions for women to be liberated—but also the challenges that must be faced in making women's liberation a reality in a postrevolutionary context. Below I briefly examine the legal achievements and also the limitations of legislation alone in achieving genuine equality for women—indicating the degree to which further struggle will be necessary *after* a socialist revolution to eradicate women's oppression.

To be sure, the revolutionary government enacted legislation establishing full social and political equality for women: the right to vote and to hold public office, the right to divorce at the request of either partner, the principle of equal pay for equal work, paid maternity leave for four months before and after childbirth, and child care at government expense. Abortion—viewed only as a health matter—was made legal in 1920, and women won the right to obtain free abortions in state hospitals. Only those who performed abortions for profit were considered criminals.

In addition, the revolution repealed all laws criminalizing homosexuality along with other laws regulating sexuality. Bolshevik Grigorii Btakis described the impact of the October Revolution on sexuality in 1923: "[Soviet legislation] declares the absolute non-interference of the state and society into sexual matters, so long as nobody is injured, and no one's interests are encroached upon—concerning homosexuality, sodomy, and various other forms of sexual gratification, which are set down in European legislation as offences against morality—Soviet legislation treats these exactly as so-called natural intercourse."[33]

But legal equality, while crucial, did not achieve liberation in everyday life within the family. As Lenin explained in 1919, "Laws alone are not enough, and we are by no means content with mere decrees. In the sphere of legislation, however, we have done everything required of us to put women in a position of equality and we have every right to be proud of it. The position of women in Soviet Russia is now ideal as compared with their position in the most advanced states. We tell ourselves, however, that this, of course, is only the beginning."[34]

Lenin commonly referred to women's oppression within the family as "domestic slavery," and he expressed alarm at its continuation in postrevolutionary Russia. In a 1920 interview with Zetkin, several years after the revolution, Lenin spoke in detail about the obstacles women continued to encounter in their domestic lives. The following quote from Lenin makes clear that Russian Marxists did not expect women's oppression to automatically disappear after the revolution, but recognized the need for continued struggle:

> Very few husbands, not even the proletarians, think of how much they could lighten the burdens and worries of their wives, or relieve them entirely, if they lent a hand in this "women's work." But no, that would go against the "privilege and dignity of the husband." He demands that he have rest and comfort. The domestic life of the woman is a daily sacrifice of self to a thousand insignificant trifles. The ancient rights of her husband, her lord and master, survive unnoticed. . . . I know the life of the workers, and not only from books. Our communist work among the masses of women, and our political work in general, involves considerable education among the men. We must root out the old slave-owner's point of view, both in the Party and among the masses. That is one of our political tasks, a task just as urgently necessary as the formation of a staff composed of comrades, men and women, with thorough theoretical and practical training for Party work among working women.[35]

Trotsky likewise argues, "To institute the political equality of men and women in the Soviet state was one problem and the simplest. . . . But to achieve the actual equality of man and woman within the family is an infinitely more arduous problem." He concludes, "All our domestic habits must be revolutionized before that can happen. And yet it is quite obvious that unless there is actual equality of husband and wife in the family, in a normal sense as well as in the conditions of life, we cannot speak seriously of their equality in social work or even in politics."[36] The Bolsheviks thus never harbored the illusion that a victorious socialist revolution is all that is required to end women's oppression. Old customs and attitudes cannot be expected to change overnight, but can only shift over time, as new generations grow up without the ideological baggage perpetuated by oppressive class societies over the course of centuries.

Indeed, it is more appropriate to appreciate the degree to which the Bolsheviks understood that the revolution was not the end, but the beginning of the struggle to win women's liberation. Most importantly, they understood the centrality of freeing women from the drudgery of "domestic slavery," however difficult, as the key to their future liberation in all spheres of life.

The Revolutionary Turning Point

The 1917 Russian Revolution had inspired a wave of revolutionary struggle across Europe. The possibility that the revolution would spread to more economically advanced societies, particularly in Germany, kept the revolutionary government's hopes alive in its first few years. That hope was erased with the final defeat of the German Revolution in 1923. Russia, its economy in shambles, was left isolated. The political terrain was thereby transformed: the decade that followed witnessed Stalinist counterrevolution in Russia and the ascendency of fascism in Europe.

The Russian Revolution also marked a turning point for the left in the United States. The SP had managed to survive the war relatively intact because it had maintained an antiwar stance. But it had already begun purging revolutionaries from its ranks in 1912 when it recalled IWW leader "Big Bill" Haywood, after he had been elected to its National Executive Committee, simply because he had publicly advocated "direct action" as a more effective tactic than voting in the class struggle. After his recall, Haywood declined to renew his membership in the SP, leading to the exodus of thousands of other revolutionary socialists who followed him out of the party.[37]

By 1919, Russian revolutionaries formed the Third, or Communist, International with the affiliation of nineteen organizations and parties. The Russian Revolution thus accelerated the already escalating conflict between the SP's left and right wings, as the party's revolutionaries cheered the Bolsheviks and the reform wing opposed them. By 1919, the SP lost its left-wing majority, which went on to form what became the Communist Party (CP) USA—affiliated with the Third International. Most IWW members—many having already left or been expelled by the SP—followed suit.

Trotskyism versus Stalinism

The 1920s, however, proved a difficult period for those seeking to uphold the Marxist tradition. The US government conducted mass raids and deportations of immigrants suspected of socialist or anarchist activity. Moreover, as Stalin consolidated his power in the Soviet Union in 1928, the CP expelled the minority in the party who supported the Trotskyist opposition to Stalinism.

The result was the emergence of two distinct socialist movements—one pro-Stalin, and the other pro-Trotsky—together comprising the political wings of the socialist left until the emergence of the New Left in the 1960s.

Some of the most dedicated and talented women leaders from the early twentieth century ended up in different organizations with opposing political views on fundamental political questions. Konikow, one of the founding members of the US Trotskyist movement, continued her work around delivering safe contraception and wrote extensively on women's right to birth control in the Trotskyist *Militant* newspaper in the 1930s and early 1940s. Gurley Flynn joined the CP in 1936 and penned a regular column for the *Daily Worker*. In this way, women veterans of the early-twentieth-century radical movements played a key role in transmitting their commitment to women's emancipation to a younger generation of women in the US left, albeit from competing organizations.

Organizing Among Women in the Great Depression: The 1936–37 Flint Strike

In the tumultuous movement for union recognition in the 1930s, the commitment to women's emancipation often played out in the course of the class struggle—without an explicit call for women's political equality.

One of the most striking examples from the labor movement is the momentous Flint, Michigan, sit-down strike during the winter of 1936–37, when Trotskyists (at that time members of the Socialist Party) and Communists worked together in brilliant cohesion to lead their strike against General Motors (GM) to victory. SP member Genora Johnson (later Genora Dollinger), at the time the twenty-three-year-old wife of strike leader Kermit Johnson, formed the Flint Women's Emergency Brigade.

While made up primarily of strikers' wives, the Emergency Brigade was far from the typical "ladies' auxiliary," consciously referring to their organization as being made up of "women" and not "ladies."[38] The women of the Emergency Brigade wore the uniform of a red beret and armband, which Dollinger later revealed was chosen partly because "it was the red flag, it's a socialist color."[39]

The Emergency Brigade could be mobilized on a moment's notice to defend the strike. As the *New York Times* noted at the time, the women of the Emergency Brigade "did not content themselves with passive resistance but used clubs the size of baseball bats, whittled down at the end to make them easy to swing and handle."[40] On more than one occasion, the Emergency Brigade faced off against the police—taunting them to beat up or shoot at a group of women.

One of the Emergency Brigade's most clever tactics was the "sound car" that was quickly dispatched when there was a sign of trouble outside the plant. The sound car would arrive to direct pickets in battle through its loudspeaker. This tactic proved indispensible in the strike strategists' diversionary battle to sidetrack police by pretending to occupy the Chevy #9 plant (while actually taking Chevy #4) on February 1. This strategy, while ultimately successful, nevertheless placed strikers' lives at stake as they fought the police at Chevy #9. As researcher Janice Hassett described, "GM police exchanged blows with the strikers, and used clubs and tear gas to move them to the back of the plant. The Emergency Brigade, 'always ready for emergencies' was on hand, and used their own clubs to break the windows and let air into the factory."[41]

Communists in Harlem

The CP, due to its larger size and consistent attention to combatting racism in the 1930s, made inroads in building a multiracial organization during that era. Black Communist women began to organize systematically among Black working-class women during the 1930s. Communist women in the Harlem neighborhood of New York City, as historian Erik S. McDuffie describes in *Sojourning for Freedom*, organized against the high prices of food in white-owned grocery stores, including the following demonstration in 1935:

> On June 3, 1935, "flying squads" of black women and children defiantly marched down Harlem's 125th Street between Seventh and Eighth Avenues, the neighborhood's main commercial thoroughfare. They were one thousand strong. Chanting, "Prices of meat must come down!" they demanded a 25 percent reduction in meat prices. Protesters held spontaneous street corner meetings about high-priced food and other pressing community concerns around high unemployment, bad housing, and inadequate social services. They meant business. Groups of women darted into

white-owned grocery stores, confronting startled white merchants about why they sold high-priced, low-quality food to their black clientele.[42]

McDuffie concludes, "The demonstration was successful. Later that evening almost fifty stores agreed to immediately reduce food prices by 25 percent."[43] The Harlem Action Committee Against the High Cost of Living, led by West Indies–born Bonita Williams, organized this immediately successful protest. Williams and Audley Moore were two of the CP's women grassroots leaders in Harlem who simultaneously organized struggles against unemployment and evictions, rent strikes, and union organizing in this turbulent period.

Williams and Moore, like many Harlem radical activists, had first entered politics as part of Marcus Garvey's movement in the 1920s, attracted by his message of nationalism and race pride. Both joined the CP through their involvement in the CP-led campaign to free the "Scottsboro Boys," nine Black teenagers who had been falsely accused of raping two white women on a train in 1931. After Williams took part in a thousands-strong multiracial march through Harlem, she recalls thinking, "If they've got a movement like that, and they're conscious of this thing [Marcus] Garvey had been speaking about, then this may be a good thing for me to get in to free my people."[44]

As the examples above show, Socialist and Communist women led important struggles involving women in the 1930s without attempting to forge a movement specifically for women's rights. In the case of Williams and Moore, their struggles were more explicitly tied to Black liberation than women's liberation. In a later interview with Hassett, Dollinger argues that a fight for "women's liberation" would have been "historically immature" in the working-class movement of 1937. But as Hassett concludes later of the Flint Women's Emergency Brigade,

> Despite the fact that the efforts of the women were not expressed in a "woman's movement," gender issues were a salient feature of the 1937 strike. Genora Johnson emphasizes that "it was a radical change. . . to give women a right to participate in discussions with their husbands, with other union members, with other women, to express their views. . . . That was a radical change for those women at that time."
>
> It was not a feminist action, and it was not a women's movement—it was a labor and class dominated phenomenon—but the events of 1936–1937 did show the nation, and the women themselves, that they were not just what they had been taught to be, that they were capable of concerted, orchestrated, and sometimes even heroic behavior. There is reason to believe that none of them was ever again "just a woman."[45]

The Communist Party in the 1940s and 1950s

Renewed interest in the politics of women's oppression began among women within the organized left in the immediate aftermath of World War II. The war era had seen the mass induction of women into high-paying manufacturing jobs in the interests of maximum war production, only to be driven out at the war's end to make room for returning vets. Many white women returned to homemaking with or without the combination of part-time work, while many Black women workers were driven back into the same full-time, low-paying domestic-labor occupations they held prior to the war.

World War II had also exposed the racist hypocrisy of fighting to extend America's "democratic freedoms" that at home excluded Black Americans from the democratic process. The civil rights movement grew in strength in the 1950s and inspired a broad radicalization in the 1960s.

Women in and around the Communist and Trotskyist movements began to reexamine theories of women's oppression, with some incorporating the effects not only of class inequality but also of racism. In so doing, they began to develop a political framework that helped to pave the way for the future fight for women's liberation.

It is worth noting that in spite of the CP's Stalinist politics, its members began to passionately discuss the problems of male chauvinism inside and outside of the party in its newspapers' letters page—pressuring the party leadership to do something to combat women's oppression in practice. The CP had begun discussing women's oppression in its publications throughout the 1940s—including a theoretical debate over whether women's household labor could be considered productive labor in Marxist discourse, a debate presaging the domestic labor debate decades later among socialist-feminists in the 1970s.

This discussion opened a floodgate of complaints, revealing that women CP members had much to complain about. At that time, the party's newspapers routinely included photos and images of scantily clad women—including what were then known as "cheesecake photos." These consisted of "bathing beauties," with captions such as "the most beautiful legs in the world." The caption to another photo described a beauty contest winner as "Mrs. New York—and She Can Cook Too." Meanwhile, the newspaper's so-called Women's Page featured a white woman dressed in high heels happily dusting her furniture—with a banner headline that read, "It's on the House" that offered a variety of household hints and dress patterns.[46]

Angry letter writers in early 1949 complained loudly and frequently about these sexist images, writing comments such as, "We feel it is very important for the *Daily* to eliminate the cheesecake pictures. These pictures have no liberating effect for women and the working class, but on the contrary, are used to perpetuate male supremacy through the idea that sex is women's only attribute."[47] Another letter reads, "For women [who are aware of the necessity for social change], "cheesecake is a slap in the face . . . I have seen many requests from readers for articles and items on the role of women in this social struggle. Surely you cannot continue to present artistic views of the female body as an answer to this demand."[48]

By June 1949, cheesecake photos had disappeared from the party's publications[49] and by 1950, the Women's Page was replaced by a "Women Today" page, with an image of two smiling women, one Black and one white, which featured articles on women's role in social and class movements. In response, letter writers urged more of the same. One writer argued, "Tear into the male supremacy that is holding back the movement almost as much as white supremacy."[50]

In response to this pressure from its rank and file, the CP expanded its attention on the issues of women's oppression, organizing classes in the early 1950s for its members on topics such as "male supremacy and family relations"—aimed at male members as well as women. As historian Kate Weigand describes, "They hoped that such classes might persuade more men to renounce the privileges they gained from male supremacy and to work for genuine egalitarianism in their relationships with their wives."[51]

Claudia Jones: "An End to the Neglect of the Problems of the Negro Woman!"

Communist Party leader Claudia Jones penned perhaps the most salient exposition of the interlocking oppressions suffered by Black women prior to rise of the Black feminist movement in the 1960s. Jones's article, "An End to the Neglect of the Problems of the Negro Woman!," published in 1949 in *Political Affairs*, first clearly asserts, "Negro women—as workers, as Negroes, and as women—are the most oppressed strata of the whole population."[52] Jones continues, "It is incumbent on progressive unionists to realize that in the fight for equal rights for Negro workers, it is necessary to have a special approach to Negro women workers, who, far out of proportion to other women workers, are the main breadwinners in their families."[53] Jones explicitly challenges "progressive white women" to recognize that this fight for equality of Negro women is in their own self-interest, inasmuch as the superexploitation and oppression of Negro women tends to depress the standards of all women. . . . Persistent challenge to every chauvinist remark as concerns the Negro woman is vitally necessary, if we are to break down the understandable distrust on the part of Negro women who are repelled by the white chauvinism they often find expressed in progressive circles.[54]

In the same pathbreaking essay, Jones emphasizes sexual assault as one of the key issues facing Black women:

> But none so dramatizes the oppressed status of Negro womanhood as does the case of Rosa Lee Ingram, widowed mother of fourteen children—two of them dead—who faces life imprisonment in a Georgia jail for the "crime" of defending herself from the indecent advances of a "white supremacist." . . . It exposes the hypocritical alibi of the lynchers of Negro manhood who have historically hidden behind the skirts of white women when they try to cover up their foul crimes with the "chivalry" of "protecting white womanhood."[55]

Jones concludes that proper attention to the plight of Black women will allow their "active participation" in fulfilling the "historic mission" of the "entire American working class": "the achievement of a Socialist America—the final and full guarantee of woman's emancipation."[56]

Jones was unable to continue her work within the CP, due to the US government's unrelenting political persecution. The Trinidad-born Jones was first imprisoned in 1948 for her political activities and jailed three more times in the following years. She was found guilty under the terms of the Internal Security Act of 1950, which banned "aliens" from Communist Party membership. She was also found guilty, along with Gurley Flynn, of "un-American activities" under the Smith Act in 1951.

In 1955 the US government deported her, but the government of Trinidad-Tobago refused to accept her. The British government agreed to accept her on "humanitarian" grounds, and she lived there until her death by massive heart attack at the age of forty-nine. While Jones continued her close involvement in the antiracist movement in Britain until her untimely death, she did not return to the theoretical work on Black women's oppression she had begun in the CP.

Other Black Communist women nevertheless continued to struggle throughout this period, campaigning for Rosa Lee Ingram and against the systematic rape of Black women—sometimes overlapping with the work of and supporting civil rights activists such as Rosa Parks. Moreover, the CP began organizing local women's commissions to help encourage women's active participation in the party. This included women's education classes in a number of localities to help them prepare to take on leadership positions. These classes provided child care and transportation to make it easier for working-class women to attend. In January 1947, for example, the Bronxville CP held a special women's dinner meeting—at which the women attendees enjoyed a lecture on "the role of women today" and discussed the problems they faced, while the men "cooked and served food, minded children, and washed dishes."[57]

Other Socialist Women Address Women's Oppression in This Era

During the postwar period, many other women on the organized left were also engaged in revisiting the issue of women's oppression. In 1952, Selma James (a former member of the Trotskyist movement[58]) coauthored the pamphlet, *A Woman's Place*, addressing the weight of family responsibilities shouldered by working-class women of that era. James and her coauthor used pseudonyms to protect themselves from losing their jobs in the face of anticommunist hysteria, although James nevertheless lost hers. The pamphlet includes the following passage, presaging Betty Friedan's observations in *The Feminine Mystique*, but with a working-class, not middle-class, wife in mind:

> Even though a woman works, it is assumed from the very beginning that the main responsibility of the house is the woman's and the main job of support is the man's. The husband is to go out and support you and the children. You are to make sure that the house is clean, the children are cared for, meals are cooked, laundry is done, etc. This seems a fair way of doing things. But soon you find that the job of staying home and taking care of the house is not the same as it is painted in the movies. Housework is a never-ending job that is monotonous and repetitious. After a while doing things in the house such as ironing or getting up early to make lunches or breakfast is not something that you want to do. It is something that you have to do.[59]

In 1954, James wrote a biweekly column called "A Woman's Place" in *Correspondence*. In one column, "Miss Universe," James described her experience watching the Miss Universe beauty contest, expressing much the same sentiment as the women's liberationists who rallied outside the Miss America pageant in 1968. James points out, for example, "The contest was supposed to be not only for beauty, the MC kept saying. It was for poise and stature as well. . . . But the most important outfit was the Catalina swimsuit in exactly the same style for each of the young women."[60] James also observed that although the contest was global, the women who paraded before television and movie viewers all shared the facial features of white American women: "As I watched the finals, it struck me that though the women were different types, every one of them looked the same. . . . Of course, there was a 'type' that wasn't represented at all. There was not one Negro woman in the beauty contest."[61]

Also in 1954, Evelyn Reed of the Socialist Workers Party (US), who frequently addressed women's oppression in the pages of the magazine *Fourth International*, argued that women's responsibilities as mothers are assumed to make them inferior to men in all aspects of life:

> It is set forth as an . . . immutable axiom that women are *socially* inferior because they are *naturally* inferior to men. And what is the proof? They are the mothers! Nature, it is claimed, has condemned the female sex to an inferior status . . . It is not nature, but class society, which robbed women of their right to participate in the higher functions of society and placed the primary emphasis upon their animal functions of maternity.
>
> And this robbery was perpetrated through a two-fold myth. On the one side, motherhood is represented as a biological affliction arising out of the maternal organs of women. Alongside this vulgar materialism, motherhood is represented as being something almost mystical. To console women for their status as second-class citizens, mothers are sanctified, endowed with halos and blessed with special "instincts," feelings and knowledge forever beyond the comprehension of men. Sanctity and degradation are simply two sides of the same coin of the social robbery of women under class society.[62]

The socialist and communist women described above did not merely keep the struggle for women's liberation alive during the decades preceding the rise of the women's liberation movement of the late 1960s. They began to advance this struggle in both theoretical and practical ways, thereby providing a continuum for those who embraced this struggle, and further advanced it, in the following generation.

From the "Old Left" to the New

As Weigand argues, "Although the women's movement of the 1960s and 1970s differed in many ways from what came before it, the movement did not emerge as a fully developed entity in the mid-1960s. Rather, second-wave feminists built upon the work of various groups that preceded them, including the work of women who inspired and were inspired by the Old Left's efforts to take women's issues seriously after 1945."[63]

In 1983, Black feminist and scholar Barbara Smith acknowledged in particular the influence of playwright Lorraine Hansberry for her early advocacy of lesbian sexuality. Hansberry, best known for authoring the acclaimed *A Raisin in the Sun* at the young age of twenty-seven, was also a left activist and Black feminist thinker. In 1957, the same year she completed *A Raisin in the Sun*, Hansberry joined the Daughters of Bilitis, the first lesbian organization in the United States. She contributed a series of letters to its publication, *The Ladder*, signing them only with the initials "L. H." to protect her privacy.

In the introduction to her book, *Home Girls: A Black Feminist Anthology*, Smith quotes one of Hansberry's letters:

> It is about time that "half the human race" had something to say about the nature of its existence. Otherwise—without revised basic thinking—the woman intellectual is likely to find herself trying to draw conclusions—moral conclusions—based on acceptance of a social moral superstructure that has never admitted to the equality of women and is therefore immoral itself. As per marriage, as per sexual practices, as per the rearing of children, etc. In this kind of work there may women to emerge who will be able to formulate a new and possible concept that homosexual persecution and condemnation has at its roots not only social ignorance, but a philosophically active anti-feminist dogma.[64]

Smith comments, "I would like a lot more people to be aware that Lorraine Hansberry, one of our most respected artists and thinkers, was asking in a lesbian context some of the same questions we are asking today, and for which we have been so maligned."[65]

Some women from the 1950s "Old Left" became participants in and theorists of the women's liberation movements in the 1960s and 1970s. Gerda Lerner, for example, who was active around the CP in the 1940s and 1950s, emerged as an eloquent women's studies scholar who was equally committed to championing the struggles of Black women against racial inequality. Selma James, after leaving the Trotskyist movement, went on to play a key role in theorizing women's domestic labor and founding the Wages for Housework campaign.

In 1970, Evelyn Reed used Engels's *Origin of the Family, Private Property and the State* for an outline of her argument, postulating that upon the rise of capitalism, women were then given two dismal alternatives. They could either seek a husband as provider and be penned up thereafter as housewives in city tenements or apartments to raise the next generation of wage slaves. Or the poorest and most unfortunate could go as marginal workers into the mills and factories (along with the children) and be sweated as the most downtrodden and underpaid section of the labor force.[66]

Like many Marxist feminists, Reed distinguishes between the reproductive roles of ruling-class versus working-class families for the owners of the means of production: ruling-class families reproduce generational wealth through inheritance, while working-class families serve to reproduce labor power.

In the same article, Reed also challenges those from other political tendencies "who say they are Marxists but refuse to acknowledge that women have to lead and organize their own independent struggle for emancipation, just as they cannot understand why Blacks must do the same." Here, she first addresses socialists who mistakenly believe that independent organizations of the oppressed pose a threat to working-class unity, which ultimately requires "the combined anti-capitalist offensive of the whole working class" to win a socialist society. Furthermore, she notes that the struggle will have to continue after the revolution to fully achieve women's liberation. As she argues,

> The reason is that no segment of society which has been subjected to oppression, whether it consists of Third World people or of women, can delegate the leadership and promotion of their fight for freedom to other forces—even though other forces can act as their allies. . . . The maxim of the Irish revolutionists—"who would be free themselves must strike the blow"—fully applies to the cause of women's liberation. Women must themselves strike the blows to gain their freedom. And this holds true after the anti-capitalist revolution triumphs as well as before.[67]

Thus, many Marxists arrived at roughly the same theoretical starting point as many socialist feminists by the late 1960s and early 1970s—and shared the same goal: using Marxist theory to better understand women's unpaid labor inside the family and its connection to women's oppression as a whole within capitalist society.

Chapter Two

The Origin of Women's Oppression

With the transfer of the means of production into common ownership, the single family ceases to be the economic unit of society. Private housekeeping is transformed into a social industry. The care and education of the children becomes a public affair; society looks after all children alike, whether they are legitimate or not. . . . Will not that suffice to bring about the gradual growth of unconstrained sexual intercourse and with it a more tolerant public opinion in regard to a maiden's honor and a woman's shame? And finally. . . . Can prostitution disappear without dragging monogamy with it into the abyss?

—Frederick Engels, 1841

Why are women oppressed? The traditional assumption is that male dominance over women is both natural and eternal: Men's greater physical strength makes them "aggressive" while motherhood makes women "nurturing" and submissive. Historically, social scientists reinforced this assumption, arguing that biological differences between men and women have led to distinct and unequal gender roles throughout human history. As historian Gerda Lerner explains, "Traditionalists, whether working within a religious or a 'scientific' framework, have regarded women's subordination as universal, God-given, or natural, hence immutable. Thus, it need not be questioned."[2]

Prejudices and Distortions in the Field of Anthropology

Sexist stereotypes have dominated the field of anthropology from its inception. Far from being an objective science, the study of human societies carries with it all the subjective baggage of its researchers' own cultural, social, and political prejudices. But both feminist and Marxist anthropologists have challenged those stereotypes since the modern women's movement emerged in the late 1960s. As socialist feminist scholars Stephanie Coontz and Peta Henderson describe,

> A number of anthropologists have recently gone back to the original anthropological sources on various cultures and found that the "masters" had reported almost exclusively on male activities and prerogatives, ignoring or downplaying equivalent female activities, rights, and prestige systems. Among the pre-colonial Ashanti, for example, "the head of state was a female position," but in accounts of Ashanti life this is often only "mentioned in passing, designated by the misnomer 'queen mother,' although she was never the king's wife, and was not necessarily his mother."[3]

Marxist anthropologist Eleanor Burke Leacock cites the following clear-cut example of sexism in her book *Myths of Male Dominance*, quoting a passage from anthropologist Robin Fox that was written as if it were only for a male audience: "For in behavior as in anatomy, the strength of our lineage lay in a relatively generalized structure. It was precisely because we did not specialize like our baboon cousins that we had to contrive solutions involving the control and exchange of females."[4]

Claude Lévi-Strauss, who pioneered the school of structuralist anthropology, goes so far as to declare that "human society . . . is primarily a masculine society." He argues that the "exchange of women" is a "practically universal" feature of human society, in which men obtain women from other men—fathers, brothers, and other male relatives. Moreover, he asserts, "the deep polygamous tendency, which exists among all men, always makes the number of available women seem insufficient." Therefore, "the most desirable women must form a minority." Because of this, "the demand for women is an actual fact, or to all intents and purposes, always in a state of disequilibrium and tension."[5] According to Lévi-Strauss, women have been the passive victims of men's sexual aggression since the beginning of human society.

Likewise, Western observers have frequently brought along their own cultural biases (including cultural chauvinism) when studying hunter-gatherer or horticultural societies. Customs are measured using a Western yardstick, rather than trying to understand the unique value system of a particular society.

As Leacock argues, for example, the traditional practice among Alaska Native women of sleeping with male household visitors was often interpreted by anthropologists as an example of women's low status—assuming that women were offered as gifts or property by their husbands.

As Leacock pointed out, however, this is an "ethnocentric reading which presumes that a woman does not (since she should not) enjoy sex play with any but her 'real' husband and which refuses to recognize that variety in sexual relations is entertaining to women (where not circumscribed by all manner of taboos) as well as to men."[6] In itself, therefore, this sexual custom reveals little about women's status in Alaska Native culture.

Male Warriors and Male Supremacy

Theories abound among anthropologists that often superimpose the features of a preclass world onto societies that have lived for centuries under colonial domination. Marvin Harris, author of a series of popular books on the evolution of human culture, is a typical example of a writer who engages in this sort of speculation.

Harris's theory rests on his assertion that "male supremacy" is a direct result of men's role in warfare and female infanticide, which he says early societies used to prevent population growth from depleting the surrounding environment. Yet he also admits, "Unfortunately, data needed to test my predictions about the rise and fall of the intensity of warfare in relation to growth and the splitting up of specific villages have not yet been collected."[7] This lack of empirical evidence in no way dampens his enthusiasm for his hypothesis.

Harris bases many of his conclusions on the cultural practices of the Yanomami, an indigenous people living in the Amazon rainforest on the border between Brazil and Venezuela. In anthropological circles, Yanomami culture is widely used as an example of a culture dominated by war and the brutal domination of women by men. But this characterization is problematic on many levels.

First, there is no single "Yanomami culture," since its people speak at least four different languages, identify primarily with their local villages over the wider population, and possess a variety of cultural practices. The particular group of Yanomami Harris and others uphold as "proof" of the warring character of "Yanomami culture" as a whole is unlikely to have developed its propensity for warfare until 1758, when the Yanomami fought off the first group of Spanish and Portuguese explorers searching for slaves—in other words, until the onset of colonialism.[8]

As cultural anthropologist R. Brian Ferguson summarizes:

> Although some Yanomami really have been engaged in intensive warfare and other kinds of bloody conflict, this violence is not an expression of

Yanomami culture itself. It is, rather, a product of specific historical situations: The Yanomami make war not because Western culture is absent, but because it is present, and present in certain specific forms. All Yanomami warfare *that we know about* occurs within what Neil Whitehead and I call a "tribal zone," an extensive area beyond state administrative control, inhabited by nonstate people who must react to the far-flung effects of the state presence.[9]

Coontz and Henderson also challenge Harris's broader conclusions about the "natural" relationship between warfare and male supremacy:

A more historically oriented study comes to quite different conclusions, showing that warfare is frequent in only eight percent of hunting and gathering societies, becoming more common in advanced horticultural systems but only "endemic" in the early agrarian states. The archeological record suggests that high levels of warfare did not follow the adoption of horticulture or agriculture *per se*, but developed only after the evolution of complex sociopolitical systems.[10]

For those interested in maintaining the sexist status quo, biological determinism offers a convenient justification. But this is an ahistorical approach to explaining gender inequality. The familiar childhood image of hairy male Neanderthals dragging their women from cave to cave is as mythical as Fred and Wilma Flintstone.

Feminist Debates on the Role of Biology

While many feminist theorists have sought to challenge biological determinism, as noted above, others have accepted that biological differences lie at the root of gender inequality. This was especially the case in the 1970s.

In the 1974 essay "Is Female to Male as Nature Is to Culture?" cultural anthropologist Sherry Ortner argues that women's low social status is tied to their capacity to give birth, which brings them symbolically closer to "nature," while men's capacity for warfare allows them to dominate in the realm of "culture." On this basis, she concludes, "everywhere, in every known culture, women are considered in some degree inferior to men."

But the evidence she offers is far from definitive. She cites, for example, a 1930s study of a matrilineal Native American society, the Crow. Although Ortner admits that in most respects Crow women hold positions of relative authority, she cites the Crow's taboo toward women during menstruation as evidence that they are nevertheless regarded as inferiors. Among other things, menstruating women are not allowed to touch either a wounded man or a man starting on a war party.[11]

Ortner's reasoning led to considerable controversy among feminist scholars and activists at the time. Lerner, who contested Ortner's approach as ahistorical, makes the following observation:

> Ortner and those who agree with her argue strongly for the universality of female subordination, if not in actual social conditions, then in the meaning systems of society. Opponents of this viewpoint object to the claim of universality, criticize its ahistoricity and reject the placing of women as passive victims. Finally, they challenge the implicit acceptance . . . of the existence of an unchanging and immutable dichotomy between male and female.[12]

The fairly common practice of isolating menstruating women in hunter-gatherer and horticultural societies has often been interpreted as evidence that women's reproductive powers are a source of contempt universally. But some such societies have no menstrual taboos at all. In others, men try to imitate women's reproductive powers. And as Coontz and Henderson point out, this interpretation of menstrual taboos leaves "the impression that women are [viewed as] unclean or evil instead of recognizing that certain substances, such as blood, are considered dangerous, whether shed by women or men" in many societies.[13]

Maria Lepowsky, who studies the sexually egalitarian society of Vanatinai, a small island southeast of New Guinea, likewise challenges the assumption that menstrual taboos reflect women's subordination. The people of this island call themselves *Vanatinai ghunoi*, which means "fruit of the motherland."[14] While menstruating women on this remote island are barred from working in a garden and planting yams in the communal garden, so too are men and women who have had sex in recent days. Women who are menstruating are neither isolated nor viewed as contaminated, and they continue to "forage, prepare food, and have sexual intercourse." Indeed, Vanatinai women do not view this taboo "as a burden or a curse but as a welcome interlude of relative leisure."[15]

If it can be shown that at least some human societies have not been based upon systematic gender inequality, then women's oppression cannot be caused *simply* by biological gender differences. Thus, women's oppression must be the result of a set of *social* developments—which can be challenged and overturned.

Marx and Engels: The Role of the Family in Women's Oppression

Marx and Engels were in many respects well in advance of their time in seeking to end women's oppression, while pursuing its relationship to class society and the family. Even in their early writings, they recognized that women's oppression is endemic to capitalism, noting the subservient role of women in property-holding families. In *The Communist Manifesto*, published in 1848, they argue that ruling-class men oppress their wives in their own families and that communists intend to free women from this oppression, stating, "The bourgeois sees in his wife a mere instrument of production. . . . He has not even a suspicion that the real point aimed at [by communists] is to do away with the status of women as mere instruments of production."[16]

In *The German Ideology*, written in 1846, Marx and Engels describe the family's historical origin in the shift from what they call the "communal economy" and communal forms of social organization that dominated in preclass societies to the rise of the "individual economy" and the rise of individual family units accompanying the onset of early agricultural societies. They wrote, "With the agricultural peoples a communal domestic economy is just as impossible as a communal cultivation of the soil."[17] Settled agricultural communities separated what was formerly communal property into individual plots of land under the private ownership of those with ample wealth to afford it—giving rise to new forms of social organization: individual family units.

They explain the connection between the early family form and class inequality as follows: "The separation of society into individual families opposed to one another, is given simultaneously the distribution, and indeed the unequal distribution, both quantitative and qualitative, of labor and its products, hence property: the nucleus, the first form, of which lies in the family, where wife and children are the slaves of the husband."[18] On this basis, Marx and Engels conclude that with the abolition of private property, "the abolition of the family is self-evident."[19]

Marx spent the final years of his life intensively researching non-Western and precapitalist societies, focusing on kinship and gender relations in particular. Between 1879 and 1882, Marx wrote over three hundred thousand words of notes, along with his own critical commentary, on the work of numerous anthropologists and other theoreticians. As Marxist scholar Kevin Anderson describes, Marx's notes covers "a wide range of societies and historical periods, including Indian history and village culture; Dutch colonialism and the village economy in Indonesia; gender and kinship patterns among Native Americans and in ancient Greece, Rome, and Ireland; and communal and private property in Algeria and Latin America."[20] Anderson also points to "the possibility that Marx's 1880–82 notebooks were concerned not so much with the origins of social hierarchy in the distant past as with the social relations within contemporary societies under the impact of globalization."[21]

Marxist humanist Raya Dunayevskaya argues of Marx's notebooks,

> What was new in these last writings from Marx's pen is that, on the one hand, he was returning to his first discovery of a new continent of thought when he singled out the Man/Woman relationship [in the *1844 Manuscripts*] as the most revealing of all relationships; and on the other hand, he was developing so new a concept of "revolution in permanence" that, in 1882, he was projecting something as startling as the possibility of revolution coming in backward lands ahead of the advanced countries.[22]

Marx was unable to develop these extensive notes into a written work before his death in 1883, and the scope of his final, ambitious project remained largely undiscovered for nearly a century afterward. Only in 1972 did ethnologist Lawrence Krader edit and transcribe *The Ethnological Notebooks of Karl Marx*, a book containing roughly half of Marx's notes in German.[23] Even then, as radical historian Frank Rosemont comments, "This last great work from Marx's pen has been largely ignored" even by "radical anthropologists."[24]

The Origin of the Family, Private Property and the State

After Marx's death, Frederick Engels sought to develop a theoretical analysis based upon some of his notebooks, along with his own ideas, resulting in the 1884 publication of *The Origin of the Family, Private Property and the State*. Engels seems to have felt a particular urgency to publish this book quickly, and it appeared less than eighteen months after Marx's death. Engels did not claim that his book provided the final word on the subject of human social development. On the contrary, he described his effort as "executing a bequest," and stated in the preface to the first edition, "My work can offer only a meager substitute for that which my departed friend was not destined to accomplish."[25]

In *Origin of the Family*, Engels explores the rise of private property and its social ramifications. As the title implies, Engels connects the rise of class society both with the rise of individual family units (in the form of the classic "patriarchal" family[26]), as the means by which propertied classes possess and pass on private wealth, and also with the rise of the state, representing the interests of the ruling class in the day-to-day running of societies. Engels argues that the family developed first among property-owning families, but eventually this family form became an economic unit of society as a whole.

Engels used portions of Marx's ethnological notebooks in writing *Origin of the Family*—primarily those discussing the anthropological data of nineteenth-century anthropologist Lewis Henry Morgan's 560-page volume *Ancient Society*, published in 1877. Morgan's anthropological research was among the first materialist attempts to understand the evolution of human social organization. While much of Morgan's anthropological data is primitive and has since been discredited by advances in the field, a wealth of more recent anthropology has provided ample evidence to support a basic evolutionary progression of human society. As Marxist historian Hal Draper argued in 1970, "There is a myth, widely accepted among the half-informed, that Morgan's anthropological work is now simply 'outmoded,' like Ptolemaic astronomy, and is rejected by 'modern anthropologists'. . . in this respect Darwin and Newton are outmoded as well."[27]

Morgan discovered, through extensive interaction with Iroquois tribes in upstate New York, a kinship system of a completely different form than the modern family form. Within this kinship system, Iroquois people lived in relative equality, and women exercised substantial authority. This discovery inspired Morgan to study other societies and, in so doing, he learned that other Native American cultures located thousands of miles from the Iroquois had remarkably similar kinship structures. This led him to argue that human society had evolved through successive stages, based upon the development of the "successive arts of subsistence."[28]

The *Origin of the Family*'s themes also borrow heavily from Swiss scholar Johan Jakob Bachofen's book *Das Mutterrecht*, published in 1861. Bachofen postulated that group marriage and tracking matrilineal descent preceded monogamy and patrilineal descent in human evolution. Engels adopted Bachofen's term "mother right," (*Mutterrecht*) to describe women's role in early matrilineal kinship systems, in which descent was traced through the mother.[29]

Engels ties the rise of the family directly to the rise of women's oppression. As he argues, the "modern individual family is founded on the open or concealed domestic slavery of the wife, and modern society is a mass composed of these individual families as its molecules." By using the term "domestic slavery," Engels links women's subservient status to their unpaid household labor.

Engels's Foresight

In addition, Engels makes two insightful observations about the consequences of women's subservient status intrinsic to their role in the patriarchal family: 1) a sexual double standard that requires monogamy *for women only* and 2) the tolerance of domestic violence against women at the hands of their husbands.

Engels makes it clear that the development of the family form based upon strict monogamy has nothing to do with morality: "Marriage according to the bourgeois conception was a contract, a legal transaction, and the most important one of all because it disposed of two human beings, body and mind, for life." He quips, "And if strict monogamy is the height of all virtue, then the palm must go to the tapeworm, which has a complete set of male and female sexual organs in each of its 50 to 200 proglottides, or sections, and spends its whole life copulating in all its sections with itself."[30]

Moreover, he argues, the monogamous family ideal is based upon a fundamental hypocrisy. From its very beginning, the family has been stamped "with its specific character of monogamy for the woman only, but not for the man."[31] In the classic patriarchal families of Rome or Greece, women were legally restricted to monogamy while men were allowed to practice polygamy. Even after polygamy was legally abolished in most societies, men continued to enjoy greater sexual freedom. Acts of infidelity on the part of women, which Victorian society condemned in Engels's time (and for which contemporary capitalist society still holds a double standard), are "considered honorable in a man, or, at the worst, a slight moral blemish which he cheerfully bears."[32]

Thus, Engels concludes of monogamous marriage: "It was not in any way the fruit of individual sex love, with which it had nothing whatever to do; marriages remained as before marriages of convenience. It was the first form of the family to be based not on natural but on economic conditions—on the victory of private property over primitive, natural communal property."[33] Even then, the requirements of monogamous marriage have been in most societies more an ideal than a reality, even for women.

Though men and women are legally equally bound to practice strict monogamy, those of both genders have been known to violate this obligation. Again, infidelity among men is more acceptable: To this day, the prevailing ideology is that men are "naturally" inclined to desire multiple sex partners while women's biology makes them more content with just one. Nevertheless, as Engels observes, with the rise of the family, "adultery became an unavoidable social institution—denounced, severely penalized, but impossible to suppress."[34]

Engels argues that the frequency of sex between married men and unmarried women became institutionalized over time. It "flourishes in the most varied forms throughout the whole period of civilization and develops more and more into open prostitution."[35] Thus, side by side with the development of monogamous marriage grew the first commodification of sex in the form of prostitution—both products of class society. "With the rise of the inequality of property," he argues, "wage labor appears . . . and at the same time, as its necessary correlate, the professional prostitution of free women side by side with the forced surrender of the slave."[36]

Monogamy and prostitution are two sides of the same coin, or, in Engels's words, "monogamy and prostitution are indeed contradictions, but inseparable contradictions, poles of the same state of society."[37] This observation by Engels is extremely perceptive, for he could probably not have imagined, living in nineteenth-century Victorian England, the degree to which the sexual commodification of women would turn into a massive and highly profitable industry in the century that followed.

In *Origin of the Family* Engels also draws attention to the frequency with which women are on the receiving end of domestic violence within the family—long before the feminist movement of the late 1960s finally made this issue a centerpiece for theory and struggle. Engels describes the drastic decline of women's status as a consequence of the rise of the classic patriarchal family and the brutality that accompanied it, arguing that the rise of this new family form brought with it a degradation of women that was unknown in preclass societies. Describing male supremacy within the patriarchal family as "the world-historic defeat of the female sex," Engels writes,

> The man took command in the home also; the woman was degraded and reduced to servitude; she became the slave of his lust and a mere instrument for the production of children. . . . In order to make certain of the wife's fidelity and therefore the paternity of his children, she is deliv-

ered over unconditionally into the power of the husband; if he kills her, he is only exercising his rights."[38]

While in this passage Engels describes the classic patriarchal family norm, domestic violence is not an archaic product of the Middle Ages, as is all too evident today. On the contrary, the right of husbands to beat their wives was legally established by law in early capitalism and continued far beyond that era. In colonial America, husbands were allowed to beat their wives—but not on Sundays or after 8:00 p.m., to avoid disturbing the peace. Not until 1911 did all US states (except Mississippi) outlaw wife beating.

Until 1973, English law permitted husbands to restrain their wives if they attempted to leave. Fathers still "give away" their daughters to their new husbands in marriage ceremonies, and "marital" or "spousal" rape was not a crime within the US legal system until 1975. Until then, every state had a "marital exemption" that allowed a husband to legally force sexual intercourse upon his wife, presumably because this was considered a husband's "right" to demand and a wife's "duty" to accept. By 1993, thanks to the 1970s-era women's movement, all fifty US states and the District of Columbia had passed laws criminalizing marital rape. Despite this legal change, however, married women still find it very difficult to prosecute their husbands for rape—due to varying state laws that require a higher standard of "proof" (such as demonstrating injuries suffered) and tend to be far less punitive for perpetrators than in cases of stranger rape.[39]

The Limitations of *Origin of the Family*

At the same time that Engels offers these valuable insights, the process he describes above is highly unlikely to have taken place as a sudden and single "world historic defeat" of the female sex resulting from the rise of the patriarchal family. Marx's ethnological notebooks also make clear that Marx, while sharing much of Engels's framework, held a more dialectical view of this historical process. As political scientist Heather A. Brown describes,

> [Marx's] notes suggest that, for Marx, the development of class society and women's oppression are part of the same historical process, but in a somewhat different way than that described later by Engels. . . . For Marx, there had been no "world historic defeat of the female sex." The condition of women in society is and has varied. This is just as true of

the time before the introduction of patriarchy as in the period of patriarchy. Instead of seeing this development in a linear way, Marx appears to have been working out a dialectical history of these processes.[40]

Engels focused almost exclusively on the relative equality that existed prior to the rise of class societies, using Morgan's research. But the Iroquois cultures Morgan studied were advanced horticultural societies, in which warfare, slavery, female monogamy, and male polygamy were already social norms. While Iroquois women experienced relative equality compared with women in developed class societies, they were not actually the social equals of men.

As Brown remarks, "While Iroquois women certainly had more power than the women in Marx's own time, their position was not ideal, however." Brown quotes Marx's notes from Morgan's text: "The husbands demanded chastity of the wives under severe penalties [which the husband might inflict], but he did not admit the reciprocal obligation . . . polygamy [was] universally recognized as the right of males [although the practice was limited from inability to support the indulgence]."[41]

Marx's notebooks focuses not only on the relative equality of preclass societies but also on the contradictions that would eventually give way to the rise of class society and a new family form. Brown comments, "While primitive communal societies were theoretically based on the equality of all members, conquest, slavery and the beginning of the trade of goods illustrated another side to the clan, as well as the potential for dissolution."[42]

Marx uses Morgan's framework, in which the evolution of family forms begins with group, or *consanguine*, marriage, in which all brothers and sisters are married to each other, and then successively narrows due to increasing restrictions. In the next family form, the *punaluan*, all women are married to their sisters' husbands and all men are married to their brothers' wives. The final family form that preceded patriarchy was the *syndyasmian*, a pairing marriage but without exclusive living arrangements.

Marx's notes, quoted in Brown, describe that because these increasing marriage restrictions limited the number of eligible partners, "'wives became scarce in place of their former abundance.' . . . As the syndyasmian family 'began to appear and the punaluan groups to disappear . . . wives came to be sought by purchase and capture. While originating in the punaluan group,' the gentile organization burst the bounds of this, its birthplace."[43]

Brown observes, "Slavery begins in the clan with the taking of women and children as captives during war, or by purchasing women from other tribes. . . . Since men were primarily responsible for hunting, and these weapons could potentially be used to capture women as well, men likely gained additional power over their choice of a partner."[44]

Women were initially captured as wives, not slaves. As Marx writes, "In seeking wives, [men] did not confine themselves to their own, nor even [to] friendly tribes, [but] captured them by force from hostile tribes; hence Indian usage to spare the lives of female captives, while the males were put to death."[45] But later, as private property expanded—and the need for exploitable agricultural labor developed—men were captured and turned into slaves.

Marx's notes describe the process by which the road was progressively paved for the rise of both the patriarchal family form and the subordination of women—before the development of large-scale agriculture actually took place. As Marx concluded, "'Paternal authority . . . began to appear as a feeble influence in the syndyasmian family, and [it became] fully established under monogamy' while it 'passed beyond all bounds of reason' in the patriarchal family of the Roman type."[46] Thus, while both Marx and Engels describe the patriarchal family as enormously oppressive to women, Marx identifies the processes that were set in motion during the latter stages of primitive communism.

Marx also differs with Engels's view of the future prospects for the institution of monogamy. Despite Engels's scathing attack on enforced monogamy described above, he nevertheless guesses that socialism will bring with it a flowering of *monogamy*, in the form of "individual sex love"—albeit in conditions of equality, in which men join women in their exclusive commitment to each other.[47] Here, Engels seems to accept the Victorian morality of his time.

Engels idealizes monogamy elsewhere in the *Origin of the Family*, echoing Bachofen. Brown describes, "Engels takes nineteenth-century norms about women and applies them to the transition from group-marriage to the pairing family, arguing that women sought the institution of the pairing family to claim the 'right of chastity.'" Quoting Engels, she writes:

> Bachofen is also perfectly right when he consistently maintains that the transition from what he calls "hetaerism" or *Sumpfzeugung* to monogamy was brought about primarily through the women. The more the traditional sexual relations lost the naive primitive character of forest life, owing to the development of economic conditions with consequent undermining of the old communalism and growing density of the population, the more oppressive and humiliating must the woman have felt

them to be, and the greater their longing for chastity, of temporary or permanent marriage with one man only, as a way of release.[48]

In contrast to Engels, Marx does not assume that the monogamous family would survive class society. On the contrary, he writes in his notes (agreeing with Morgan),

> As the *monogamanian* family has improved greatly since the commencement of capitalism, and very sensibly in modern times, it must be supposable that it is still capable of further improvement until the equality of the sexes is attained. Should the *monogamanian* family in the distant future fail to answer the requirements of society, assuming the continuous progress of civilization, it is impossible to predict the nature of its successor.

Brown comments on this passage, "Marx emphasizes, through his use of underlining, the need and possibility for the 'equality of the sexes [to be] attained.'"[49]

The integration of some key conclusions found in Marx's ethnological notebooks has helped to advance our understanding of the processes involved in the rise of women's oppression. And Brown is undoubtedly correct in asserting, "Engels remains within a relatively deterministic and unilinear framework, whereas Marx's formulation allows for greater variety in outcomes and for a much greater degree of human agency, especially for women."[50] Marxist feminist Lise Vogel, moreover, analyzes the theoretical contradictions of Engels's preface, in which he argues,

> According to the materialist conception, the determining factor in history is, in the final instance, the production and reproduction of immediate life. This, again, is of a twofold character: on the one side, the production of the means of existence, of food, clothing and shelter and the tools necessary for that production; on the other side, the production of human beings themselves, the propagation of the species."[51]

This passage, taken at face value, provides a useful description of early human societies. At the same time, it can be interpreted that Engels is describing two separate social systems: one for production and another for reproduction.

Vogel argues that Engels's passage unintentionally presents what can be interpreted as a "dual systems" approach, in which "two powerful motors drive the development of history: the class struggle and the sex struggle."[52] In the 1970s, a wing of socialist feminists credited Engels's passage as validating a dual-systems methodology that distinguishes between two separate and parallel systems, "capitalism" and "patriarchy." Engels's approach was often viewed at the time as a departure from

Marx's emphasis on the economic base (relations of production) versus the superstructure (social and political institutions, including kinship and family relations, which uphold the economic base). These necessary criticisms do not diminish Engels's profound contribution, which I hope to demonstrate below. Taken together, Marx and Engels provide a broad theoretical framework that locates the source of women's oppression primarily in their reproductive role within the family and the family's role as an economic unit in class society.

In order to fully appreciate the pathbreaking contribution of Marx and Engels's work, it is only necessary to realize that Charles Darwin had laid out his theory of human evolution just two decades before Engels wrote his book—first with the publication of *Origin of Species* in 1859, followed by *Descent of Man* in 1871. The first early human skeletal remains had only been discovered in 1856![53] Marx and Engels's theoretical framework, outlined below and corrected when necessary using more recent research, continues to provide a broad understanding of the crucial connection between class society and women's oppression.

The Evolution of Human Society

The strength of the Marxist method lies in its materialist approach and its dialectical understanding of human history—an understanding that human beings are both products of the natural world and at the same time, producers, who, in the process of interacting with their natural surroundings, change themselves and the world around them.

It is true that there are some aspects of early human societies that we will never know about because there are no written records. Nevertheless, by studying tools, bones, and other fossils, it is possible to see what distinguished our human ancestors from apes. In the first instance, it was humans' ability to plan their actions in order to gain greater control over their natural environment. This enabled them to eke out a means of subsistence in a wider range of climates and circumstances, eventually enabling them to spread all over the world.

Marxist Chris Harman argues that apes "are genetically programmed in narrow ways that provide them with the behavior appropriate to a limited range of environments." In contrast, humans possess an immense flexibility in behavior

> that enables us, virtually alone in the animal world, to thrive on any part
> of the globe. . . . So gorillas are not to be found outside tropical rain

forests, chimps outside wooded regions in sub-Saharan Africa, gibbons outside the tree tops of Southeast Asia, orangutans outside a few islands in Indonesia; by contrast, humans have been able to live across a vast swath of Africa, Europe, and Asia for at least half a million years. Our genetic "specialty" is precisely that we are not specialized, not constrained by any limited range of instinctive behavior.[54]

In order to survive in different environments, humans were required to plan hunting, building shelter, and other activities. These necessitated coordination and communication, which led to the development of the larynx and the possibility for verbal communication. Toolmaking required manual dexterity and intelligence, which led to the development of the hand and the enlargement of the brain. In his unfinished article, "The Part Played by Labor in the Transition from Ape to Man," Engels writes, "Thus, the hand is not only the organ of labor, it is also the product of labor."[55]

Human anatomy thus evolved according to the needs of the labor process. But in turn, the evolution of the human anatomy helped to advance labor processes further still, leading to improvements in both the tools used to master the environment and also to more complex forms of communication. As Engels puts it, "In a sense, we have to say that labor created man himself."[56] This same course of development applies to human society as a whole.

Before class society, the idea of a strictly monogamous pairing of males and females living with their offspring—the nuclear family—was unknown to humans. For more than a hundred thousand years, humans lived in groups made up of people who were mostly related by blood, knowing only who their mothers were, in conditions of relative equality. Using Morgan's framework, Engels outlines three distinct periods, each a progressive stage of social development. Like Morgan, Engels called them "savagery, barbarism, and civilization," reflecting the terminology of the Victorian period. The names have changed since then, but the basic outline remains valid: the stage he calls "savagery" refers to hunter-gatherer or foraging societies; "barbarism" is a stage in which agriculture predominated, first with "slash-and-burn" agriculture or horticulture and later using advanced techniques, such as plowing and large-scale irrigation; "civilization" is a term still used, which refers to the development of urban society and the beginnings of industry. Morgan's research helped support Marx and Engels's long-held contention that a long period of "primitive communism" preceded class society, but it also helped to clarify how women's oppression developed with the rise of class society. Morgan's study of the Iroquois showed two things: 1) Iroquois women and men had a rigid division of labor between the sexes and 2) women not only held autonomy over their own responsibilities but also considerable decision-making power within society as a whole.

The earliest evidence for the egalitarianism common in Native American cultures came largely from an unlikely source: seventeenth- and eighteenth-century Jesuit missionaries who kept written records of their encounters with the Montagnais-Naskapi of Eastern Canada. The Jesuits were generally appalled by the egalitarianism and sexual freedom common among the Montagnais-Naskapi. As one missionary reported, "I told him that it was not honorable for a woman to love anyone else except her husband, and that, this evil being among them, he himself was not sure that his son, who was there present, was his son." But the Naskapi were equally appalled by the Jesuit's comments. The man replied, "Thou hast no sense. You French people love only your own children; but we love all the children of our tribe."[57]

The Jesuits recorded their disbelief at the fact that the Naskapi neither had, nor apparently desired, a social hierarchy. Father Paul Le Jeune, writing in 1634, wrote: They "cannot endure in the least those who seem desirous of assuming superiority over the others; they place all virtue in a certain gentleness or apathy." Le Jeune and other missionaries set out, of course, to change this state of affairs. "Alas," he complained, "if someone could stop the wanderings of the savages, and give authority to one of them to rule the others, we could see them converted and civilized in a short time." But the obstacles were many. "As they have neither political organization, nor offices, nor dignities, nor any authority, for they only obey their chief through good will toward him, therefore they never kill each other to acquire these honors. Also, as they are contented with a mere living, not one of them gives himself to the Devil to acquire wealth."[58]

In Iroquois societies, women elders participated in the deliberations of the decision-making council. As one nineteenth-century observer noted: "They exercised a negative, or what we call a veto power, in the important question of the declaration of war. They had the right also to interpose in bringing about a peace."

Feminist anthropologist Judith Brown argues that because women controlled the planting and cultivating in Iroquois societies, they commanded a great deal of authority, even over men's activities:

> It was not only in the domestic realm that the matrons controlled the dispensing of food. By supplying the essential provisions for male activi-

ties—the hunt, the warpath, and the Council—they were able to control these to some degree. Thus Randle writes, "Indirectly, too, it is stated that the women could hinder or actually prevent a war party which lacked their approval by not giving the supplies of dried corn and the moccasins which the warriors required."[59]

Thus, women's role in production afforded them—women elders in particular—considerable political power within Iroquois society as a whole. More recent research has provided substantial data on other cultures indicating that, despite the commonality of a gender-based division of labor, women enjoyed relative equality with men in at least some pre-class societies. As Lerner argues,

> When feminist anthropologists have done their own fieldwork, they have found male dominance to be far from universal. They have found societies in which sexual asymmetry carries no connotation of dominance or subordination. Rather, the tasks performed by both sexes are indispensible to group survival, and both sexes are regarded as equal in status in most aspects. In such societies, the sexes are considered "complementary"; their roles and status are different—but equal.[60]

For example, anthropologist Patricia Draper's studies of !Kung bush people in the Kalahari Desert draw similar conclusions. Draper finds that in !Kung hunter-gatherer societies, women contributed equally, if not more, to the food supply. She describes the two sexes living in equality, noting, "Among the !Kung there is an extremely low level of cultural tolerance for aggressive behavior by anyone, male or female. In societies where aggressiveness and dominance are valued, these behaviors accrue disproportionately to males, and the females are common targets, resulting in the lowering of their status. !Kung women are not caught by this dimension of sex-role complementarity. They customarily maintain a mild manner, but so do their men."[61]

In a similar vein, Lepowsky, whose research on menstruation practices on the island of Vanatinai is described above, concludes, "On Vanatinai males are not dominant over females in either ideology or practice." She added, "This also challenges the assumption that male dominance, or sexual asymmetry, is universal and that only its form and intensity vary."[62]

The Rise of Agricultural (and Class) Society

Human evolution has taken place over a very long time. The earliest human ancestors (*Homo habilus*) probably appeared some two million or more years ago, while anatomically modern humans (*Homo sapiens*) appeared roughly 100,000 to 200,000 years ago. The earliest forms of agriculture began 10,000 years ago, and it is only over the last thousand years that human society has experienced much more rapid technological development.[63]

For most of human history, it would have been impossible to accumulate wealth and there likely would not have been much motivation to do so. For one thing, there would have been no place to store it. People lived first in nomadic bands—hunter-gatherer societies—sustaining themselves by some combination of gathering berries, roots, and other vegetable growth, and hunting or fishing. They produced what they could immediately consume. In most such societies, there would have been no point in working more than the hours per day it took to produce what was necessary for subsistence. But even among the first societies to advance to horticulture, it wasn't really possible to produce much more than what was to be immediately consumed by members of the band.

With the onset of more advanced agricultural production—through the use of the plow and/or advanced methods of irrigation—and the beginnings of settled communities, in some societies human beings were able to extract more than the means of subsistence from the environment. This led to the first accumulation of surplus, or wealth. As Engels argues in *Origin of the Family*: "Above all, we now meet the first iron plowshare drawn by cattle, which made large-scale agriculture, the cultivation of fields, possible and thus created a practically unrestricted food supply in comparison with previous conditions."[64] This marked a turning point in human society, for it meant that, over time, production for use could be replaced by production for exchange and eventually for profit—leading to the rise of the first class societies some six thousand years ago (first in Mesopotamia, followed a few hundred years later by Egypt, Iran, the Indus Valley, and China).[65]

Engels argues that the rise of class society brought with it rising inequality—between the rulers and the ruled, and between men and women. At first the surplus was shared with the entire clan, so no one individual or group of individuals accumulated wealth. But gradually, as settled communities grew in size and became more complex social organizations, and most importantly, as the surplus grew, the distribution of wealth became unequal—and a small number of men rose above the rest of the population in wealth and power.

The crux of Engels's theory of women's oppression rests on the relationship between the gendered division of labor and the mode of production, which underwent a fundamental transformation with the onset of agricultural production. In hunter-gatherer and early horticultural societies, there was a gender-based division of labor, involving rigidly defined sets of responsibilities for women and men. But both sexes were allowed a high degree of autonomy in performing those tasks. Moreover—and this is an element that has been learned since Engels's time—women not only provided food for the band in hunter-gatherer societies but also, in many cases, provided most of the food.[66]

Women in preclass societies were able to combine motherhood and productive labor, as there was no strict demarcation between reproductive and productive activities. Women could in many cases carry small children with them while they gathered or planted, or leave the children behind with other adults for a few hours at a time. Likewise, many goods could be produced in the household. This arrangement was upended over time by the development of settled agriculture. Men had traditionally taken charge of big game hunting, so it made sense for them to oversee the domestication of cattle. Likewise, men tended to take on heavier agricultural jobs, like plowing, since it was more difficult for pregnant or nursing women and might endanger small children being carried along. Engels argued that the domestication of cattle preceded the use of the plow in agriculture, although it is now accepted that these two processes developed at the same time. Nevertheless, his explanation as to why control over cattle fell to men is convincing.

The Sexual Division of Labor and Gender Inequality in Early Class Societies

As production shifted away from the household, the role of reproduction changed substantially. Technological advances in agricultural production sharply increased the productivity of labor. This, in turn, increased the demand for labor: The greater the number of field workers, the higher the surplus. Thus, unlike hunter-gatherer societies, which sought to limit the number of offspring, agricultural societies sought to maximize women's reproductive potential, so the family would have more children to help out in the fields. Therefore, at the same time that men were playing an increasingly exclusive role in production, women were required to play a much more central role in reproduction.

The gendered division of labor remained the same, but production shifted away from the household in property-holding families. The family came to serve a primarily reproductive function in this rising ruling class—and as such, it became an economic unit of consumption. These women became much more confined by their role as the biological reproducers of children, increasingly cut off from playing a key role in production. Although these changes took place first among the property-owning families, eventually, the family became an economic unit of society as a whole—even among women who continued to participate in agricultural production. It is important to understand that these changes did not take place overnight, but over a period of many centuries. Moreover, greed was not responsible in the first instance for the unequal distribution of wealth. Nor was male chauvinism the reason power fell into the hands of (some) men while the status of women fell dramatically. There is no evidence that men coerced women into their gendered role in the family. As Lerner comments, "I have tried to show how it might have come to pass that women agreed to a sexual division of labor, which would eventually disadvantage them, without having been able to foresee the later consequences."[67]

For property-owning families in an agricultural society, a larger surplus would have been in the interest of all household members. Engels says of the first male "property owners" of domesticated cattle, "What is certain is that we must not think of him as a property owner in the modern sense of the word." He owned his cattle in the same sense that he owned the other tools required to obtain food and other necessities. But "the family did not multiply so rapidly as the cattle."[68] Agricultural output also increased sharply—some of which needed to be stored to feed the community in case of a poor harvest, and some of which could be traded for other goods.

Obviously, every society across the globe did not experience an identical succession of changes in the mode of production. Nor do changes in the mode of production automatically lead to precise changes in the sphere of reproduction. Engels's personal knowledge was vast but limited to Germany and classical Mediterranean and Asian societies. He relied primarily on Morgan's data to evaluate non-Eurasian societies. But since Engels's time, as Leacock maintains, "Archeological researches have yielded an undeniable picture of [hu]mankind's development from 'savage' hunters to 'barbarian' agriculturists and finally to 'civilizations' of the Ancient East."[69] Likewise, Harman writes, "The exact route from hunter-gathering through horticulture and agriculture to civilization did vary considerably from one society to another." But

> the divergent forms under which class society emerged must not make us forget the enormous similarities from society to society. Everywhere there was, in the beginning, primitive communism. Everywhere, once settled agricultural societies were formed, some lineages, lineage elders, or "big men" could begin to gain prestige through their role in undertaking the redistribution of the little surplus that existed in the interests of the group as a whole. Everywhere, as the surplus grew, this small section of society came to control a greater share of the social wealth, putting it in a position where it could begin to crystallize out into a social class.[70]

The old communal forms of organization weren't transformed overnight, nor were they transformed uniformly from one society to the next. But as Coontz and Henderson note, "Chiefs were traditionally expected to give more than they received. . . . They were also expected to work harder than anyone else, all in return for an amorphous prestige that gave them no control over the lives of others aside from that they exerted through their persuasive powers."[71] They add, "Wealth produced at the lowest level appears to be the 'work of the gods,'" and those accruing wealth commonly gained a reputation as closer to the gods:

> By the egalitarian principles of reciprocity, such wealth, given by the ancestors/gods to a local lineage, must be redistributed through feasting. But if one or another lineage consistently feasts the rest of the community, it acquires quite naturally a reputation for special proximity to the ancestors and to the supernatural. . . . The leading lineage, then, feasts the community and, by the rules of reciprocity, gains back more gifts and bridewealth from the rest of the community. . . . More and more of the surplus flows to the leading lineage, and when other groups cannot repay the lineage's circulation of that surplus they begin to pledge labor instead.[72]

Gift giving was traditionally an egalitarian form of mutual exchange. But if the gift giver becomes wealthy while the receiver is without property, it eventually becomes impossible for the receiver to reciprocate. In such conditions, the gift giver can easily become an exploiter or a tax collector. A chief who wields little or no authority in a foraging band can later turn into a priest or a bureaucrat standing over the rest of society once classes emerge. And a man who owns a few heads of cattle or a fertile patch of land can, under the right conditions, become a wealthy and powerful landlord.

The Rise of the Family and the Oppression of Women

It was under these circumstances that the family began to take form. Its primary purpose was to establish ownership and inheritance of private property from one generation to the next. Feminist anthropologist Karen Sacks summarizes the impact of private property on women's overall standing in society as follows:

> Private property transformed the relations between men and women within the household only because it also radically changed the political and economic relations in the larger *society*. For Engels the new wealth in domesticated animals meant that there was a surplus of goods available for exchange between productive units. With time, production by men specifically for exchange purposes developed, expanded, and came to overshadow the household's production for use. . . . As production of exchange eclipsed production for use, it changed the nature of the household, the significance of women's work within it, and consequently women's position in society.[73]

Engels understood the hypocrisy of ruling-class marriage and the degradation of women that came with it. In *Origin of the Family*, he describes ruling-class marriage as typically "a conjugal partnership of leaden boredom, known as 'domestic bliss.'"[74] Using Marx's notes, Engels also traces the rise of the family as a property relationship from the meaning of the term *family* in the Roman Empire:

> The original meaning of the word "family" (*familia*) is not the compound of sentimentality and domestic strife which forms the ideal of the present-day philistine; among the Romans it did not at first even refer to the married pair and their children but only to the slaves. *Famulus* means domestic slave, and *familia* is the total number of slaves belonging to one man. As late as the time of Gaius, the *familia, id est patrimonium* (family, that is the patrimony, the inheritance) was bequeathed by will. The term was invented by the Romans to denote a new social organism whose head ruled over wife and children and a number of slaves, and was invested under Roman paternal power with rights of life and death over them all.[75]

Engels adds, quoting Marx, "The modern family contains in germ not only slavery (*servitus*) but also serfdom, since from the beginning it is related to agricultural services. It contains in miniature all the contradictions which later extend throughout society and its state."[76] That the emergence of this new family form was a consequence of class society is central to Engels's argument.

Leacock describes how the rise of the modern family developed in response to the needs of a rising class society:

> The separation of the family from the clan and the institution of monogamous marriage were the social expressions of developing private property; so-called monogamy afforded the means through which property could be individually inherited. And private property for some meant no property for others, or the emerging of differing relations to production on the part of different social groups. The core of Engels's formulation lies in the intimate connection between the emergence of the family as an economic unit dominated by the male and this development of classes.[77]

Without strict monogamy, a property-holding man could not be certain that his wife's children were also his own and that his wealth would be passed on to his biological children. Engels writes, "Thus, on the one hand, in proportion as wealth increased it made the man's position in the family more important than the woman's, and on the other hand created an impulse to exploit this strengthened position in order to overthrow, in favor of his children, the traditional order of inheritance. . . . Mother right, therefore, had to be overthrown, and overthrown it was."[78]

Here, Engels overstates both the dominance of matrilineal descent ("mother right") in all preclass societies and also its significance in determining women's status in society. It is true that Iroquois societies tended to be matrilineal. But Engels wrongly concluded that this necessarily meant that all horticultural societies must also have been matrilineal. As Lerner observed using more recent research, while early hunter-gatherer societies tended to be matrilineal, "in the horticultural societies studied, most are patrilineal, despite women's decisive economic role." But, Lerner adds, "Patrilineal descent does not imply subjugation of women nor does matrilineal descent indicate matriarchy."[79]

Thus, it is likely that matrilineal descent gave way to patrilineal descent earlier than Engels (and Morgan) realized. What is indisputable, however, is that class society eventually produced a near-universal shift to patrilineage—and the prescribed role of men as "heads" of their households. Most importantly, Engels correctly understands that this shift corresponded to the systematic oppression of women.

The sexual division of labor that existed in preclass societies, when production for use was the dominant mode of production, carried no necessary implication of gender inequality. Women were able to combine their reproductive and productive roles, so both sexes were able to perform productive labor. But with the rise of class society, when production for exchange began to dominate, the sexual division of labor helped to erode equality between the sexes. Production and trade increasingly occurred away from the household, so that the household became a sphere primarily for reproduction.

As Coontz and Henderson argue,

> The increasing need for redistribution (both within local groups and between them) and the political tasks this creates have consequences for sex roles in that these political roles are often filled by males, even in matrilineal/matrilocal societies. Presumably this flows from the division of labor that associates males with long-distance activities, external affairs, and products requiring group-wide distribution, while females are more occupied with daily productive tasks from which they cannot be absented.[80]

This began the development of a "public" versus a "private" sphere in property-holding families, with women increasingly trapped in the household. The rise of the family itself explains women's subordinate role within it. For the first time in human history, women's ability to give birth kept them from playing a significant part in production. Indeed, Lerner concludes,

> In the course of the agricultural revolution the exploitation of human labor and the sexual exploitation of women become inextricably linked. . . . Sometime during the agricultural revolution relatively egalitarian societies with a sexual division of labor based on biological necessity gave way to more highly structured societies in which both private property and the exchange of women based on incest taboos and exogamy were common. The earlier societies were both matrilineal and matrilocal, while the latter surviving societies were predominantly patrilineal and patrilocal. Nowhere is there any evidence of a reverse process, going from patriliny to matriliny. The more complex societies featured a division of labor no longer based only on biological distinctions, but also on hierarchy and the power of some men over other men and all women.[81]

Women's Oppression under Capitalism

Marx and Engels no doubt would have marveled at the many ways in which women's lives have changed and advanced over the last century. In the United States today, women make up half the labor force and men do more domestic labor than they did decades ago. Moreover, technology has advanced so that the time spent on household chores, like laundry, has been reduced to a fraction of what it was in Marx and Engels's time. Store-bought prepared foods make it possible for women to spend less time cooking. Public schooling means that the time women spend on childrearing is greatly reduced from the days when many women with young children barely left the home.

Yet, despite all these changes, women are still oppressed. Women's wages are markedly lower than men's throughout the world. Sexual harassment is a well-documented problem for women workers. Substantial numbers of women still suffer from rape and domestic violence. Massive profits are made each year not only from pornography, but even more so through the sexual objectification of women in advertising and throughout the mass media. And, although most women hold jobs outside the home, society still holds them responsible for the bulk of childrearing and housework.

The fundamentals of Engels's analysis of women's oppression still hold. He locates the source of women's oppression as stemming primarily from their reproductive role within the family and the family's role as an economic unit in society. Moreover, he takes note of the "double burden" of paid labor and unpaid domestic labor carried by working-class women in the following passage:

> In the old communistic household, which comprised many couples and their children, the task entrusted to women of managing the household was as much a public, a socially necessary industry as the procuring of food by the men. With the patriarchal family and still more with the single monogamous family, a change came. Household management lost its public character. It no longer concerned society. It became a private service; the wife became the head servant, excluded from all participation in social production. Not until the coming of modern large-scale industry was the road to social production opened to her again—and then, only to the proletarian wife. *But it was opened in such a manner that, if she carries out her duties in the private service of her family, she remains excluded from public production and unable to earn; and if she wants to take part in public production and earn independently, she cannot carry out family duties.* . . . The modern individual family is founded on the open or concealed domestic slavery of the wife, and modern society is a mass composed of these individual families as its molecules.[82] (Emphasis added.)

Engels's insight is profound. At the same time, his analysis of the family does not sufficiently address the class differences between women in modern capitalism. Even in Engels's time, a staff of servants relieved wealthy women of many of the domestic tasks necessary for reproduction, while boredom and a sense of uselessness traditionally characterized their oppression. Ruling-class women tended to be little more than showpieces, whose main social contribution was considered to be the birth of a son to inherit the family's wealth.

Moreover, Engels vastly underestimates the extent to which middle- and ruling-class women would enter into professional and managerial careers in the last century, and even more so in the last few decades. Women in the upper echelons of corporate management and women political leaders do often encounter sexist attitudes and a "glass ceiling," but they also wield considerable class and social power in their own right. Their situation is therefore far more complex than Engels foresaw, since they face oppression as women yet also play a role in the system of exploitation.

More importantly from a theoretical standpoint, neither Marx nor Engels fully anticipated the degree to which capitalism would manage to incorporate working-class women into the labor force without diminishing their centrality to the reproduction of labor power. This is certainly understandable, since women only began to enter the workforce on a mass scale in the twentieth century, when the development of reliable birth control made it possible to limit childbearing.

Finally, Engels also held an almost romantic vision of the proletarian household, as if the lack of property removed the basis for working-class women's oppression inside the family:

> Here there is no property, for the preservation and inheritance of which monogamy and male supremacy were established; hence there is no incentive to make this male supremacy effective. What is more, there are no means of making it so. Bourgeois law, which protects this supremacy, exists only for the possessing class and their dealings with the proletarians.... And now that large-scale industry has taken the wife out of the home onto the labor market and into the factory ... no basis for any kind of male supremacy is left in the proletarian household, except, perhaps, for something of the brutality toward women that has spread since the introduction of monogamy.[83]

This passage, besides dismissing the importance of the "brutality" suffered by women in working-class households, also greatly overestimates the degree to which their participation in "large-scale industry" raised their social status, as if they suffered less severe oppression than women in property-holding families.

But the oppression experienced by working-class women is far more severe than that of wealthy women precisely because their families have no property. (This was undoubtedly also true in Engels's day.) The difference is not only one of degree. Although all nuclear families remain centers for privatized reproduction, *ruling-class families exist to reproduce the next ruling class, while working-class families reproduce generations of workers.* Thus, the very character of the oppression suffered by women of different classes is also quite different. As Vogel remarks,

> While Engels underscores the simultaneous emergence of sex and class conflict, he never achieves a clear picture of their connection. The two developments remain historically parallel phenomena, whose theoretical relationship is best characterized as one of autonomy. For the propertied family, women's oppression has its source in the husband's need to preserve and transmit his private property. Obviously, the absence of private property should be accompanied by an absence of sex conflict. In fact, as Engels is forced to acknowledge, women occupy a subordinate place in property-less households. Engels offers no theoretical basis for this historic oppression, although the preface's concept of systematic "production of human beings themselves" hints obliquely at a distinct mechanism.[84]

Since Engels's time, the lives of working-class women have changed, but they have not improved in any fundamental way. Capitalists still take precious little responsibility for the legion of workers whose labor produces their profits. The consistent lack of affordable childcare and the drastic cuts in public education have only increased this burden on working-class families. As Marxist feminist Martha Gimenez argues, "The class that controls the means of production also controls the conditions for the physical and social reproduction of the property-less classes and sets the parameters within which the empirically observable forms of sexual inequality develop and change."[85]

The responsibility for the reproduction of labor power still lies primarily with the working-class family, enabling today's generation of workers to replenish themselves so they can return to their jobs each day while also rearing the next generation of workers through childhood. The working-class family thus remains the preferred means for reproducing labor power by those who own and control the capitalist system.

The large-scale entry of women into the labor force hasn't changed that fact. Engels understood that working-class women who hold jobs are nevertheless also expected to fulfill their family duties. But while Engels implied that working women would have to make a choice between the two roles, the experience of advanced capitalism has proven otherwise. Working-class women are expected to do both. The result is that working-class women return home at the end of each workday only to face all their family responsibilities. Each day is a never-ending battle to fulfill both sets of responsibilities.

Women's participation in the labor force in advanced capitalism has allowed for greater financial independence, making it possible to leave unhappy marriages—leading to the prevalence of divorce and single parenting. The importance of this relative independence should not be underestimated, even if single-parent households headed by women are far more likely to live in poverty. It is also the case, however, that women in single-parent households bear an even heavier burden in fulfilling their responsibilities as workers and mothers. Thus, although women play a productive role in advanced capitalism, this alone hasn't translated into greater equality with men as it did in preclass societies.

Engels makes clear that women's liberation requires supplanting privatized reproduction with the socialization of domestic labor—which in turn requires a socialist transformation of society. Only then can the material conditions be created, with far-reaching social ramifications that will make it possible for women to win genuine equality:

> With the transfer of the means of production into common ownership, the single family ceases to be the economic unit of society. Private housekeeping is transformed into a social industry. The care and education of the children becomes a public affair; society looks after all children alike, whether they are legitimate or not. . . . Will not that suffice to bring about the gradual growth of unconstrained sexual intercourse and with it a more tolerant public opinion in regard to a maiden's honor and a woman's shame? And finally. . . . Can prostitution disappear without dragging monogamy with it into the abyss?[86]

Engels incorporated many aspects of women's oppression—including domestic abuse, the alienation of sexuality, the commodification of sex, the drudgery of housework, and the hypocrisy of enforced monogamy—into his analysis. And most importantly, he emphasized the inequality among those performing gendered roles within the family. Moreover, he did so in the Victorian era, when such ideas were far less common than they have become in the aftermath of the modern women's liberation movement.

Indeed, while Marx and Engels's analysis of the nuclear family does not include its relationship to LGBT (lesbian, gay, bisexual, transgender) oppression, they nevertheless provide a framework that more recent theorists have used to do so. These theorists have located the roots of LGBT oppression in the imposition of the rigid heterosexual norms that accompany the nuclear-family ideal.[87]

Despite the historical constraints of his own era, Engels put forward a vision of the future that should inspire all those seeking a world without sexual oppression of any kind:

> What we can now conjecture about the way in which sexual relations will be ordered after the impending overthrow of capitalist production is mainly of a negative character, limited for the most part to what will disappear. But what will there be new? That will be answered when a new generation has grown up: a generation of men who never in their lives have known what it is to buy a woman's surrender with money or any other social instrument of power; a generation of women who have never known what it is to give themselves to a man from any other considerations than real love or to refuse to give themselves to their lover from fear of the economic consequences. When these people are in the world, they will care precious little what anybody today thinks they ought to do; they will make their own practice and their corresponding public opinion about the practice of each individual—and that will be the end of it.[88]

Chapter Three

Modern Women's Movements

*Those of us who are poor, who are lesbians, who are black, who are older,
know that survival is not an academic skill. It is learning how to stand
alone, unpopular and sometimes reviled, and how to make common cause
with those other identified as outside the structures, in order to define and
seek a world in which we can all flourish. . . . For the master's tools will
never dismantle the master's house. They may allow us to temporarily beat
him at his own game, but they will never enable us to bring about genuine
change. And this fact is only threatening to those women who still define the
master's house as their only source of support.*

—Audre Lorde[1]

In the 1960s, conditions were ripe for a movement to fight for women's
rights. Women encountered legal and social inequality in virtually every
sphere of life. In 1963, the President's Commission on the Status of
Women reported that in many states, a wife has "no legal rights to any
part of her husband's earnings or property during the existence of the
marriage, aside from a right to be properly supported."[2] Women were
expected to surrender their surnames upon marriage and could not obtain credit cards without their husbands' written permission. Upon divorce, homemakers in most states in 1963 were also denied any rights to
share in the husband's income during the years they had been married.[3]

The "help wanted" section of newspapers typically noted which
jobs were intended for men (such as "heavy manufacturing" or "managerial" positions) and for women (low-paid "clerical" or "light industrial" work). Many of the wanted ads for females included descriptions
such as "pretty" and "attractive" as job requirements. Open racism was
also on display in some ads for domestic labor placed by white, middle-class families. One such ad sought, for example, a servant who was
"White, well-experienced." Meanwhile, ads from firms such as the

"Miss Dixie Employment Agency" offered to provide Northern families with a supply of "dependable" (and presumably Black) live-in domestic helpers.[4]

This outrageous level of discrimination extended to the treatment of women who filed charges of rape in this era. Twentieth-century legal standards espoused standards of "proof" that assumed women who filed rape charges claimed to have said "no" when they actually meant "yes": The *Yale Law Journal* argued in 1952,

> When her behavior looks like resistance although her attitude is one of consent, injustice may be done the man by the woman's subsequent accusation. Many women, for example, require as a part of preliminary "love play" aggressive overtures by the man. Often their erotic pleasure may be enhanced by, or even depend upon, an accompanying physical struggle. The "love bite" is a common, if mild, sign of the aggressive component in the sex act. And the tangible signs of struggle may survive to support a subsequent accusation by the woman.[5]

Nearly fifteen years later, the same approach remained intact. As the *Stanford Law Review* claimed in 1966,

> Although a woman may desire sexual intercourse, it is customary for her to say, "no, no, no" (although meaning "yes, yes, yes") and to expect the male to be the aggressor. . . . It is always difficult in rape cases to determine whether the female really meant "no." . . . The problem of determining what the female "really meant" is compounded when, in fact, the female had no clearly determined attitude—that is, her attitude was one of ambivalence. . . . Furthermore, a woman may note a man's brutal nature and be attracted to him rather than repulsed.[6]

Abortion, which remained illegal until 1973, was out of reach for the vast majority of US women. Those who were desperate to end an unwanted pregnancy were often forced to risk their lives in illegal "back-alley" abortions, then fear arrest if complications arose and they needed emergency hospitalization. The death toll during this time is unknown, but the number is certainly large. A University of Colorado study done in the late 1950s reported that three hundred and fifty thousand women experienced postoperative complications each year from illegal abortions in the United States.[7]

Because of both the economic and social consequences of racism, the lives of Black women, Latinas, and other racially oppressed working-class women were most at risk when abortion was illegal. Before abortion was legalized in 1973 in the United States, Black women and

Latinas made up the majority of the five thousand abortion-related deaths per year.[8]

But reliable contraception was also out of reach for millions of women during the 1960s. Until 1965, thirty states still outlawed or restricted the right even for married couples to use birth control. In the early 1970s, many states required married women to get their husbands' permission to use contraception. And only in 1972 did the Supreme Court finally strike down a Massachusetts law making it illegal to distribute birth control to unmarried people.[9]

Throughout the 1950s and early 1960s, a host of "experts" persistently disseminated opinions assuming women's natural destiny could only be fulfilled in their role as wives and mothers. As such, all white, middle-class women were expected to prioritize their commitment, first, to obtaining a husband, followed immediately by uninterrupted devotion to their husband and children. Betty Friedan's widely acclaimed *The Feminine Mystique*, published in 1963, quotes a typical report from a marketing firm with its patronizing view of the average housewife:

> She "finds in housework a medium of expression for femininity and individuality." . . . She still feels "lazy, neglectful, haunted by guilt feelings" because she doesn't have enough work to do. The advertiser must manipulate her need for "a feeling of creativeness" into the buying of his product. . . . "Creativeness is the modern woman's dialectical answer to the problem of her changed position in the household. Thesis: I'm a housewife. Antithesis: I hate drudgery. Synthesis: I'm creative!" This means essentially that even though the housewife may buy canned food . . . she doesn't let it go at that. She has a great need for "doctoring up" the can and thus prove her personal participation and her concern with giving satisfaction to her family.[10]

Despite this ideological onslaught, the labor force participation rate for married women with young children grew dramatically after 1950. In 1950, only 12 percent of women with children under age six worked outside the home. That number doubled between 1950 and 1965, and then doubled again between 1965 and 1985. By 1988, over 57 percent of women with children under the age of six were participating in the labor force.[11]

Black women's labor force participation has been historically higher than white women's. In 1960, 47 percent of Black women were in the labor force, compared with 36 percent of white women. But the gap closed in the following decades. In 1970, 49 percent of Black women were in the labor force compared to 43 percent of white women. By

1987, Black women's labor force participation was 58 percent compared with 56 percent of white women's.[12]

The doors to higher education had finally opened to women on a large scale during the 1960s. The rate of female high-school graduates attending college nearly doubled, from 14.1 percent in 1947 to 26.3 percent in 1970.[13] Women college graduates' expectations soared, as they resumed that university educations would lead to higher-status professional careers. But most of those expectations went unfulfilled in that decade, as they entered the corporate world only to find new doors slammed in their faces.

In 1963, full-time women workers earned just 61 percent of men's earnings, while Black women earned just 43 percent. Moreover, women made up only about 15 percent of all managers in 1960.[14] In 1970, women numbered fewer than 8 percent of all physicians; in 1972, women made up only 3 percent of licensed attorneys.[15] Women professionals faced sexist and racist attitudes and limited opportunities for advancement—often referred to as "the glass ceiling" that kept the upper echelons of the corporate and political world overwhelmingly white and male.

The Role of Racism

At the same time, it is not the case that all men fared better than all women. On the contrary, in 1960, Black men earned just 55.5 percent of white men's salaries, and Black women (many trapped in paid domestic labor) earned just 60.5 percent of white women's. Black male college graduates—like their female counterparts—earned less than white male high school graduates in 1963.[16] Moreover, financial security eluded even Black families with middle-class incomes. As Stephanie Coontz observes,

> Black families with the same annual incomes as whites had, on average, only one-tenth as many assets, and they were far less likely to receive the kind of government aid that subsidized upward mobility for white families during the 1950s. In his study of the fight to integrate the Levittown suburbs of New York and Pennsylvania, David Kushner points out that of the $120 billion in new housing underwritten by the federal government between 1934 and 1960, less than 2 percent went to minorities.[17]

Added to that, the unemployment rate for African Americans, which has historically persisted at roughly double that of whites, is a constant feature of financial insecurity that plagues the Black working-class population to this day.

Furthermore, the same "experts" who prescribed a life of happy homemaking for white suburban women blamed Black women for their failure to conform to this model. Because Black mothers have traditionally worked outside the home in much larger numbers than their white counterparts, they were blamed for a range of social ills on the basis of their economic independence.

Coontz describes "Freudians and social scientists," among them African Americans, who "insisted that Black men had been doubly emasculated—first by slavery and later by the economic independence of their women." A 1960 *Ebony* magazine article stated plainly that the traditional independence of the Black woman meant that she was "more in conflict with her innate biological role than the white woman."[18]

This theme emerged at full throttle in 1965, when the US Department of Labor issued a report entitled "The Negro Family: The Case for National Action." The report, authored by future senator Daniel Patrick Moynihan, described a "Black matriarchy" at the center of a "tangle of pathology" afflicting Black families, leading to a cycle of poverty. "A fundamental fact of Negro American family life is the often reversed roles of husband and wife," in which Black women consistently earn more than their men, argued Moynihan.[19]

The report stated, "In essence, the Negro community has been forced into a matriarchal structure which, because it is to [*sic*] out of line with the rest of the American society, seriously retards the progress of the group as a whole." The report went on to explain why this was ostensibly the case:

> There is, presumably, no special reason why a society in which males are dominant in family relationships is to be preferred to a matriarchal arrangement. However, it is clearly a disadvantage for a minority group to be operating on one principle, while the great majority of the population, and the one with the most advantages to begin with, is operating on another. This is the present situation of the Negro. Ours is a society which presumes male leadership in private and public affairs. The arrangements of society facilitate such leadership and reward it. A subculture, such as that of the Negro American, in which this is not the pattern, is placed at a distinct disadvantage.[20]

For the reasons described above, gender discrimination cannot be effectively understood without factoring in the role of racism and racial segregation.

Racial Segregation

Indeed, the 1950s and 1960s was a period of intensive racial polarization in the United States, and a period of intensive struggle against
racism—as the massive civil rights movement struggled to end Jim
Crow segregation throughout the South and the de facto racial segregation of the North. Interracial marriage was still banned in sixteen states
until 1967, when the Supreme Court finally ruled that such bans were
unconstitutional in its *Loving v. Virginia* decision.

Urban rebellions swept the country from the early to late 1960s,
touched off by police brutality and other forms of racial discrimination
in poverty-stricken Black ghettoes. In 1967, the National Advisory
Commission on Civil Disorders, also known as the Kerner Commission,
was established to investigate the root causes of urban rebellions. In
1968, the commission issued a report that included a scathing indictment of racism and segregation in US society. The report concluded,

> Our nation is moving toward two societies, one black, one white—sepa-
> rate and unequal. . . . Segregation and poverty have created in the racial
> ghetto a destructive environment totally unknown to most white Amer-
> icans. What white Americans have never fully understood but what the
> Negro can never forget—is that white society is deeply implicated in the
> ghetto. White institutions created it, white institutions maintain it, and
> white society condones it.[21]

The Kerner Commission emphasized, "Frustrated hopes are the residue
of the unfulfilled expectations aroused by the great judicial and legislative
victories of the Civil Rights Movement and the dramatic struggle for
equal rights in the South." Much of the problem was rooted in "pervasive
discrimination and segregation in employment, education and housing,
which have resulted in the continuing exclusion of great numbers of Negroes from the benefits of economic progress."[22] The commission concluded that the degree of housing segregation was such that, "to create an
unsegregated population distribution, an average of over 86 percent of all
Negroes would have to change their place of residence within the city."[23]

Racial segregation is not an aberration from the past, but a constant
feature of US society that continues today. As Black feminist Patricia
Hill Collins describes, "Yet for African-American women, the effects of
institutionalized racism remain visible and palpable. Moreover, the institutionalized racism that African-American women encounter relies
heavily on racial segregation and accompanying discriminatory practices designed to deny US Blacks equitable treatment."[24] She adds,

"Most Black women do not have the opportunity to befriend White women and men as neighbors, nor do their children attend school with White children. Racial segregation remains a fundamental feature of the US social landscape, leaving many African-Americans with the belief that "the more things change, the more they stay the same."[25]

The Multiple Women's Movements of the 1960s and 1970s

The history of racial segregation in the United States has effectively prevented the development of a unified women's movement that recognizes the manifold implications of the historic racial divide. No movement can claim to speak for *all* women unless it speaks for women who also face the consequences of racism, which also place women of color overwhelmingly in the ranks of the working class and the poor. Race and class must be central to the project of women's liberation if it is to be meaningful to those women who are the most oppressed by the system.

The assertions above are not intended to belittle the very real oppression facing *all* women under capitalism. Nor are they meant to be "divisive," as some claim—as if acknowledging the differences that exist between women inevitably leads to separation, which it does not. On the contrary, they are a proposal for *inclusion*: the integration of the struggles against racism and against all forms of oppression and exploitation with the fight for women's liberation.

The history of the struggles for women's liberation in the 1960s is thus complex. The history presented here recognizes the consequences of the race and class divides that existed from the early phases of the modern women's movement—without disparaging the importance of the struggles for women's liberation that have benefited all women and influenced mass consciousness in lasting and fundamental ways.

Indeed, the achievements of the women's liberation movement of the 1960s and 1970s were enormous, articulating a vast range of preconditions for women's liberation. These included: 1) women's right to choose their own reproductive destinies; 2) freedom from sexual objectification, with all its dehumanizing and violent trappings; 3) rejection of rigid gender roles and women's second-class citizenship in traditional marriage and in society at large; and 4) equal opportunity in the workplace and in higher education. But the demands above do not mean the same things to all women as a single group. Unfortunately, there was no single women's movement that represented the interests of all women in the

1960s and 1970s. Rather, there were a number of different women's movements that progressed on parallel tracks, largely separated not only on the basis of politics but also on the basis of race, sexuality, and class.

Each movement will be described in turn below: first, the emergence of the largely white women's liberation movement—which was born united but quickly became divided into liberal and radical wings; second, the struggles by Black and other racially oppressed women to organize around their own demands—which were often neglected by nationalist and antiracist organizations as well as predominantly white women's groups. Each of these movements made its own contribution to advancing the interests of women, although often in quite different ways. Each also led to particular political and theoretical developments, which will be examined in the chapters that follow.

The Women's Liberation Movement: Feminism without Apology

In the late 1960s, the women's liberation movement emerged, involving mostly young white women who as students had already committed themselves to the New Left, civil rights, and/or antiwar movements. In the context of this broad radicalization, new women's liberation groups began meeting in 1967. By 1969, groups had been established in more than forty cities across the United States.

As unapologetic fighters for women's equality, radical feminists in many ways defined the women's liberation movement during this period. They deserve substantial credit for bringing the issues of women's sexual objectification, unequal pay, lack of child care, and the criminalization of abortion into the political mainstream. Redstockings, the New York–based radical feminist group founded in 1969, introduced the term "Sisterhood Is Powerful," which became one of the most popular slogans of women's liberation in its early years.

As feminist scholar Linda Nicholson observes, radical feminists sought to distinguish themselves politically from "liberal feminism":

> In the late 1960s there existed at least two very different movements. The mass media recognized this difference in their distinction between what they called the "women's rights" movement versus what they dubbed "women's lib," the latter a pejorative shortening of the term "women's liberation." The "women's rights" movement was composed primarily of those professional women who initiated activities in the mid-1960s and who were involved in such organizations as the Na-

tional Organization for Women. "Women's liberation," on the other hand, was largely constituted by younger women who were active in the 1960s' protest movements of the New Left and whose concern with women's issues began to receive national attention only toward the latter part of the decade. It is from within "women's liberation" that the tendency "radical feminism" emerged, the label intended as a means of distinguishing it from the "liberal feminism" expressed in the "women's rights" movement.[26]

With an eye toward gaining publicity, women's liberationists successfully staged many lively protests in quick succession that confronted and parodied their sexist opponents while TV cameras rolled—bringing the struggle for women's liberation into living rooms all over the United States, fundamentally affecting mass consciousness in the process.

New York Radical Women organized one of the most noteworthy protests of the early women's liberation movement outside the 1968 Miss America Pageant in Atlantic City, New Jersey, when roughly 150 protesters from six cities staged a "No More Miss America" rally. As Jo Freeman recalls, "A live sheep was crowned Miss America. Objects of female oppression—high-heeled shoes, girdles, bras, curlers, tweezers—were tossed into a Freedom Trash Can. . . . Women sang songs that parodied the contest and the idea of selling women's bodies: 'Ain't she sweet; making profits off her meat.' A tall, Miss America puppet was auctioned off." Meanwhile, sixteen activists went inside to the pageant, unfurling a "Women's Liberation" banner and shouting "Freedom for Women."

Freeman adds, "This action was quickly followed by the release of two stink bombs on the floor of the hall.[27]

Although the organizers of the "No More Miss America" protest had planned to burn the contents of the "Freedom Trash Can," they were unable to get a fire permit. So no undergarments were burned at this protest (or at any other women's liberation protest).[28] Yet the movement's detractors quickly pounced on this opportunity to stamp "women's libbers" with the nickname of "bra burners." Nevertheless, the protest struck a chord with millions of women who were also disgusted by the sexual objectification of women and began to identify with the demands of women's liberation.

Fighting for Abortion Rights

Likewise, radical feminists played a key role in the struggle to legalize abortion as a central demand of the women's liberation movement—

organizing angry protests demanding the right to repeal, not reform, laws criminalizing abortion. These protests gained substantial media attention and played a role in publicizing the plight of women forced to undergo illegal abortions.

Members of Redstockings, for example, disrupted a 1969 hearing on abortion by the New York state legislature after learning that the witnesses would consist of fourteen men and one woman—who was a nun. The protesters shouted down the speakers, demanding that women's voices be heard—and the legislators responded by moving the hearing to another room where the protesters were not allowed.[29]

On March 21, 1969, Redstockings launched a new type of protest known as a "speakout," attended by several hundred people. The speakout featured women telling their own stories about the pain and humiliation of dangerous illegal abortions or their inability to get an abortion and experiences carrying an unwanted fetus to term.[30] Speakouts soon spread all across the United States as a means of standing up for abortion rights between the years of 1969 and 1973, when the US Supreme Court issued its *Roe v. Wade* decision repealing the nation's abortion bans.

But protests began to lead to victories well before the *Roe v. Wade* decision. As Katha Pollitt noted about abortion rights, "What's missing from [most of] these accounts of legalization is the feminist activism that made it happen." Indeed, Redstockings' disruption of the legislative hearings on abortion led to fast-paced change, and in 1970 the New York state legislature repealed its law that had made nearly all abortions illegal, legalizing abortion through the twenty-fourth week of pregnancy.

Pollitt observes, "This dramatic action was widely, if not always respectfully, reported—Gals Squeal for Repeal was one headline. 'The very moderate reform law of 1969 failed to pass,' notes Ellen Willis, who took part in that disruption, 'yet just a year later the same legislature passed the most liberal law in the country. Guess all those guys just had a spontaneous change of heart.'"[31]

Sit-in at the *Ladies' Home Journal*

The year 1970 witnessed the women's liberation movement's first major sit-in, when a group of one hundred feminists from ten women's organizations sat in for eleven hours at the offices of the *Ladies' Home Journal* on March 18. Drawing attention to women's magazines' incessant focus on beauty products and the wonders of housework, the protesters brought their own proposal along with a mockup for a revamped magazine, hanging a banner reading "Women's Liberated Journal" outside the office windows. As participant Minda Bikman described at the time, "No more articles like Poor Woman's Almanac, no more Bettelheims and Rubins telling women they are guilty and must change, no more stories about Elizabeth Taylor's pearls and Jackie Onassis's diamonds, no more articles on how to get a face-lift and the fabulous life of Mrs. Henry Ford II."[32]

Participant Susan Brownmiller later recalled a list of suggested titles for articles that would be more relevant to their female contemporaries, ranging from "How to Get a Divorce," "How to Have an Orgasm," and "How to Get an Abortion" to "What to Tell Your Draft-Age Son" and "How Detergents Harm Our Rivers and Streams."[33] While many of the protesters' demands asked for a drastic increase in women personnel on the editorial staff, from a woman editor in chief to women columnists, other demands spoke also to the issues of race and class.

> We demand that the magazine hire non-white women at all levels in proportion to the population statistics. We demand that all salaries immediately be raised to a minimum of $125 a week. We demand that editorial conferences be open to all employees so the magazine can benefit from everyone's experience and views. Since this magazine purports to serve the interests of mothers and housewives, we demand that the *Journal* provide free day-care facilities on the premises for its employees' children, and that the policies of this day care center be determined by employees.[34]

Raising Mass Consciousness for Women's Liberation

The women's liberation movement's impact on larger society was far greater than its activist base, and its ideas raised both the consciousness and the expectations of millions of women, as indicated by the results of Harris opinion polls in 1972 and 1976. Harris's 1972 poll showed that significantly more Black women (62 percent) supported "efforts to strengthen and change women's status in society" than white women (45 percent). As Louis Harris and Associates reported in 1972, "American women, in a relatively short period, have accelerated their desires for a changed role in society. Those who are most concerned with strengthening women's status represent an essentially urban coalition of young, well-educated, and black women."[35]

By 1976, a Harris survey reported that 65 percent of all women (and

63 percent of all respondents) supported "efforts to strengthen and change women's status in society."[36] As medical ethicist Harriet A. Washington noted, "In 1970, social activist Donald Bogue found that 80 percent of the Black women he surveyed in Chicago approved of birth control and 75 percent were using it."[37]

The survey results above indicate that Black women supported many of the goals of the women's liberation movement, yet that support did not by and large result in common organizing efforts—or necessarily in a sense of mutual solidarity. Why this is the case will be explored below.

Movements of Black and Other Racially Oppressed Women

The racial disconnect among women's organizations was not due only to what many women of color rightly regarded as racist attitudes within predominantly white feminist groups but also because many were already politically committed to civil rights or nationalist movements and wished to remain in racially separate organizations. Indeed, many women of color chose to prioritize the struggle against racism over that against sexism, while others identified themselves as feminists.

Nor is it the case that women of color began organizing *after* white women's liberationists. On the contrary, a variety of organizations sprung up simultaneously among women seeking to address the particular forms of racism and sexism in society at large—including against the myth of the Black matriarchy—as well as sexism they encountered within activist movements. Black women from the Student Nonviolent Coordinating Committee (SNCC) formed a Black Women's Liberation Caucus inside SNCC to address issues of sexism inside the organization in 1969.

The caucus split from SNCC, which was already in decline in 1969, to form the Black Women's Alliance, calling for "a true revolutionary movement [that] must enhance the status of women" that would combat both racism and sexism.[38] The organization soon thereafter adopted opposition to imperialism as part of its program and began admitting other racially oppressed women—including Puerto Rican, Chicana, Native American, and Asian American women—as members, changing its name to the Third World Women's Alliance.[39]

In 1973, a group of notable Black feminists, including Florynce Kennedy, Alice Walker, and Barbara Smith, formed the National Black Feminist Organization (NBFO). In 1974, Smith joined with a group of other Black lesbian feminists to found the Boston-based Combahee

River Collective as a self-consciously radical alternative to the NBFO. The Combahee River Collective itself was named to commemorate the successful Underground Railroad Combahee River Raid of 1863, planned and led by Harriet Tubman, which freed 750 slaves.

Women of Color Organizing

Likewise, issues of women's rights were already percolating among Chicanas, who organized women's workshops at the 1969, 1970, and 1971 Chicano Youth Liberation Conferences and organized a women's caucus at the 1970 convention of the Mexican-American Political Association (MAPA). In October 1970, participants in a workshop on women at the Mexican-American National Issues Conference held in Sacramento voted to form the Comisión Femenil Mexicana Nacional, an independent Chicana feminist national organization. Its founding statement included the following resolutions:

> The effort and work of Chicana/Mexican women in the Chicano movement is generally obscured because women are not accepted as community leaders, either by the Chicano movement or by the Anglo establishment.
>
> The existing myopic attitude does not prove that women are not capable or willing to participate. It does not prove that women are not active, indispensable (representing over 50% of the population), experienced and knowledgeable in organizing tactics and strategy of a people's movement.
>
> THEREFORE, in order to terminate exclusion of female leadership in the Chicano/Mexican movement and in the community, be it RESOLVED that a Chicana/Mexican Women's Commission be established at this conference which will represent women, in all areas where Mexicans prevail, and;
>
> That this commission be known as the Comisión Femenil Mexicana, and;
>
> That the Comisión direct its efforts to organizing women to assume leadership positions within the Chicano movement and in community life, and;
>
> That the Comisión disseminate news and information regarding the work and achievement of Mexican/Chicana women, and;
>
> That the Comisión concern itself in promoting programs which specifically lend themselves to help, assist and promote solutions to female type problems and problems confronting the Mexican family, and;
>
> That the Comisión spell out issues to support, and explore ways to establish relationships with other women's organizations and movements.
>
> VIVA LA RAZA![40]

At the first national conference of Raza women, held in 1971, a survey of the roughly six hundred Chicanas in attendance showed that 100 percent agreed that women were expected to do all the housework, child care, laundry, and cooking even while attending school. An overwhelming 72 percent said they felt there was discrimination toward women within La Raza, and *no respondents* said they had never experienced discrimination (28 percent did not give an opinion).[41]

As noted above, during the 1960s and 1970s, many Black women and other women of color felt sidelined and alienated by the lack of attention to women's liberation inside nationalist and other antiracist movements. As bell hooks described of the black liberation movement,

> The 60s movement toward black liberation marked the first time in which black people engaged in a struggle to resist racism in which clear boundaries were erected which separated the roles of women and men. Black male activists publicly acknowledged that they expected black women involved in the movement to conform to a sexist role pattern. They demanded that black women assume a subservient position. Black women were told that they should take care of household needs and breed warriors for the revolution.[42]

Due to the racist history of the birth-control movement in the United States, described below, birth control and abortion were also contentious issues within most nationalist organizations in the late 1960s and early 1970s. Women were to be found on either side of this debate for a variety of reasons, from religious beliefs to fears of genocide after experiencing decades of sterilization abuse.

It is important to note, however, that opinions often changed dramatically during this period, as women of color pursued an agenda of reproductive rights. For example, whereas the Black Panther Party initially opposed birth control and abortion as being tools of genocide, by 1975 they were firmly in the pro-choice camp. As women's studies scholar Jennifer Nelson describes, "As black feminists became increasingly outspoken in their support for abortion rights, the Black Panthers followed their lead. Like black feminists, the Panthers addressed the particular needs of poor and black women."[43]

Likewise, Puerto Rican women in the New York City–based Young Lords successfully fought for the organization to add a range of feminist demands to its program between 1969 and 1974. While these women first met with resistance, by 1970 the Young Lords adopted a position supporting Puerto Rican women's reproductive rights that demanded their right to bear as many children as they desired and to raise living standards above the poverty line.

As Nelson describes, "The reproductive rights agenda developed by the female Young Lords between 1969 and 1974 was inclusive: it encompassed access to voluntary birth control, safe and legal abortion, a quality public health care system, free day care, and an end to poverty among Puerto Ricans and other people of color."[44]

Nevertheless, many women of color were reluctant to identify themselves as feminists because of their alienation from the predominantly white women's movement. Native American women's organizations, for example, had no wish to organize separately from men.[45] They worked inside the American Indian Movement (AIM), founded in 1968, which identified the struggle to achieve self-determination as its overriding goal. In the context of the historic genocide against Native Americans, AIM regarded attacks on Indian women's reproductive rights as a means of destroying Native culture. On this basis, women and men from AIM combated coercive reproductive practices as part of the project to defend Indian culture from extermination.

When women AIM activists formed Women of All Red Nations (WARN) in 1978, they did so not in opposition to AIM but to advance AIM's mission. Phyllis Young, a cofounder of WARN made this clear: "Our creation of an Indian women's organization is not a criticism or division from our men. . . . Only in this way can we organize ourselves as Indian women to meet our responsibilities, to be fully supportive of the men, to work in tandem with our partners in a common struggle for the liberation of our people and our land."[46]

All women of color face racism and discrimination as a constant feature of daily life, but often in different ways. Black women's oppression dates back to slavery and is thoroughly embedded in the foundations of US society. Many Latinas are immigrants, living in communities under the constant disruption and threat of deportation; Puerto Rican women are oppressed as residents of a US colony. Women of Asian descent are lumped together as the "model minority," despite the widespread impoverishment of Asian American communities. Arab and Muslim women are regarded in the US political mainstream as part of a culture prone to "terrorism," while those who choose to wear headscarves are derided as aiding in their own oppression.

Racially oppressed women involved in women's rights organizing during the 1960s and 1970s chose the paths they regarded as most appropriate for themselves. The result was the proliferation of organizations, operating with different sets of principles and goals.

Critiquing Racism among White Feminists

It must be acknowledged that many women of color who identified as feminists in the 1970s and 1980s were justifiably critical of mainstream white feminists' refusal to challenge racism, homophobia, and other forms of oppression, relegating women and lesbians of color to the status of outsiders and tokens "invited" occasionally to "join" into their movement activities.

Chicana feminists Gloria Anzaldúa and Cherríe Moraga describe their own experiences with tokenism in the introduction to their groundbreaking book of essays, *This Bridge Called My Back: Writings by Radical Women of Color*, first published in 1981.[47] After being invited and offered a scholarship to attend a workshop at a women's retreat in 1979, "the management and some of the staff" made Anzaldúa feel like

> an outsider, the poor relative, the token woman of color. And all because she was not white nor had she paid the $150 fee the retreat organizers had set for the workshop. . . . What had happened at the women's retreat was not new to our experience. Both of us had first met each other working as the only two Chicanas in a national feminist writers organization. After two years of involvement with the group, which repeatedly refused to address itself to its elitist and racist practices, we left the organization and began work on this book.[48]

The same volume includes a speech by Black lesbian feminist and celebrated poet Audre Lorde, addressing the Second Sex Conference at the New York University Institute for the Humanities in 1979, in which she lambasts the tokenism she experienced: "I stand here as a black lesbian feminist, having been invited to comment within the only panel at this conference where the input of black feminists and lesbians is represented. What this says about the vision of this conference is sad, in a country where racism, sexism and homophobia are inseparable."[49]

Elsewhere in *This Bridge Called My Back*, Japanese American feminist and poet Mitsuye Yamada describes repeatedly encountering outsider status from "women's organizations [that] tell us they would like to have us 'join' them and give them 'input'" while maintaining "the passive, sweet, etc. stereotype of the 'Oriental' woman." Yamada adds that, despite Asian women's activism, "we continue to hear, 'Asian women are of course traditionally not attuned to being political,' as if most other women are; or that Asian women are too happily bound to their traditional roles as mothers and wives, as if the same cannot be said of a great number of white American women among us."[50]

In her book, *Ain't I a Woman? Black Women and Feminism*, bell hooks describes the invisibility of Black women among many white women's liberationists, who continued "sexist-racist practice":

> The most glaring example of their support of the exclusion of black women was revealed when they drew analogies of "women" and "blacks" when what they were really comparing was the social status of white women with that of black people. Like many people in our racist society, white feminists could feel perfectly comfortable writing books or articles on "the woman question" in which they drew analogies between "women" and "blacks".... [And] by continuously making this analogy, they unwittingly suggest that to them the word "woman" is synonymous with "white women" and the term "blacks" synonymous with "black men."[51]

In a clear challenge to white, middle-class, heterosexual feminists, Combahee River Collective cofounder Barbara Smith argued for the *inclusion of all the oppressed* in a 1979 speech: "The reason racism is a feminist issue is easily explained by the inherent definition of feminism. Feminism is the political theory and practice to free all women: women of color, working-class women, poor women, physically challenged women, lesbians, old women, as well as white economically privileged heterosexual women. Anything less than this is not feminism, but merely female self-aggrandizement."[52]

Chapter Four

Mainstream Feminism: From Women's Liberation to "Power Feminism"

There are going to be times when woman to woman aggression is a healthy, even energizing corollary of our having reached full participation in society. . . . Women are managing, criticizing and firing other women, and their employees sometimes, understandably, hate their guts.

—Naomi Wolf, 1994[1]

Betty Friedan's *The Feminine Mystique*, published in 1963, gave voice to the anguish of white middle-class homemakers who were trapped in their suburban homes, doomed to a life revolving around fulfilling their families' every need. Friedan made a conscious decision to target this particular audience of women, despite her own radical background. Friedan had traveled in left-wing labor circles during the 1930s and 1940s but decided in the mid-1950s (at the height of the anticommunist witch hunts of the McCarthy era) to reinvent herself as an apolitical suburban housewife.[2]

As Stephanie Coontz notes, "The content of *The Feminine Mystique* and the marketing strategy that Friedan and her publishers devised for it ignored Black women's positive examples of Friedan's argument." Few Black women or working-class women of any race would have been able to afford Friedan's proposal that women hire domestic workers to perform their daily household chores while they were at work. Thus Coontz adds, "Black women who did read the book seldom responded as enthusiastically as did her white readers."[3] Coontz also argues, however, that "using the word 'boredom' to describe the doubts and insecurities of these middle-class women unfairly trivializes their pain,"[4] which is undoubtedly correct. There is no need to disparage the loneliness and pain of middle-class housewives in order to also understand that they face dramatically different challenges from working-class women—whose lives are governed by pressing financial concerns that usually place the goal of career fulfillment out of reach.

At the same time, Friedan was wrong to ignore the importance of the very real issues that confront working-class women when she surely knew better. Indeed, Friedan wrote a 1952 article, "UE Fights for Women Workers," during her days in the labor movement.[5] Yet Friedan makes clear from the beginning that *The Feminine Mystique* limits its discussion to the problems of suburban housewives. In the chapter called "The Problem That Has No Name," she writes, "It is not caused by lack of material advantages; it may not even be felt by women preoccupied with desperate problems of hunger, poverty or illness."[6] She makes no further comment on the plight of those women who *are* preoccupied by problems of poverty, hunger, or illness.

Friedan praises those women who had shown the courage to break from their traditional roles to seek well-paying careers, writing sympathetically that these women "had problems of course, tough ones—juggling their pregnancies, finding nurses and housekeepers, having to give up good assignments when their husbands were transferred."[7] Yet she doesn't deem it worthy to comment on the lives of the nurses and the housekeepers these career women hire, who also work all day but then return home to face housework and child-care responsibilities of their own.

Soon after *The Feminine Mystique* was published, left-wing civil rights activist and women's historian Gerda Lerner wrote to Friedan, praising the book but also expressing "one reservation": Friedan had addressed the book "solely to the problems of middle-class, college-educated women." She noted that "working women, especially Negro women, labor not only under the disadvantages imposed by the feminine mystique, but under the more pressing disadvantages of economic discrimination."[8]

Veteran socialist and feminist Evelyn Reed put forward an even sharper class critique, while first acknowledging, "Betty Friedan's findings have a wider relevance than the well-to-do housewives she has investigated. . . . [D]istorted ideas and values seep down to infect masses of women, including some working women who wonder whether they might not lead a better life as a full-time housewife. This book should help settle their doubts."[9] But, Reed continued,

> Betty Friedan's diagnosis of the disease is superior to her remedy for it. She suggests that more serious education and study, together with interesting, well-paying jobs, will open the door of the trap. This is the same kind of limited, individual solution that the feminists formerly proposed—

and that subsequently proved so ineffective. Some fortunate women can do what the author has done—turn around, make a "new life plan" and escape the domestic cage. But the life-plans for the great majority of women are determined for them by forces outside their personal control—the ruling powers.[10]

In addition, Friedan introduced a profoundly antigay theme in *The Feminine Mystique* that would reverberate in her organizing efforts. She argues that "the homosexuality that is spreading like a murky smog over the American scene" has its roots in the feminine mystique, which can produce "the kind of mother-son devotion that can produce latent or overt homosexuality. . . . The boy smothered by such parasitical mother-love is kept from growing up, not only sexually, but in all ways."[11]

Thus, while Friedan introduced the very real problems of suburban women's oppression to a mass audience, she also consciously excluded those of working-class women (especially Black women)—while also denouncing homosexuality and blaming "smothering" mothers for its occurrence.

The National Organization for Women

Despite Friedan's political flaws, she aimed to build a mass women's movement and devoted her life singlemindedly to this project. Perhaps no other single figure played such an influential role in shaping the politics and character of early mainstream feminism as Friedan. She was instrumental in forming the National Organization for Women (NOW) in 1966, and served as its first president until 1970. In 1969, she played a key role in founding the National Association for the Repeal of Abortion Laws (NARAL), the precursor to NARAL Pro-Choice America, and in 1970, she helped form the National Women's Political Caucus.

The social and political repression of the 1950s gave way to a rise in social struggle in the 1960s, as the civil rights movement and antiwar movements grew in size and strength. The women's liberation movement was born in their wake, as part of the mass radicalization of the 1960s—raising demands that would have been unthinkable only a few years earlier, yet attracting a sizeable following.

NOW was organized in the midst of this rise in struggle, and its stated aims reflected the changed political climate. NOW sought to fight for equal opportunity for women in the workplace and in society at large. By 1974 its membership swelled to more than forty thousand nationally. When NOW called a national "Women's Strike for Equality" on August 26, 1970, more than fifty thousand people came out to demonstrate for women's rights across the country. As *Nation* columnist Katha Pollitt described, these demonstrations "called for twenty-four-hour childcare centers, abortion on demand and equal opportunity in education and employment."[12]

NOW's stated commitments in its early years included demands specific to women workers, and it called explicitly for the legalization of abortion. Its second conference in 1967 approved a "Women's Bill of Rights in 1968," which it planned to present to the platform committees of both the Democratic and Republican Parties prior to the 1968 presidential elections. The Bill of Rights consisted of the following demands:

I. Equal Rights Constitutional Amendment
II. Enforce Law Banning Sex Discrimination in Employment
III. Maternity Leave Rights in Employment and in Social Security Benefits
IV. Tax Deduction for Home and Child Care Expenses for Working Parents
V. Child Day Care Centers
VI. Equal and Unsegregated Education
VII. Equal Job Training Opportunities and Allowances for Women in Poverty
VIII. The Right of Women to Control Their Reproductive Lives
We Demand:
I. That the United States Congress immediately pass the Equal Rights Amendment to the Constitution to provide that "Equality of rights under the law shall not be denied or abridged by the United States or by any State on account of sex" and that such then be immediately ratified by the several States.
II. That equal employment opportunity be guaranteed to all women, as well as men by insisting that the Equal Employment Opportunity Commission enforce the prohibitions against sex discrimination in employment under Title VII of the Civil Rights Act of 1964 with the same vigor as it enforces the prohibitions against racial discrimination.
III. That women be protected by law to insure their rights to return to their jobs within a reasonable time after childbirth without loss of seniority or other accrued benefits and be paid maternity leave as a form of social security and/or employee benefit.
IV. Immediate revision of tax laws to permit the deduction of home and child care expenses for working parents.
V. That child care facilities be established by law on the same basis as parks, libraries and public schools adequate to the needs of children, from the pre-school years through adolescence, as a community resource to be used by all citizens from all income levels.

VI. That the right of women to be educated to their full potential equally with men be secured by Federal and State legislation, eliminating all discrimination and segregation by sex, written and unwritten, at all levels of education including college, graduate and professional schools, loans and fellowships and Federal and State training programs, such as the Job Corps.

VII. The right of women in poverty to secure job training, housing and family allowances on equal terms with men, but without prejudice to a parent's right to remain at home to care for his or her children; revision of welfare legislation and poverty programs which deny women dignity, privacy and self respect.

VIII. The right of women to control their own reproductive lives by removing from penal codes the laws limiting access to contraceptive information and devices and laws governing abortion.[13]

NOW's expansive set of demands, as described above, included "the right of women to control their reproductive lives"—a call for abortion rights. A more conservative group of members who objected to demanding legal abortion defected from NOW to form the Women's Equity Action League, a group with the singular goal of winning an equal rights amendment.[14] But NOW did not back down from its support for legal abortion, even in the face of this defection.

NOW Opts for the Mainstream

Despite its sweeping set of demands, however, NOW did not share the opposition to capitalism and imperialism of its radical counterparts even in the late 1960s. On the contrary, mainstream feminists rejected radical politics and embraced a strategy of pressuring the capitalist system from within to fight for equality—including an increasing focus on influencing politicians and elections as a means for advancing women's rights.

Moreover, NOW's stated commitments to the struggle for racial equality and working women's rights outlined in its 1968 Bill of Rights was not reflected in its practice. It sought first and foremost to remove the obstacles preventing professional women from career advancement, while neglecting other issues it believed might jeopardize this endeavor. As political scientist Janet A. Flammang described, "A 1974 survey of NOW members showed that 66 percent had bachelor's degrees, 30 percent had advanced degrees, and 25 percent were professionally employed. Only 8 percent were clerical workers, despite the fact that clerical workers made up 35 percent of the employed female population, and 10 percent were women of color."[15]

By 1972, NOW had embarked on what would turn out to be a failed ten-year, multimillion-dollar campaign to pass an Equal Rights Amendment (ERA) to the US Constitution, which exposed the flaws inherent in its electoral strategy. The ERA was a straightforward amendment, stating simply, "Equal rights under the law shall not be denied or abridged by the United States or any state on account of sex." In the wake of the social upheavals of the late 1960s, such a statement seemed quite mild and destined for victory.

At the same time, many labor activists criticized the proposed amendment as too compatible with the needs of the capitalist class because it would invalidate hard-won protective legislation for women workers. Protective legislation provided not only minimum wages and limits on hours but also legal requirements for toilet facilities, rest areas, mandatory meal breaks, and other crucial safety regulations. These benefits were won for women workers, but often tended to also benefit the men who worked alongside them at particular workplaces.

Most employers would have liked nothing better than to remove these protections via an ERA, evidenced by the fact that, as socialist and feminist Marilyn Danton argued at the time, "several state Chambers of Commerce and employers' organizations are campaigning for its passage.[16]

Many socialist feminists and labor radicals, like Danton, believed in and fought for women's liberation. They argued in favor of an ERA in principle but against the legislation as worded in NOW's proposal—proposing instead that the wording be changed to reflect the needs of working-class women. As Danton argued in 1970, "Instead of supporting an amendment which will certainly invalidate protective laws, one could propose an amendment which would either retain existing legislation, or, even better, extend this legislation to men."

These arguments from activists in the labor movement fell on deaf ears, and NOW proceeded with the ERA proposal as worded. In so doing, NOW chose its class allegiance, leaving "no alternative available but to oppose the present ERA, no matter how unfortunate it might seem to do so," as Danton concluded.[17]

From Activism to Electoralism: How the ERA Was Lost

Nevertheless, the ERA seemed destined for success. In March 1972, the Senate passed it overwhelmingly, by a vote of eighty-four to eight. Even President Richard Nixon endorsed it. By August 1974, thirty-three states had ratified the ERA, leaving only five more to reach the thirty-eight required for passage. Throughout the ten-year period of NOW's campaign for the ERA, opinion polls showed a majority consistently voicing support for it. Yet on June 30, 1982, the deadline for ratification passed with only thirty-five states having ratified—three states short of passage. Not a single state ratified after January 1977.

The ERA's fate was clearly tied up with the activist strength of the women's liberation movement, which peaked in the early 1970s. As the activism of the women's movement dwindled, so did momentum for the passage of the ERA. But NOW's leadership did not renew NOW's commitment to activism in the face of its losing battle for the ERA. Instead, as time wore on, NOW's strategy became *more conservative*, in the hopes of winning more friends among state legislators.

NOW's single-minded focus on the ERA also alienated many African American members, who complained about the organization's lack of attention to combating racial inequality. NOW's first statement of purpose in 1966 was coauthored by a Black woman, veteran civil rights activist Dr. Pauli Murray, and contained a commitment to fighting around issues of importance to African American women.

Thirteen years later little progress had been made. In 1979, after an all-white slate was nominated to lead the organization for the second year in a row, Aileen Hernandez, a founding member and the second president of NOW, resigned from the organization and urged other Black members to do the same. Hernandez, a veteran civil rights and labor activist, called NOW "too white and middle-class" and urged Black women not to join until "NOW takes meaningful action to eliminate racism."[18]

In the wake of the Hyde Amendment, which banned federal Medicaid funding for poor women's abortions beginning in 1977 (and in effect ever since), NOW's newly elected president Eleanor Smeal argued that lawyers appealing the Hyde Amendment should not link the Fourteenth Amendment's equal-protection clause to abortion. To do so, she reasoned, could frighten away potential pro-ERA legislators who opposed abortion funding.[19] By the close of the 1970s, the overall picture was that of a rapidly growing antiabortion, antifeminist, Christian, conservative base of the Republican Party—and a women's movement that was declining and growing more conservative in its aims and strategy. If the women's movement had lost its militancy, Christian conservatives had only begun to fight.

NOW had not expressed a commitment to lesbian rights in its original platform, but in 1971 the organization adopted a resolution stating that "a woman's right to her own person includes the right to define and express her own sexuality and to choose her own lifestyle."[20] But its stated support was not immediately translated into action, and the organization was divided in its first decade over whether to support lesbian rights at all.

Friedan, who allegedly referred to "out" lesbian activists as a "lavender menace," is known to have played a role in omitting the New York chapter of the Daughters of Bilitis from the list of sponsors on its press release for the First Congress to Unite Women in November 1969.[21] NOW's New York branch was nearly destroyed over the issue in 1970. Lesbian author and activist Rita Mae Brown, who went on to help found the direct-action organization Lesbian Menace, wrote that year in New York NOW's newsletter, "Lesbianism is the one word which gives New York NOW a collective heart attack."[22]

As its quest to win the ERA dragged on, NOW became increasingly reluctant to allow either a visible lesbian or socialist presence at ERA events, fearing that it might alienate more conservative supporters. While early ERA marches and demonstrations had been open to all who wished to participate, NOW eventually banned lesbian and socialist contingents from carrying banners or identifying markers at marches.[23]

NOW's class bias emerged at full throttle in the 1980s. By then, NOW was unabashed in its commitment to championing the interests of women seeking to enter the corporate and political elite. In 1987, two-time NOW president Eleanor Smeal founded the Feminist Majority Foundation to focus more attention on electoral and legislative campaigns. The Feminist Majority spawned its own political action committee (Feminist Majority PAC) in 2002, with its stated aim being "to support Congressional candidates who will carry the banner of women's rights. We continue to help feminist candidates across the country with donations, contacts and campaign advice." The Feminist Majority describes its mission, in part, as "to empower feminists, who are the majority, and to win equality for women at the decision making tables of the state, nation, and the world."[24]

To be sure, women are grossly underrepresented in the upper echelons of business and politics, despite significant gains in entering professions and middle management since the 1970s. But the vast majority of women remain stuck in low-paying, working-class jobs with little hope for career advancement. Yet by the 1980s, NOW had abandoned the fight to win reforms such as paid parental leave—even though the United States remains one of only a few countries in the world that does not offer paid maternity leave to its women workers.

In 1986, NOW formally took a stand *against* the right to unpaid maternity leave in the case of a woman bank worker who was fired from her job after she took time off—without pay—after having a baby. In the case *California Savings and Loan v. Guerra*, NOW filed a friend-of-the-court brief agreeing with the bank that allowing a woman to take maternity leave discriminates against men with "similar disabilities." NOW took the side of the bank management over that of the woman worker—on the basis that special protections for women harm their employment opportunities when competing with men in the job market.[25] This concern, while real for those women seeking to climb the corporate ladder, ignores the needs of the much larger number of working-class women for whom losing a job due to pregnancy and childbirth—an obvious act of gender discrimination—can be devastating.

The Mainstream Pro-Choice Movement Endorses the Democrats' Antichoice Policies

This conservative turn occurred not only with NOW but also with the mainstream abortion-rights movement, which could have—and should have—pursued a strategy that could galvanize the pro-choice majority into a fighting force to defend abortion rights. On April 9, 1989, at least three hundred thousand pro-choice activists demonstrated in Washington, DC, to show their determination to fight for the right to legal abortion. In 1992, an even larger crowd—at least half a million—turned out to defend the right to choose. The potential for building a mass movement tying the fight for abortion rights to the fight for women's equality was as clear then as it is now.

But the leaders of the largest pro-choice organization, NARAL, made a conscious choice to shift its polemic on choice to one that would "play" on Capitol Hill—and with swing voters. NARAL issued a "talking points" memo to its affiliates in 1989, instructing staffers specifically not to use phrases such as "a woman's body is her own to control." Rather, the right to choose was to be cast as a right to "privacy."[26] Increasingly, pro-choice organizations emphasized that being pro-choice also meant being "pro-family"—giving up crucial ideological ground to the main slogan of the Christian right.

No national pro-choice marches took place in Washington, DC, between the election years of 1992 and 2004—even though the anti-abortion movement rallied by the tens of thousands there each January 22, the anniversary of the *Roe v. Wade* decision. When the "pro-choice" Democrat Bill Clinton broke his campaign promise to pass a Freedom of Choice Act, the pro-choice movement did not organize mass protests to hold him accountable. And when Clinton fulfilled his campaign promise to "end welfare as we know it" in 1996, signing Republican-sponsored legislation eliminating the federal welfare program, Aid to Families with Dependent Children (AFDC), pro-choice leaders did not lend activist support to the many thousands of poor women and children thrown off welfare.

Clinton's first term as president witnessed the most antichoice voting record in Congress's history until then, yet Clinton's only attention to the abortion issue in his second term was to promote sexual abstinence among teens to lower the country's abortion rate. In 1997, Hillary Clinton urged the pro-choice movement to reject "extremism" and start forging unity with abortion foes on points of agreement, such as lowering the abortion rate in the United States.[27]

Yet mainstream pro-choice organizations continued to take their lead from the Clinton administration. Throughout Clinton's presidency, pro-choice "protests" were by and large limited to issuing press releases against the multitude of new restrictions on abortion, while "activism" revolved around campaigning for pro-choice Democrats. For example, NARAL embarked on a campaign in 1997 to help the Clinton administration in reducing the number of unplanned pregnancies by 30 percent. "People would like to see fewer abortions," echoed NARAL leader Kate Michelman at the league's annual luncheon celebrating the twenty-fourth anniversary of the right to legal abortion.[28]

Clinton's 1996 reelection campaign ads emphasized that he had signed a ban on gay marriage, the Defense of Marriage Act, and "required teen mothers on welfare to stay in school or lose benefits." Yet the pro-choice movement's support for Clinton's reelection never wavered.[29] By the end of Clinton's second term, women's right to choose was far more restricted than when he took office in 1993. Clinton's presidency shows why politicians cannot be relied upon to defend abortion rights—whatever their campaign rhetoric. Rather than an advance for abortion rights, Clinton's presidency witnessed a significant rise in legislation eroding this constitutional right.

The downward spiral in reproductive rights has continued ever since, not only under the administration of George W. Bush but also under Barack Obama's. Michelman did not call for protests when Congress first passed the Partial-Birth Abortion Ban Act of 2003, signed into law by Bush. Without pressure from mainstream feminists to defend the right to abortion, the Democratic Party steadily retreated on choice.

Retreat finally turned to surrender after John Kerry's defeat in 2004. In January 2005, on the thirty-second anniversary of *Roe v. Wade*, Senator Hillary Clinton called abortion a "sad, even tragic choice" that shouldn't "ever have to be exercised, or only in very rare circumstances."[30] Soon after, Howard Dean, then chairman of the Democratic National Committee, argued, "I don't think we need to be the pro-abortion party. Nobody's pro-abortion."[31] Michelman—who assumed the role of Democratic Party strategist after retiring as NARAL's president—quickly voiced her approval. In a letter to the *New York Times*, Michelman stated, "Senator Clinton deserves praise for reaching out to anti-choice Americans."[32]

Like Bill Clinton, Barack Obama pledged to pass a Freedom of Choice Act while on the campaign trail, which also never materialized once he took office as president. Instead, Obama has further extended the strict restrictions on federal funding for abortion outlined in the Hyde Amendment to apply to the Affordable Care Act. Whereas the Hyde Amendment targeted poor women's right to abortion funding, Obama has targeted the rights of all women receiving medical care from companies participating in the "Obamacare" health-insurance program. On March 24, 2010, the White House issued an executive order announcing:

> Following the recent enactment of the Patient Protection and Affordable Care Act (the "Act"), it is necessary to establish an adequate enforcement mechanism to ensure that Federal funds are not used for abortion services (except in cases of rape or incest, or when the life of the woman would be endangered), consistent with a longstanding Federal statutory restriction that is commonly known as the Hyde Amendment. . . .
>
> The Act maintains current Hyde Amendment restrictions governing abortion policy and extends those restrictions to the newly created health insurance exchanges. Under the Act, longstanding Federal laws to protect conscience . . . remain intact and new protections prohibit discrimination against health care facilities and health care providers because of an unwillingness to provide, pay for, provide coverage of, or refer for abortions.[33]

Yet in 2012, NOW's political action committee glowingly endorsed Obama for reelection, applauding his defense of contraception but without mentioning his betrayal on abortion rights. As NOW wrote, "President Obama's record on women's issues speaks for itself. . . . And the president stood up to the U.S. Conference of Catholic Bishops when they demanded restrictions on birth control, ensuring access to contraception coverage for the millions of women insured through religiously affiliated schools, hospitals and nonprofits throughout the country."[34]

Imperialist Feminism Cannot "Liberate" Women

Mainstream US feminists have not limited their support to the political establishment's domestic policies, but also to its imperialist projects. Beginning in the late 1990s, the Feminist Majority Foundation set its sights far beyond US borders, on Afghanistan—while proclaiming Western cultural superiority and, wittingly or not, bolstering US imperialism's domestic and global aims, all under the guise of freeing women from "Islamic terrorism."

Shortly after the Taliban came to power in Afghanistan in 1996, Feminist Majority activist Mavis Leno (wife of celebrity Jay Leno) launched a publicity-driven campaign on behalf of Afghan women. The Lenos donated $100,000 to get this campaign off the ground, through the Feminist Majority Foundation's global women's rights program.[35] Smeal joined this campaign enthusiastically and, along with Mavis Leno, became one of its main spokespersons for years in the late 1990s.

In this role, Smeal was key in whipping up support for George W. Bush's war on Afghanistan in 2001, helping the Bush administration to promote the fiction that the war aimed to "liberate" Afghan women. When First Lady Laura Bush declared, "The fight against terrorism is also a fight for the rights and dignity of women," Smeal embraced this claim, adding to the general post–September 11 hysteria by putting forward her own version of the "domino theory":

> We argued that the Talibanization of society would not stop in Afghanistan. We could see it moving into Pakistan, into Algiers and all through the Middle East to Turkey. We argued that it would lead to regional instability, and that this had much larger world ramifications than just what is happening to women there. . . . The link between the liberation of Afghan women and girls from the terrorist Taliban militia and preservation of democracy and freedom in America and worldwide has never been clearer.[36]

In the immediate aftermath of September 11, this illusion helped Bush gain support among a wide swathe of liberals and even some antiwar activists in the United States for the invasion that launched the "war without end" in Afghanistan, creating the path for the US invasion and occupation of Iraq in 2003.

Smeal appeared as a regular guest on television news programs in that decisive period, ratcheting up anti-Muslim racism while the USA PATRIOT Act sailed through Congress and thousands of Arabs and Muslims were rounded up and "detained indefinitely" without charges or the right to legal representation in the name of "fighting terrorism." In a typical racist rant, Smeal stated, "We have become the bad guys; they are blaming all of their economic ruin on the West. They think we don't like Muslims, so instead, they become more fundamentalist: 'We'll show you, we'll be more Muslim.'"[37]

When Bush (prematurely) declared the war over in November 2001, the Feminist Majority even circulated a petition thanking his administration for its commitment to restoring the rights of women in Afghanistan. And feminists applauded Secretary of State Colin Powell when he proclaimed in November 2001, "The rights of women in Afghanistan will not be negotiable," as television cameras zoomed in to show smiling Afghan women lifting their veils.[38]

More than a decade later, US media outlets have rarely returned to report on the fate of women in post-Taliban Afghanistan. If they did, they would find that the majority of Afghan women continue to wear the burqa, the head-to-toe Islamic covering. As Mariam Rawi of the Revolutionary Association of Women of Afghanistan (RAWA) argued in 2004, "The U.S. has replaced one misogynist fundamentalist regime with another."[39]

The Taliban's Department of Vice and Virtue was soon resurrected under the name of the Ministry of Religious Affairs. Warlords responsible for a reign of terror between 1992 and 1996, including the mass rape and murder of women, remain in power throughout the countryside, enriching themselves through opium production. Then-president Hamid Karzai appointed fundamentalist Fazl Hadi Shinwari as the chief justice of the Supreme Court. "Shinwari has packed the nine-member Supreme Court with 137 sympathetic mullahs and called for Taliban-style punishments to implement Shari'a law."[40]

This outcome should have been easy to predict. But the Feminist Majority has never challenged the ridiculous notion that a right-wing

Republican like Bush was taking a genuine interest in advancing women's rights, even as the war continued and the Obama administration picked up where Bush left off, with no end in sight. In February 2015, the Afghanistan Independent Human Rights Commission (AIHRC) announced that it had recorded 4,250 cases of violence against women in the previous nine months—including beheadings and other murders, gang rape, the selling of women, forced childhood marriages, and other acts of brutality.[41]

"Power Feminism"

Mainstream feminism was transformed by its rightward trajectory after the 1970s, described above. By the 1990s, some mainstream feminists made their final break from the movement's 1960s roots, downplaying the role of discrimination and arguing instead that if women want rights, they should stop seeing themselves as victims and begin taking responsibility for their actions.

Naomi Wolf outlines this changed approach in her 1994 book *Fire with Fire*. In it, she coins the term "power feminism" as an alternative to what she calls "victim feminism," which she described as "old habits left over from the revolutionary left of the 1960s—such as reflexive anti-capitalism, an insider-outsider mentality, and an aversion to 'the system.'"[42] Wolf admits that capitalism "does oppress the many for the few,"[43] but that "enough money buys a woman out of a lot of sex oppression." Wolf advises women to embrace capitalism and accumulate as much money and power as they can. She argues, bastardizing Marxism, that "pending the 'revolution,' women are better off with the means of production in their own hands. . . . Women's businesses can be the power cells of the 21st century."[44] But according to Wolf, women can only accomplish this goal if they stop seeing themselves as victims. After all, she writes, "If we stay hunkered down, defensive and angry, we waste our energies."[45] She adds, power feminism means "practicing tolerance rather than self-righteousness."[46]

Wolf maintains that women should stop focusing on all the things that are wrong with their lives and start thinking of themselves as powerful human beings, while using the many opportunities to raise themselves up as entrepreneurs and high-ranking politicians. As an example, she offers, "An advertisement that shows the swearing in of a woman president can have as much or more power to advance women's historical progress as can the passage of the Equal Rights Amendment on the political level."[47]

Wolf argues that discrimination is not the primary reason women are held back from career advancement, but that women hold themselves back because of the "fear of having too much." Women are no longer hampered by economic or political obstacles in the way of equality, but quite simply by their own psychological negativity. "The question to ask," she wrote, "is not whether society is ready to yield to women their rightful places, but whether women themselves are ready to take possession of them."[48] If only women would stop seeing themselves as victims, her logic goes, they would stop being victimized. If only women would embrace capitalism, they would stop being oppressed by it. If only women would stop being angry, they would be happy.

This "self-help" approach to approach to feminism is based upon acceptance of even the most barbaric aspects of capitalist society, including war. Wolf offers American women combat soldiers during the 1991 Persian Gulf War as a concrete example of power feminism. "Images of women wielding real firepower shook loose the blinkers that keep women from imagining themselves as beings who can elicit not just love and desire, but respect and even fear," she gushed.[49] The two hundred thousand Iraqis, many of them women and children civilians, who were killed by the United States and its allies in the carpet bombing of Iraq during the 1991 Gulf War do not merit even a mention by Wolf.

Wolf embraces not only the pursuit of profits but also the class antagonism that goes with it. Although she does not dwell on the subject, she admits that for every woman who succeeds in business, there are many other women who cannot. This is, of course, the nature of capitalism—workers must produce profits, or there would be no managers. But class differences between women are not a cause for concern: Wolf argues that power feminists should welcome any and all antagonisms that might be produced by the scapegoating and discrimination that take place in class society: "We are maturing into the understanding that women of different classes, races and sexualities have different, and often competing, agendas. Those conflicts should not be a source of guilt to us. They do not represent a breakdown of sisterhood. In the fullness of diversity, they represent its triumph."[50]

What is abundantly clear from the remarks quoted above is that Wolf is concerned only with that minority of women who are in the process of climbing the corporate ladder. Working-class women are mentioned only in passing. They are the women getting fired by or cleaning the homes of power feminists. Yet power feminism allows women managers to convince themselves that they are bettering humanity through their powerful positions in business or government. Wolf recalls that the first sizable check she wrote to a women's organization

> made me feel powerful in a way that felt right. . . . I began to tithe my income. Paradoxically, the more steadily I did this, the greater the sense of possession and entitlement I then felt . . . learning about money, trying to make money yield money, and even trying to negotiate for more. Money was not just a selfish, dirty indulgence that made me part of an oppressive system. It was an agent of change. . . . Not only was it permissible to learn to ask for more, always more, but it was a political act. It was imperative."[51]

Changing Sides

A brief examination of Wolf's career since the publication of *Fire with Fire* demonstrates how power feminism can lead easily to the right wing of the political spectrum—including on abortion rights. Wolf has espoused her views on the issue of choice numerous times, and each time she appears more in opposition to abortion rights than before. In *Fire with Fire* she writes, "The other side of having reproductive rights is taking reproductive responsibility." Furthermore, she argues, "some of the most thoughtful feminists are beginning to describe abortion as violence against women."[52]

In a 1997 op-ed in the *New York Times*, Wolf stated, "What if we called policies that sustain, tolerate and even guarantee the highest abortion rate of any industrialized nation what they should be called: crimes against women?" In the editorial, she called for supporters of choice to join forces with those who are against abortion, to "reject extremism," and to lower the "shamefully high rate of abortion" in the United States.[53] After this article appeared, Wolf became an unpaid adviser to President Bill Clinton. She then landed a job as a paid adviser to presidential candidate Al Gore during his 2000 campaign. "How did Wolf start out as Betty Friedan and end up as Dick Morris?" asked Jodi Kantor in *Slate* during Gore's campaign. Kantor wrote that Wolf "coached each [Clinton and Gore] to emphasize his manly strengths, relying on hoary, tired gender stereotypes. She reportedly told Gore that he is the 'beta male' who must fight Clinton's 'alpha male' for dominance."[54]

In a 2005 article called "Female Trouble," published in *New York* magazine, Wolf critiques the Kerry campaign for allowing his wife, Teresa Heinz, to publicly "emasculate" him in her convention speech:

> It has been well established that modern women maddeningly long for men who are tender in private but authoritative in public. Unfortunately, Teresa Heinz Kerry's speech, which all but ignored her husband, did more to emasculate him than the opposition ever could. By publicly shining the light on herself rather than her husband, she opened a symbolic breach in Kerry's archetypal armor. Listen to what the Republicans are hitting Kerry with: Indecisive. Effete. French. They are all but calling this tall, accomplished war hero gay.[55]

Besides resurrecting the alpha-male stereotype and old-school homophobia, in the same article Wolf also turns on pro-choice *mainstream* feminists, writing, "Abortion is an issue not of *Ms. Magazine*-style fanaticism or suicidal Republican religious reaction, but a complex issue on which 'good people can disagree.'"[56]

By 2010, Wolf was singing the praises of the right-wing Tea Party movement. In the article "Tea Time in America," Wolf argues:

> To be sure, the Tea Party's brand of aggrieved populism—and its composition of mostly white, angry, middle-class voters—has deep roots in the United States, flaring up during times of change. But observers who have drawn comparisons to the Know-Nothings, the racist, paranoid, anti-Catholic, and anti-immigrant party that surged in the 1850s are reading the movement far too superficially.
>
> Indeed, those who deride and dismiss this movement do so at their peril. . . . While some Tea Partiers may be racist or focused on eccentric themes—such as the validity of Barack Obama's birth certificate—far more of them, those who were part of the original grass-roots effort, are focused on issues that have merit.[57]

Addressing Tea Party support for states' rights, she continued, "the Tea Party activists' focus on supporting states' autonomy—and even on property rights and the right to bear arms—can seem like a prescient effort to constrain overweening corporate and military power in national government."[58]

"Women, Money, Power"

Beginning in 2009, the Feminist Majority Foundation established an annual "Women, Money, Power" summit and luncheon. In 2013, discounted tickets for students and seniors for the "luncheon only" option started at $100 (nearly fourteen hours of work at the federal minimum wage). Nondiscounted tickets started at $200, while "sponsorship packages" for the luncheon and summit ranged as high as $25,000.[59] The class vantage point of power feminism couldn't be clearer.

Chapter Five

From Radical Feminism to Separatism

> *Reactionary separatism is rooted in the conviction that male supremacy is an absolute aspect of our culture, that women have only two alternatives: accepting or withdrawing from it to create subcultures. This position eliminates any need for revolutionary struggle, and it is in no way a threat to the status quo.*
>
> —bell hooks[1]

Radical feminists organized some of the most visible and unapologetic protests for women's liberation in the late 1960s and early 1970s. But within a few short years, many reached the conclusion that sexism was insurmountable and turned toward a strategy based on separate organizations for women. Separatism ultimately privileged the fight against women's oppression over the fight against class exploitation and all other forms of oppression, including racism. While the label "radical feminism" remained, it devolved from its initial commitment to transformative social change, turning decisively rightward—toward a more conservative worldview—despite its sometimes-radical terminology and slogans.

But radical feminism was a product of its time, and it would be wrong to assume that women radicals who later became separatists began their political journey favoring separatism over other forms of struggle. On the contrary, the history of the 1960s movements from which radical feminists emerged shows that many women radicals *first* unsuccessfully sought to integrate the struggle for women's liberation inside the broader activist left before splitting. Many of these young women, who were predominantly white, had been involved in the civil rights and antiwar movements, and Students for a Democratic Society (SDS)—which formed in 1960 and issued what became a historic document, the Port Huron Statement, in 1962.[2] SDS went on to become the organizational center of the New Left until it split in 1969.

It is an unfortunate but significant fact that many men from the New Left reacted with hostility or indifference to attempts by women to call attention to and raise demands around their oppression within the larger movement. As early as 1964, when women active in the Student Non-violent Coordinating Committee (SNCC) wrote a position paper called "The Position of Women in SNCC," activist Stokely Carmichael (reportedly attempting humor) offered the following reply: "The only position for women in SNCC is prone."[3]

At an SDS conference in 1965 a discussion of "women's issues" elicited "catcalls, storms of ridicule and verbal abuse."[4] The following year, women who proposed a plank supporting women's liberation were reportedly "pelted with tomatoes and thrown out of the convention."[5] In 1967, at the National Conference for a New Politics, when women's liberation activists Jo Freeman and Shulamith Firestone proposed from the speakers' podium that the conference discuss issues of sexism, male leaders told them there were more important issues to discuss and the conference decided not to deal with the women's "trivial complaints." One women's liberation activist reportedly was patted on the head and told to "calm down, little girl."[6] In a similar vein, a Berkeley underground newspaper stated in 1968, "Our line on the women's trip—LET THEM EAT COCK."[7]

◆ ◆ ◆

In 1968, SDS finally adopted a position on women's oppression, acknowledging the need to fight against "male supremacy." This was too little, too late for women's liberation activists like Freeman and Firestone, who had already exited SDS to found separate women's liberation groups. But even after the 1968 statement on women's oppression, old habits inside SDS died hard. A group of New Left women reported that they were still the movement's "shit workers," while men continued to hold most leadership positions.[8] One chapter of the organization put out a pamphlet in 1969 that stated, "The system is like a woman; you have to fuck it to make it change."[9]

For some New Left women, the 1969 counter-inauguration protest against Richard Nixon was the last straw, as Ruth Rosen documents in her book *The World Split Open: How the Modern Women's Movement Changed America*.[10] Two women's liberation activists—one Marilyn

Salzman Webb, the other Shulamith Firestone—were among those chosen to represent the struggle for women's liberation (by the male organizers) from the podium.

Webb started to deliver her speech, which began, "We as women are oppressed. We, as women [who] are supposedly the most privileged in this society, are mutilated as human beings so that we will learn to function within the capitalist system." As Webb spoke, however, her speech was drowned by hecklers shouting, "Fuck her! Take her off the stage! Rape her in a back alley!" and jeers to "Take it off!"[11] After this experience, Webb concluded, "We had to make a break from SDS and become an autonomous movement."[12]

Women's liberationist and journalist Ellen Willis, who had been sitting on the stage wondering why the event organizers did not attempt to quell the heckling, wrote, "A genuine alliance with male radicals will not be possible until sexism sickens them as much as racism. This will not be accomplished through persuasion, conciliation, or love, but through independence and solidarity; radical men will stop oppressing us and make our fight their own when they can't get us to join them on any other terms."[13]

In this atmosphere, it is perfectly understandable that many women's liberationists decided to exit the New Left and form separate women's liberation organizations.

Distortions of Marxism in the New Left

Thus, many radical feminists turned away from the New Left at least partly because of the denunciations of women's liberation that so often came from New Left radicals—many of them self-proclaimed Marxists. But those claiming Marxism as their theoretical worldview often belonged to Maoist or Stalinist organizations that had distorted classical Marxist theory beyond recognition. While Marx had defined socialism as "the self-emancipation of the working class," the dominant politics of the New Left effectively rejected this central tenet. While some 1960s-era Marxists were critical of the Soviet Union, China, and Cuba, they were a small minority of the left in that era. By the time of the SDS's final split conference in 1969, various factions of Maoism and Stalinism had come to dominate its politics.

Writing in 1969, Jack Weinberg and Jack Gerson of the Independent Socialists—who were critical of SDS's dominant politics—explained why these political tendencies came to influence the New Left. First, "It has been only too easy for the U.S. left to cast longing glances elsewhere for its own salvation,"[14] rather than setting its sights on the self-mobilization of the US working class. Second, the global polarization of the Cold War era between the United States and the Soviet Union led many 1960s-era radicals to identify with the enemies of American imperialism. As Weinberg and Gerson remarked, "Acceptance of the methodology, 'The enemy of my enemy is my friend' (patriotism in reverse), allows U.S. imperialism to define (negatively) the models toward which revolutionaries should aspire."[15]

Finally, the Vietnam War played a key role in shaping the political consciousness of the New Left. The powerful struggle of the National Liberation Front (NLF) in Vietnam led many in SDS to identify anti-imperialism as the key component in transforming society. Thus, Weinberg and Gerson observed, "Since its earliest days, the majority of the new left has reflected a strong affinity with Castro and Che Guevara, with Ho Chi Minh, with Mao, and with others similarly locked in combat with American imperialism and involved in a real or imagined process of revolutionizing their society."[16]

As New Left activist Max Elbaum later recalled, "With a few exceptions, Maoist groups had an unfriendly attitude toward the rapidly growing women's liberation movement (dismissing it as petty bourgeois) and were intensely hostile to homosexuality and the emerging lesbian/gay rights movement."[17]

In historian Alice Echols's description,

> Neither Weathermen nor the Progressive Labor Party [PL]—the dominant factions within SDS in the late '60s—was sympathetic to women's liberation. In their atavistic embrace of the labor metaphysic, PL'ers insisted that racism and sexism were "secondary contradictions" which would be resolved by socialist revolution. In Weathermen's apocalyptic vision, the system would be brought down by the Vietnamese abroad and Black militants at home (with support from white revolutionaries and the white youth they organized).[18]

Many women's liberationists also questioned the role of women in so-called existing socialist or communist societies of the time, where women remained oppressed. In 1968, activist Anne Koedt argued in New York Radical Women's *Notes from the First Year* that the Soviet Union had "simply transferred male supremacy, paternalism and male power onto a new economy."[19] That same year, women's liberationists Beverly Jones and Judith Brown coauthored a document, "Toward a Female Liberation Movement," which argued that existing socialist societies had not led to the equality of women:

> In female liberation literature, we hear about three groups of women who allegedly "won their freedom" or are winning equality by picking up guns and fighting for the national liberation of one or another country. Cuba, the most often cited case, did use women as troops, much as they are used in SDS. In the war, women had much the same status as the female in SDS, and now that the Cuban revolution has moved into its cultural phase, we know what Castro wants them to do: go home, cook, take care of the kids.[20]

Despite their misgivings, however, many radical feminists who formed separate women's liberation groups initially remained committed to participating in the New Left and/or maintained their commitment to fighting imperialism and capitalism. As Linda Nicholson describes, "The early organizers of radical feminism shared with the rest of the New Left a belief in the systemic nature of much of political injustice. Thus when these women began to perceive the situation of women as representing a case of this injustice, they employed the adjective 'radical' to describe their stance. It signified a commitment to look for root causes."[21] Echols likewise notes, "And while feminists like Firestone argued that women should form their own movement, they did not suggest that as individuals women should withdraw from the left."[22] Freeman also envisioned both "organizing all women around issues which directly affect their lives" and "organizing other women into the [New Left] Movement."[23] Historian Sara Evans makes a similar point in her history of the development of the 1960s women's movement, *Personal Politics*: "Separatism was in the cards logically, for the New Left was focused on the need for all oppressed groups to organize themselves.... But women in the New Left also resisted. They kept trying to find a way to be equal within the very insurgency that had built the foundation for their growing self-consciousness."[24]

In January 1968, for example, members of New York Radical Women took part in the Jeannette Rankin Brigade, named after the first woman elected to the US Congress and the only member of Congress to vote against US entry into both the First and Second World Wars. The Rankin Brigade held an antiwar protest and conference against the Vietnam War on the first day of the congressional session, attended by five thousand women. But New York Radical Women also brought women's liberation issues to the fore, leading a group of four hundred that evening to Arlington National Cemetery, where they buried a dummy representing "Traditional Womanhood."[25]

Radical Feminists versus "Politicos"

There were a significant number of women activists who did not join the feminist exodus from SDS. Indeed, some of the most forceful objections to radical feminism came from women "politicos," who belonged to one or another of the factions within SDS described above. Bernardine Dohrn was an outspoken politico from one of the Revolutionary Youth Movement factions of SDS (which later formed the Weathermen, an organization that viewed political violence as an end in itself). The Weathermen's road to women's liberation required women to demonstrate their "equal" ability to engage in political violence: "Political power grows out of the barrel of a gun, and the struggle to gain and use political power against the state is the struggle for our liberation."[26]

The Weathermen accused radical feminists of "accept[ing] the chauvinism of men as unchangeable—and thus their strategy is to weaken men and revolutionary male leadership so that women (in the weakness they have accepted as unchangeable) can be equal or superior."[27] In this context, Dohrn called women's liberation groups "bourgeois, unconscious, or unconcerned with class struggle and the exploitation of working class women."[28] Thus, many of the loudest arguments from New Left women against radical feminism came from women politicos like Dohrn. Firestone later countered: "Contemporary politicos see feminism as only tangent to 'real' radical politics, instead of central, directly radical in itself; they still see male issues, e.g. the draft, as universal, and female issues, e.g., abortion, as sectarian."[29]

Nicholson noted that the basis of the disagreements between radical feminists and Marxists shifted somewhat as many of those from the New Left who had been hostile came to accept the importance of women's oppression:

> The derogatory stance of many Marxists to the women's movement diminished somewhat by the early 1970s. Gender joined the ranks of race to become a worthy organizing issue. Persisting for a longer time was the question of how gender oppression was best to be explained. While many Marxists came to accede to radical feminism's claim that gender oppression was a significant type of oppression, the argument remained that radical feminism lacked an adequate explanation of its cause. [30]

Socialist Feminists and Marxist Feminists

There were also many women radicals from the New Left era who have received far less attention from historians, but who were in the process of gravitating toward classical Marxist theory or who had also been won to joining a Marxist organization, albeit of a different variety than the Weathermen or PL. Although these Marxist women remained in a minority in the early years of the women's liberation movement, they played their own role in the movement, mobilizing for legal abortion, equal pay, subsidized child care, union organizing, and the Equal Rights Amendment—from working-class women's perspective.

Many of these socialist feminists and Marxist feminists took part in the founding convention of the Coalition of Labor Union Women (CLUW) in 1974. CLUW's founding statement prioritized its four main goals: "to promote affirmative action in the workplace; to strengthen the role of women in unions; to organize the unorganized women; and to increase the involvement of women in the political and legislative process."[31] Afterward, the Illinois-based Direct Action for Rights in Employment (DARE) reported, "The striking fact about the founding convention was that the large majority of participants (at least 2,000 out of the 3,000) were not left women, nor were they union staff women. They were rank & file women whose presence indicated that there are enormous numbers of women who are angry and that those numbers can be brought together."[32]

Despite its promising start, CLUW's founding meeting took place just as the decline in social and class struggle began in the United States, and it never reached its potential in organizing a rank-and-file working women's movement. Nevertheless, this example demonstrates the possibilities of socialist feminists and Marxist feminists' orientation on working-class women and their efforts to help mobilize these women in their own interests. In addition, left-wing and socialist feminists formed women's organizations such as Bread and Roses in Boston and the Chicago Women's Liberation Union (CWLU), that consciously oriented to the needs of working-class and poor women. Some of these women incorporated an analysis of class society into the struggle for women's liberation. And many of these activists had an enormous impact on the struggle for women's liberation at the grassroots level.

For example, an offshoot of CWLU was a project known as the Jane collective, in which women activists trained themselves to perform abortions at both a far lower cost and a much higher level of safety than what was generally available to women in conditions of illegality. Between

1969 and 1973, Jane performed hundreds of safe and low-cost abortions, without encountering medical complications. The collective offered free abortions to poor women because it believed that every woman should have the right to abortion, whatever their financial status.[33]

Radical Feminism and Patriarchy Theory

After radical feminists established themselves outside of the New Left, however, many gravitated toward separatism, and "women-only" organizing became their preferred route to fighting women's oppression. Patriarchy theory provided separatism's political center, based on two assumptions: first, locating the source of women's oppression in men's innate propensity to dominate women; second, the need for alternatives to Marxism in explaining women's oppression.

The notion of the "patriarchy" is widely accepted today. But there is a difference between the popular use of the term *patriarchy* as a description of sexism and radical feminists' *theory* of patriarchy in the 1970s, which described a distinct social system through which all men oppress all women. While this might seem like hairsplitting, a system of sexism and a system of patriarchy are theoretically worlds apart.

The theory of patriarchy was a relatively recent development in feminist thought. Before the women's liberation movement of the 1960s, patriarchy referred to a specific family form among ancient Greeks and Romans, of absolute rule by the male head of the household over its male and female dependent members. The notion of "*the* patriarchy" as a social system, coupled with hostility to Marxism, originated with radical feminists. As Nicholson argues, "In counter to Engels' argument, radical feminists claimed that male domination, labeled 'patriarchy,' extends further back than even to the beginnings of class society. . . . This specific criticism was conjoined with a more generalized suspicion of traditional Marxism's focus on the 'economic.'"[34]

Susan Brownmiller, a widely read radical feminist of the time, wrote (inaccurately) in *Against Our Will: Men, Women and Rape* that "the great socialist theoreticians Marx and Engels and their many confreres and disciples who developed the theory of class oppression and put words like 'exploitation' into the everyday vocabulary, they, too were strangely silent about rape, unable to fit it into their economic constructs."[35] (Brownmiller clearly had not actually read Engels's classic *Origin of the Family, Private Property and the State*, discussed in chapter 2 of this volume, in which he argues of the rise of the family and women's oppression in class society: "The man took command in the home also; the woman was degraded and reduced to servitude; she became the slave of his lust and a mere instrument for the production of children. . . . She is delivered over unconditionally into the power of the husband; if he kills her, he is only exercising his rights."[36])

But, as Marxist feminist Martha Gimenez observes, the "Marx" many patriarchy theorists rejected was based more on a straw figure than reality: "Second wave feminist thought developed largely in a dialog with Marx; not with the real Marx, however, but with a 'straw Marx' whose work is riddled with failures (e.g., failure to theorize childbirth, women's labor, the oppression of women), determinisms and reductionisms (e.g., class reductionism, economic determinism, vulgar materialism), disregard for 'agency,' 'sex blind categories,' and 'misogyny.'"[37]

◆ ◆ ◆

Different variants of patriarchy theory emerged during this era. Some rooted women's oppression in biological differences, while others emphasized psychological or cultural phenomena. But all privileged women's oppression over other forms of oppression, while the possibility that women and men might share a common interest in the fight against racism, homophobia, national oppression, and class exploitation was ruled out.

The New York Radical Feminists described male chauvinism in psychological terms in its founding statement in 1969: "We believe that the purpose of male chauvinism is primarily to obtain psychological ego satisfaction, and that only secondarily does this manifest itself in economic relationships. For this reason we do not believe that capitalism, or any other economic system, is the cause of female oppression, nor do we believe that female oppression will disappear as a result of a purely economic revolution."[38]

Feminist Kate Millett's *Sexual Politics*, published in 1970, describes the system of patriarchy as cultural, with the role of the family as paramount:

> Patriarchy's chief institution is the family. It is both a mirror of and a connection with the larger society; a patriarchal unit within a patriarchal whole. . . . Serving as an agent of the larger society, the family not only encourages its own members to adjust and conform, but acts as a unit in the government of the patriarchal state which rules its citizens through its family heads. Even in patriarchal societies where they are granted legal citizenship, women tend to be ruled through the family alone and have little or no formal relation to the state.[39]

But biological explanations also loomed large. Shulamith Firestone argued explicitly in *The Dialectic of Sex: A Case for Feminist Revolution*, "I have attempted to take the class analysis one step further to its roots in the biological division of the sexes."[40] Firestone hypothesizes that women could not achieve true gender equality until science freed women from physically bearing children, perhaps through constructing an artificial womb.

Brownmiller described the root of women's oppression in the crudest of biological terms, based on men's physical ability to rape: "When men discovered that they could rape, they proceeded to do it. . . . Man's discovery that his genitalia could serve as a weapon to generate fear must rank as one of the most important discoveries of prehistoric times, along with the use of fire and the first crude stone axe. From prehistoric times to the present, I believe, rape has played a critical function."[41] On this basis, Brownmiller concluded that men use rape to enforce their power over women, writing, "It is nothing more and nothing less than a conscious process by which all men keep all women in a state of fear."[42]

Brownmiller furthermore located the source of all inequality in society as originating with male power over women:

> It seems eminently sensible to hypothesize that man's violent capture and rape of the female led first to the establishment of a rudimentary mate-protectorate and then sometime later to the full-blown solidification of power, the patriarchy. As the first permanent acquisition of man, his first piece of real property, woman was, in fact, the cornerstone, of the "house of the father." Man's forcible extension of his boundaries to his mate and later to their offspring was the beginning of the concept of ownership. Concepts of hierarchy, slavery and private property flowed from, and could only be predicated upon, the initial subjugation of women.[43]

Radical Feminism Abandons Radicalism and Turns Right

If the patriarchy is paramount, then the centrality of women's oppression diminishes the importance of all other forms of oppression and exploitation. Firestone argued explicitly, for example, "Racism is sexism extended."[44]

This theoretical framework allowed some radical feminists to justify reactionary assumptions in the name of combating women's oppression. Brownmiller's analysis, for example, easily led her to reach openly racist conclusions in her account of the 1955 lynching of Emmett Till. Fourteen-year-old Till, visiting family in Jim Crow Mississippi that summer, committed the "crime" of whistling at a married white woman named Carolyn Bryant, in a teenage prank. Till was tortured and shot before his young body was dumped in the Tallahatchie River.

Despite Till's lynching, Brownmiller describes Till and his killer as sharing power over a "white woman," using stereotypes that Black activist and scholar Angela Y. Davis calls "the resuscitation of the old racist myth of the Black rapist."[45] Brownmiller's own words illustrate Davis's claim:

> Rarely has one single case exposed so clearly as Till's the underlying group male antagonisms over access to women, for what began in Bryant's store should not be misconstrued as an innocent flirtation. . . . Emmett Till was going to show his black buddies that he, and by inference, they could get a white woman and Carolyn Bryant was the nearest convenient object. In concrete terms, the accessibility of all white women was on review.[46]

Elsewhere, Brownmiller writes, "And what of the wolf whistle, Till's gesture of adolescent bravado?. . . The whistle was no small tweet of hubba-hubba or melodious approval for a well turned ankle. . . . It was a deliberate insult just short of physical assault, a last reminder to Carolyn Bryant that this black boy, Till, had in mind to possess her."[47] The acclaimed novelist, poet, and activist Alice Walker responded in the *New York Times Book Review* in 1975, "Emmett Till was not a rapist. He was not even a man. He was a child who did not understand that whistling at a white woman could cost him his life."[48]

Davis describes the contradictions inherent in Brownmiller's analysis of rape: "In choosing to take sides with white women, regardless of the circumstances, Brownmiller herself capitulates to racism. Her failure to alert white women about the urgency of combining a fierce challenge to racism with the necessary battle against sexism is an important plus for the forces of racism today."[49]

In 1976, *TIME* named Susan Brownmiller one of its women of the year, praising her book as "the most rigorous and provocative piece of scholarship that has yet emerged from the feminist movement."[50] The objections to Brownmiller's overtly racist standpoint from accomplished Black women such as Davis and Walker went largely unnoticed by the political mainstream.

Brownmiller had played a key role in the *Ladies' Home Journal* occupation in 1970, described in chapter 3. Yet she penned her racist remarks on Emmett Till just five years later, illustrating the rapid shift rightward of many radical feminists who embraced separatism in the 1970s.

Joining Forces with the Christian Right to Make Pornography Illegal

By the start of the 1980s, the most visible wing of radical feminism was unapologetically right-wing in its political aims. Separatists Catharine MacKinnon and Andrea Dworkin initiated a campaign to criminalize the production and sale of pornography on the grounds that it "violates the rights of women." Their campaign, called "Women Against Pornography," succeeded in winning an ordinance outlawing pornography in the cities of Minneapolis and Indianapolis in 1983 and 1984, but both laws were eventually overturned by a Supreme Court decision on the grounds that they were unconstitutional.

Far from challenging the then-rising Christian right, MacKinnon and Dworkin enlisted them in their campaign. In Indianapolis, for example, Women Against Pornography drew the enthusiastic support of a city council member active in the Stop ERA (Equal Rights Amendment) crusade and from the city's mayor, police department, and the local Christian right. The ordinance was pushed through the city council with the overwhelming support of Republicans. These right-wingers wanted to outlaw pornography for reasons that had nothing to do with advancing women's right. Criminalizing pornography, rather, fit nicely with their interest in finding any way to legitimize the routine police practices of raiding gay and lesbian bars, harassing prostitutes, and committing acts of police brutality. Yet MacKinnon and Dworkin were pleased to have these right-wingers on board. As Dworkin explained in a *New York Times* interview in 1985, "When Jerry Falwell [leader of the Moral Majority] starts saying there's harm in pornography, that is valuable to me."[51]

In the early 1990s, Dworkin and MacKinnon's antipornography legislation was put into practice in Canada. In 1992, the Canadian Supreme Court adopted the substance of a legal brief submitted by MacKinnon in its *Regina v. Butler* decision. The court declared that the right to freedom of expression can be suspended when sexually explicit material promotes "harm" or is "degrading" or "dehumanizing," particularly to women.

The new law backfired badly, however. The ruling vastly increased the jurisdiction of Canadian customs officials, who used their new censorship powers primarily *against* feminist and LGBT publications. Indeed, officials seized cases of books en route to small feminist and LGBT bookstores, while often allowing the same titles to proceed smoothly to mainstream commercial bookstores.[52] Soon after the ruling, border guards seized a plethora of literature. The books withheld included such titles as *Black Looks: Race and Representation*, by bell hooks, assigned for university courses—along with those of literary figures such as Oscar Wilde, Langston Hughes, and Audre Lorde.[53] Zealous border guards even withheld an issue of the liberal *Nation* magazine in 1993.

Andrea Dworkin herself was targeted: her books *Woman Hating* and *Pornography: Men Possessing Women* were confiscated "because they illegally eroticized pain and bondage."[54] Canadian customs officials even confiscated a cookbook, *Hot, Hotter, Hottest*.[55] A satirical feminist cartoon book, *Hothead Paisan*, was banned for being "degrading to men." A publication called *Weenie Toons* was banned for "degradation of the male penis."[56]

A Vancouver-based LGBT bookstore named Little Sister's spent many years unsuccessfully seeking to overturn the Supreme Court's 1992 ruling on the basis that it violates freedom of expression. In 2000, the Supreme Court acknowledged that border agents had been singling out LGBT bookstores for harassment, but it maintained the law's constitutionality. Little Sister's appealed again but finally ran out of money when the court refused to advance the legal costs necessary to continue the appeal. In 2007, Little Sister's co-owner Jim Deva finally acknowledged, "We have to put our case to bed and declare defeat."[57]

Separatism and Lifestyle Politics

The social movements of the late 1960s and early 1970s had produced a mass radicalization; their decline by the mid-1970s produced widespread disorientation and political retreat. Separatism as a lifestyle exacerbated this tendency among radical feminists. During the 1970s, as activism declined, radical feminist collectives became more fragmented and demoralized and whole organizations turned inward, leading to irreparable splits—including women-only collectives that often lasted less than a few years. As Alice Echols described, "By 1973, the radical feminist movement was actually in decline. The groups responsible for the important theoretical breakthroughs were either dead or moribund."[58]

Both Redstockings and New York Radical Women had splintered by the early 1970s. In the words of one feminist, "When you stop looking out, and turn exclusively inward, at some point you begin to feed on each other. If you don't direct your anger externally—politically—you turn it against yourselves."[59] Separatism promoted fragmentation rather than unity, particularly when combined with the high degree of moralism that existed. One participant described in hindsight, "In the name of anti-elitism, they were trying to pull off the most elite thing possible. The meeting ended with charges and counter-charges and a distinct lack of a feeling of sisterhood."[60] Separatism never attracted large numbers of working-class and Black women or other women of color because the need to fight alongside men against racism or in the class struggle made separatist ideas unappealing. The Combahee River Collective, for example, stated in 1977,

> Although we are feminists and Lesbians, we feel solidarity with progressive Black men and do not advocate the fractionalization that white women who are separatists demand. Our situation as Black people necessitates that we have solidarity around the fact of race, which white women of course do not need to have with white men, unless it is their negative solidarity as racial oppressors. We struggle together with Black men against racism, while we also struggle with Black men about sexism.[61]

Black feminist bell hooks wrote, "The separatist notion that women could resist sexism by withdrawing from contact with men reflected a bourgeois class perspective."[62] She also argued that this perspective alienated many women of color and lesbians:

> [The] affirmation of bonding between Black women and men was part of anti-racist struggle. It could have been part of feminist struggle had white women's liberationists stressed the need for women and men to resist sexist socialization that teaches us to hate and fear one another. They chose instead to emphasize hate, especially male woman-hating, suggesting that it could not be changed. Therefore no viable political solidarity could exist between women and men. Women of color from various ethnic backgrounds, as well as women who were active in the gay movement, not only experienced the development of solidarity between women and men in the resistance struggle, but recognized its value.[63]

In conclusion hooks noted, "Reactionary separatism is rooted in the conviction that male supremacy is an absolute aspect of our culture, that women have only two alternatives: accepting or withdrawing from it to create subcultures. This position eliminates any need for revolutionary struggle, and it is no way a threat to the status quo."[64]

Somewhat unexpectedly, a reincarnated radical feminism rooted in ostensibly "natural" biology has surged in influence in recent years—with a reactionary antitransgender agenda. This group of feminists issued a 2013 statement, "Forbidden Discourse: The Silencing of Feminist Criticism of 'Gender,' an Open Statement from 37 Radical Feminists

from Five Countries," in which they claimed to be victimized for asserting "the right of women to organize for their liberation separately from
men, including M>F (male to female) transgendered people." In the
statement they conclude,

> We look forward to freedom from gender. The "freedom for gender"
> movement, whatever the intentions of its supporters, is reinforcing the
> culture and institutions of gender that are oppressing women. We reject
> the notion that this analysis is transphobic. We uphold the radical femi-
> nist principle that women are oppressed by male supremacy in both its
> individual and institutional forms. We continue to support the radical
> feminist strategy of organizing an independent power base and speaking
> the basic truths of our experience out of earshot of the oppressor. We
> hold these principles and strategies essential for advancing toward
> women's liberation.[65]

Radical feminism, which had propelled the women's liberation movement
forward in the late 1960s, was derailed by its own theoretical shortcomings. Its recent antitransgender resurgence places itself firmly outside
today's movements that seek to end LGBT oppression in all its forms.

Other Conceptions of "the Patriarchy"

As described above, the term *patriarchy*, though widely adopted since
the 1970s, does not necessarily refer to a separate system of male domination as defined by separatist feminists. Black feminist bell hooks, for
example, has used the term *patriarchy* for decades, but in a very different
way than either separatists or dual-systems theorists. Like others in the
Black feminist tradition, hooks incorporates patriarchy as one of numerous and simultaneous oppressions, arguing, "I often use the phrase 'imperialist white-supremacist capitalist patriarchy' to describe the
interlocking political systems that are the foundation of our nation's
politics."[66] Moreover, hooks approaches the idea of patriarchy without
hostility toward men, offering this definition in 2003: "Patriarchy is a
political-social system that insists that males are inherently dominating,
superior to everything and everyone deemed weak, especially females,
and endowed with the right to dominate and rule over the weak and to
maintain that dominance through various forms of psychological terrorism and violence."[67] But hooks argued that *men do not run the patriarchy*.
On the contrary, they are also victimized by it. Thus, she states, "patriarchy is the single most life-threatening social disease assaulting the

male body and spirit in our nation."[68]

There is not space here to provide adequate consideration of the many arguments that unfolded at the time—including attempts to incorporate capitalism and patriarchy into a single system, the *capitalist-patriarchy*, which socialist feminist Zillah R. Eisenstein defined as the "mutually reinforcing dialectical relationship between capitalist class structure and hierarchical sexual structuring."[69] The comments below are therefore directed specifically at those socialist feminists who embraced the concept of "patriarchy" as a *separate* system from capitalism.

"Dual-Systems" Theory: Capitalism and Patriarchy

A number of socialist feminists in the 1970s attempted to formulate a theory describing capitalism and patriarchy as two distinct social systems, the former being one of exploitation and the latter one in which men oppress women.

Socialist-feminist Heidi Hartmann gave voice to those who had become frustrated with attempts by domestic-labor theorists to unite Marxist and feminist theories (discussed in chapter 6). She circulated a paper in 1975, "The Unhappy Marriage of Marxism and Feminism," a revised draft of which appeared in the influential book, *Women and Revolution: A Discussion of the Unhappy Marriage of Marxism and Feminism*, first published in 1979. In the essay, Hartmann argues, "The 'marriage' of Marxism and feminism had been like the marriage of husband and wife depicted in English common law: Marxism and feminism are one, and that one is Marxism."[70]

Hartmann concluded, "Who benefits from women's labor? Surely capitalists, but also surely men, who as husbands and fathers receive personalized services at home. The content and extent of the services may vary by class or ethnic or racial group, but the fact of their receipt does not."[71] This observation is undoubtedly correct, in that women's responsibility for domestic labor and childrearing produces significant inequality in the life conditions between women and men, who do not have to carry this burden. This will not change without a struggle to change conditions inside the family—including, as Lenin, Kollontai, and other Bolsheviks noted, after a revolution that transfers power to the working class.

At the same time, however, working-class men and women both have an objective interest in combating all forms of oppression as part of the fight for socialism. This is a necessary precondition for the self-emancipation of the working class, if the fight for a socialist society is to succeed. As Marx and Engels argued in *The German Ideology*, "The revolution is necessary, therefore, not only because the *ruling* class cannot be overthrown in any other way, but also because the class *overthrowing* it can only in a revolution succeed in ridding itself of all the muck of ages and become fitted to found society anew."[72] Hartmann, however, separates family relations from the system of capitalism as two entirely separate phenomenon—assigning all men, regardless of class, to a shared system of patriarchy, through which they "control women's labor power." Hartmann described patriarchy as

> a set of social relations between men, which have a material base, and which, though hierarchical, establish or create interdependence and solidarity among men that enable them to dominate women. Though patriarchy is hierarchical and men of different classes, races, or ethnic groups have different places in the patriarchy, they are also united in their shared relationship of dominance over their women; they are dependent on each other to maintain that domination.... The material basis of patriarchy is man's control over women's labor power ... [and] does not rest solely on childrearing in the family, but on all the social structures that enable men to control women's labor.[73]

The essence of this approach became known as "dual-systems theory," and its advocates fell within the broader context of socialist feminism.

Regarding Marxism, Hartmann argues, "either we need a healthier marriage or we need a divorce."[74] In particular, she notes, "Though aware of the deplorable situation of women in their time the early Marxists failed to focus on the differences between men's and women's experiences under capitalism. They did not focus on the feminist questions—how and why women are oppressed as women. They did not, therefore, recognize the vested interest men had in women's continued subordination."[75]

Hartmann is correct in stating that Marx and Engels did not focus on the "feminist questions" that emerged in the 1970s. Marx and Engels were a product of their own times. Indeed, Marx and Engels's feminist contemporaries didn't challenge certain Victorian assumptions about women's roles either. Elizabeth Cady Stanton, a key figure in the radical suffrage movement, delivered a speech at Seneca Falls, New York, in 1892 listing four points regarding the rights of women. The last point stated, "Fourthly, it is only the incidentals of life, such as mother, wife, sister, daughter, that may involve some special duties and training."[76]

Like Stanton, Marx and Engels accepted some ideas about women that have since been successfully challenged. This alone does not negate their contribution toward providing a materialist explanation for women's oppression. Vogel argued that the questions Marx and Engels confronted in their lifetimes were quite different from those confronting 1970s socialist feminists, who then overlooked their substantial insights:

> The frustration many socialist-feminists experience derives also from the fact that Marx and Engels did not say what these modern critics wanted to hear. Or, to put it another way, today's questioners often ask, and try to answer, a different set of woman questions. . . . Because they are asking different questions, however important, those socialist-feminist theorists and activists who today chide Marx and Engels for their failings often cannot hear what they are actually saying. And yet a substantial amount of material is there, waiting to be developed."[77]

Marxist feminist Martha Gimenez likewise argued that the focus of many 1970s feminists on the aspects of women's oppression that Marx neglected to analyze led to a dismissal of the *analytical tools* he provided for future generations:

> I believe that Marx's most important potential contributions to feminist theory and politics reside precisely in the aspect of his work that most feminists ignored: his methodology. Exclusive focus on what he said and did not say about women kept feminist theorists from exploring the potential of his methodological insights to deepen our understanding of the phenomena called "the oppression of women" or, in earlier times, the "woman question."[78]

In addition, many dual-systems theorists assumed that Marx made a moral judgment in distinguishing between "productive" and "unproductive" labor, as if he regarded unproductive labor as unimportant. But *productive labor* in Marxist economics refers merely to labor that produces *surplus value* and has nothing to do with its usefulness, or *use value*, to human society.

Socialist feminist Nancy Holmstrom argues that distinguishing between "productive" and "unproductive" labor was merely an attempt to understand the role of surplus value in the workings of capitalism: "It was not sexism that led Marx to say that in capitalism women's household labor was unproductive for he said the same thing about a carpenter working for the government. Although both are obviously productive in a general sense, Marx was seeking to understand what is productive from the point of view of capitalism—that only labor produces surplus value."[79] Indeed, Marx's definition of productive labor had been key to locating women's domestic labor as a crucial component of social reproduction, as advanced by Vogel and other domestic-labor theorists, described later.

Attempts to integrate patriarchy and capitalism as parallel systems proved difficult, both in theory and in practice. While all women are oppressed, class differences also often divide women from each other. Moreover, because of the virulence of racism, the gender oppression faced by Black and other racially oppressed women is different in crucial respects than that faced by white women. Likewise, it is impossible to separate where sexism ends and homophobia begins in the oppression faced by lesbians and trans people. Accounting for these differences requires a more complex approach to analyzing women's oppression, while also providing a strategy for the liberation of all women.

Indeed, a fundamental set of contradictions plagued dual-systems theory, which became more evident with the passage of time. By embracing the theory of patriarchy, dual-systems theorists reproduced many of the same shortcomings of separatist feminism. As Gimenez notes, "feminist rejection of Marx's 'economic determinism' led to the production of ahistorical theories of patriarchy that sought the origins of male domination outside modes of production."[80]

Vogel criticizes dual-systems theory for its lack of attention to racism and national oppression specifically:

> Socialist-feminist theory has focused on the relationship between feminism and socialism, and between sex and class oppression, largely to the exclusion of issues of racial or national oppression. At most, sex, race, and class are issues of racial or national oppression whose parallel manifestations harm their victims more or less equally. Strategically socialist feminists call for sisterhood and a women's movement that unites women from all sectors of society. Nonetheless, their sisters of color often express distrust of the contemporary women's movement and generally remain committed to activity in their own communities. The socialist-feminist movement has been unable to confront this phenomenon either theoretically or practically.[81]

Similarly, Holmstrom comments, "Socialist feminists of the 1970s had criticized liberal and Marxist writers for using categories that were 'gender-blind': 'the individual' in liberalism, 'the working class' in Marxism. . . . But women of color could and did make the same criticism of feminism, including socialist feminism, for using race-blind categories: 'working class women,' or simply 'women.'"[82]

In an essay in *The Unhappy Marriage of Marxism and Feminism,* Black feminist Gloria Joseph focuses her arguments on this lack of attention to racism in an essay, critiquing Hartmann while explaining the vastly different experiences of Black women from those Hartmann was addressing. Joseph argues that Hartmann was "speaking about a specific but unlabeled and apparently middle-class group of feminists." She continued, "So while Hartmann's essay represents an attempt to transcend the limitations and shortcomings of both Marxist analysis and feminist analysis, I lament the absence of an analysis of the Black woman and her role as a member of the wedding."[83]

Joseph goes on to examine the very different relationship between Black women and men because of their shared experience of racism: "The slave experience for Blacks in the United States made an ironic contribution to male-female equality. Laboring in the fields or in the homes, men and women were equally dehumanized and brutalized." In modern society, she concludes, "The rape of Black women and the lynching and castration of Black men are equally heinous in their nature."[84]

Describing the theoretical difficulties of "the anti-Marxist version of socialist-feminism," Holmstrom argues: "To accommodate race oppression (and heterosexism and other forms of oppression), there seemed to be two choices. If we need to posit 'a system of social relations' to explain sexism as they argued, then to explain racism (and other forms of oppression) . . . we would have to posit systems beyond capitalism and patriarchy." She adds, "The other option was to go back to a theory like Marxism which aims to be all inclusive. . . . This did not seem an attractive option, but neither did the multiplication of systems."[85]

Vogel remarks, "The idea of two different systems—capitalism and patriarchy—soon became hegemonic in socialist-feminist theorizing" adding, "Yet this meant that Marxist theory remained untouched by feminist insight."[86] It also meant that patriarchy theory retained all the theoretical problems inherent in separatist feminism—most notably, privileging women's oppression over other forms of oppression, racism in particular—while downplaying the importance of class divisions central to Marxism.

By the end of the 1970s, dual-systems theory had faded in importance, even among socialist feminists. Although the term *patriarchy* has lived on, its meaning evolved to reference male dominance without privileging women's oppression over racism or other forms of oppression.

◆ ◆ ◆

Despite the fragmentation of the women's liberation movement in the 1970s, the impact of its rapid rise in the late 1960s should not be underestimated. Its unapologetic, protest-based brand of feminism brought women's oppression into the national spotlight after forty years of gross neglect. The women's liberation movement introduced concepts that had never before been put forward—including the right of women to control their own bodies and reproductive lives, an end to the sexual objectification of women, and an end to rape and violence against women. Meanwhile, the rise of the gay liberation movement brought forth the first demand for lesbian and gay liberation. Combined with the massive civil rights movement and the Black liberation movement, the social struggles of the late 1960s transformed consciousness in fundamental ways which are still felt today.

Chapter Six

Women and the Family:
The Domestic-Labor Debate

From the late 1960s into the 1970s, socialist feminists sought to analyze women's unpaid family work within a framework of Marxist political economy. Such an analysis would provide a foundation, they thought, for understanding women's differential positioning as mothers, family members, and workers, and thereby for a materialist analysis of women's subordination. . . . Women's liberationists studied Marxist texts, wrestled with Marxist concepts, and produced a range of original formulations combining, or at least intermingling, Marxism and feminism. Their enthusiasm for this work is hard today to recapture. It turned out, moreover, to be relatively brief. By the end of the 1970s, interest in domestic labor theorizing had dramatically declined.

—Lise Vogel[1]

While many of their contemporaries were in the process of pursuing patriarchy theory to explain women's oppression, women's liberationists involved in the 1970s domestic-labor debate explicitly attempted to locate its economic roots in capitalism. This was not an easy task, since Marx implied a theoretical framework for this understanding but did not pursue it himself. Moreover, while Marx and Engels understood the role of women in property-holding families in maintaining and reproducing generations of the capitalist class and its wealth, their approach to the role of women in working-class families was less developed and more contradictory.

Capitalism and the Family

Marx argued somewhat caustically in *Capital*, Volume 1, "The maintenance and reproduction of the working class is, and must ever be, a necessary condition to the reproduction of capital. But the capitalist may safely leave its fulfillment to the laborer's instincts of self-preservation and of propagation."[2] This is not the case historically, however. The family structure of preclass societies did not seamlessly evolve into the family ideal appropriate to capitalism.

Before the era of industrialization introduced laws regulating marriage norms for all classes in society, common law marriage was the custom. As socialist feminist Stephanie Coontz argues, "For most of Western history . . . marriage was a private contract between two families. . . . For 16 centuries, Christianity also defined the validity of a marriage on the basis of a couple's wishes. If two people claimed they had exchanged marital vows—even out alone by the haystack—the Catholic Church accepted that they were validly married."[3] Historian Joseph Martos likewise describes, "Before the eleventh century there was no such thing as a Christian wedding ceremony in the Latin Church, and throughout the Middle Ages there was no single church ritual for solemnizing marriage between Christians."[4]

The rise of capitalism prompted government regulation of marriage—and its prescribed family form. British Marxist Joan Smith wrote in the 1970s,

> Because the class of free wage-laborers is the essential pre-condition for capitalism, all capitalists have sought to intervene in the reproduction of this class. The Family system under which this class is reproduced is one of the first and most important areas of State intervention. The formless common law marriage of England (established purely by consent) was 'reformed' in 1753 into a stipulated Church ceremony after the calling of banns on three successive Sundays, and then in 1836 the office of Superintendent Registrar was established. (Prior to this legislation marriage law was merely canon law.) From the beginning of Capitalism the organization of reproduction in the privatized Family is massively controlled by the laws, repressive apparatus and ideological structures of the State.[5]

The same process Smith describes above took place elsewhere—including the United States, while it was still a British colony. In 1769, American colonies adopted the principles of English common law, making women legally invisible upon marriage: "By marriage, the husband and wife are one person in the law. The very being and legal existence of the woman is suspended during the marriage, or at least is incorporated into that of her husband under whose wing and protection she performs everything."[6] Until the mid-nineteenth century, US states continued to recognize marriages based on cohabitation. As Coontz noted, "By the later part of that century, however, the United States began to nullify common-law marriages and exert more control over who was allowed to marry."[7]

In the colonial era, individual colonies exerted their own interest in maintaining marriages once performed. Courts tended to allow divorce only in cases of extreme cruelty, infidelity, or abandonment—with the burden of proof on the accuser.[8] Only in the 1970s did divorce law loosen significantly, allowing couples to end their marriages simply over irreconcilable differences in states across the country. The liberalization of divorce laws led to a sharp rise in divorce rates in the 1980s. Today nearly 40 percent of children are born to parents who are unwed, either because of divorce or because they were never married to begin with.[9]

In addition, US marriage laws historically incorporated the explicitly racist interests of a capitalist class that was brought into being through a genocidal war against Native Americans and developed its Northern industrial centers through the chattel slavery of Africans. By 1691, Virginia had passed a law stating that any couple composed of a white person and a Black, mixed, or American Indian person would be banished from the colony. In 1724, Louisiana forbade marriages between enslaved people without the approval of the slave master. In 1865, Mississippi banned Black people from marrying whites, punishable by life imprisonment.[10] Even in 1967, interracial marriage was still banned in sixteen states when the US Supreme Court finally legalized it.

Because the institution of marriage under capitalism has relied upon rigidly defined gender roles, the legal system has until recently banned same-sex couples from marrying. In recent years, the struggle for equal marriage has been successful in many states, and it is likely to follow the trajectory of continued legalization state by state (as was the case with interracial marriage, divorce, and abortion law) and eventually achieve federal legalization. Nevertheless, the demand for legalizing same-sex marriage has met with resistance every step of the way. A 2006 decision by the Washington State Supreme Court exposed the motivations behind this resistance. In overturning a lower court's ruling that a state law banning same-sex marriage was unconstitutional, the Washington Supreme Court ruled,

> Under this standard, DOMA (the Defense of Marriage Act) is constitutional because the legislature was entitled to believe that limiting marriage to opposite-sex couples furthers procreation, essential to survival of the human race, and furthers the well-being of children by encouraging families where children are reared in homes headed by the children's biological parents. . . . DOMA bears a reasonable relationship to *legitimate state interests—procreation and child-rearing*.[11] (Emphasis added.)

The US Supreme Court has since overturned key parts of DOMA as "unconstitutional."[12] The history of marriage law, described above, demonstrates the degree to which the capitalist class, using its legal apparatus, maintains its allegiance to "traditional" marriage—but also how it is susceptible to pressure from below.

Marx and Engels on the Working-Class Family

Both Marx and Engels mistakenly believed 1) that the route to equality for working-class women lies exclusively in their participation in paid, productive labor and 2) that the working-class family was in the process of disappearing, because the participation of whole families in factory labor made family life impossible. Neither of these predictions materialized, yet neither is outlandish given the deteriorating conditions of working-class families and the corresponding changes in gender relations in their time.

At that point in English history, many working-class children were literally being worked to death before reaching adulthood. In *Capital*, Volume 1, Marx quotes a report by the Medical Officer for Health in 1875, describing "the average age at death of the Manchester . . . upper middle class was 38 years, while the average age at death of the laboring class was 17; while at Liverpool those figures were represented as 35 against 15. It thus appeared that the well-to-do classes had a lease of life which was more than double the value of that which fell to the lot of the less favored citizens."[13]

Marx also quotes a study commissioned by the Privy Council in 1863 into the health and nourishment of silk-weavers, needlewomen, kid-glovers, stocking-weavers, glove-weavers, and shoemakers. The study found widespread poverty and hunger, observing that the worst conditions were those of "the needle-women, silk-weavers and kid-glovers," living

> in quarters where commonly there is least fruit of sanitary supervision, least drainage, least scavenging, least suppression of public nuisances, least or worst water supply, and, if in town, least light and air. Such are the sanitary dangers to which poverty is almost certainly exposed, when it is poverty enough to imply scantiness of food. . . . These are painful reflections, especially when it is remembered that the poverty to which they advert is not the deserved poverty of idleness. In all cases it is the poverty of working populations. . . . And on a very large scale the nominal self-support can be only a circuit, longer or shorter, to pauperism."[14]

Writing decades earlier in *The Condition of the Working Class in England in 1844*, Engels noted that women and children had wholly replaced men in many textile jobs in Manchester, leaving hundreds of married men unemployed. The young Engels responded with a certain degree of shock at the gender-role reversal in these families, in which women became the breadwinners and the men performed the domestic labor: "In many cases the family is not wholly dissolved by the employment of the wife, but turned upside down. The wife supports the family, the husband sits at home, tends the children, sweeps the room and cooks."[15]

But Engels also makes the following astute observation: "We must admit that so total a reversal of the position of the sexes can have come to pass only because the sexes have been placed in a false position from the beginning. If the reign of the wife over the husband, as inevitably brought about by the factory system, is inhuman, the pristine rule of the husband over the wife must have been inhuman too."[16]

As Marx and Engels matured politically, they also concluded that women's involvement in productive labor played a role in raising their status within the family. As Marx writes, "However terrible and disgusting the dissolution, under the capitalist system, of the old family ties may appear, nevertheless, modern industry, by assigning as it does an important part in the process of production, outside the domestic sphere, to women, to young persons, and to children of both sexes, creates a new economic foundation for a higher form of the family and of the relation between the sexes."[17]

Likewise, Engels writes in *The Origin of the Family, Private Property and the State*,

> The peculiar character of man's domination over woman in the modern family, and the necessity as well as the manner of establishing real social equality between the two, will be brought out into full relief only when both are completely equal before the law. *It will then become evident that the first premise for the emancipation of women is the reintroduction of the entire female sex into public industry; and that this again demands that the quality possessed by the individual family of being the economic unit of society be abolished.*[18] (Emphasis added.)

The "Double Burden" of Women Workers

Since Marx and Engels's time, women have entered the workforce on a mass scale. While women's participation in paid employment does make them less reliant on a (male) partner for their means of subsistence, this alone has not made them the equals of men either in the family or in society at large. Capitalism has proven itself capable of incorporating women into the workforce without abandoning their centrality to performing domestic labor inside the family, resulting in a daily double burden of responsibilities. Moreover, the responsibility for the reproduction of labor power remains privatized, on the shoulders of individual working-class families.

Even in Marx's time, the capitalist class was in the process of bolstering the British working-class family because the impoverishment of the working class was endangering its ability to reproduce itself, as described above. Employers increased male workers' wages enough to provide for their dependent family members, in what became known as "the family wage."

As Joan Smith puts it,

> In the first half of the nineteenth century in Britain the workforce in the industrial towns failed to reproduce themselves and were constantly augmented by workers from the rural areas. Marx quotes many sources on the absolutely horrific conditions under which wage-workers lived and died in early Capitalism. At the demand of the most class-conscious Capitalists and at the demand of the wage-workers themselves, the Capitalist State had to intervene in order to impose restricted working hours on both women and children."[19]

Smith concludes, "Within the capitalist system there is thus a contradiction between the demands of production (women into the labor force) and the demands of reproduction (women into the home). It is this contradiction that is at the heart of women's double burden of woman and worker."[20] Capitalists hold an interest both in reducing payments to their workers as much as possible in order to increase their own profits but also in investing enough resources to ensure that the working-class family is able to reproduce labor power for the system.

Thus, the British government set and enforced marriage laws to encourage workers to live in nuclear family units, while setting the wheels in motion for the state to take on some of the responsibility for providing skills and services for the next generation of workers that had formerly been left to the family—including the establishment of free and compulsory public education.

But the needs and wants of the capitalist class have never singlehandedly determined the terms of class and social relations—including those of families. Rather, these have always been negotiated via class and social struggle, as workers advance their interests against those who own and control the means of production, and all those oppressed by the system fight for the betterment of their own conditions of life.

Vogel argues, "The processes of reproduction of labor power in class society ordinarily constitute an important terrain of battle." She argues that the results can be mixed—even, at times, reinforcing backward prejudices and ideas: "Migrant workers may fight against their isolation from kin. Native-born workers may oppose the use of foreign labor. Women may refuse to stay home to bear and raise children. Men may resist the participation of women in the labor force. Workers may support legislation banning child labor. Women and men may organize to defend the existing forms of their institutions of family life."[21]

As socialist feminist Johanna Brenner argues,

> The welfare state is a major arena of class struggle, within limits imposed by capitalist relations of production. Those limits can accommodate substantial reforms. However, these reforms have not been handed down from above as part of a strategy to impose the bourgeois family form on the working class. Welfare state policies have been achieved as political concessions to working-class movements and middle-class reformers. On the other hand, to regard the welfare state as a direct expression of working-class needs would be to ignore the constraints within which reform movements have operated.[22]

The Changing "Family"—Still Reproducing Labor Power for the System

The 1960s women's liberation movement successfully challenged the notion that marriage and childrearing should be the sum total of all women's life ambitions, responding to the dramatic rise in working mothers but also to advancing changes in families themselves. For example, fewer women today take their husbands' last names upon marriage than ever before. Likewise, thanks to the LGBT movement, more same-sex couples are raising children, challenging gender stereotypes not only inside families but also in society as whole.

The rise in divorce has produced many more single-parent households, typically headed by women and living in poverty. Other low-income households bring extended families under the same roof for survival. As more women have taken on jobs outside the home, they are having fewer children on average and doing so later in life.

The responsibilities of domestic labor have tended to decrease compared with decades past. While improved household technology is a contributing factor, less time is spent cooking and cleaning because standards of cleanliness are less rigid and home-cooked meals less frequent. Meanwhile, as more middle-class women take on higher-paying and professional jobs, there is an increased tendency for domestic work to be turned into paid labor—with the hiring of nannies and house cleaners for those families with the means to afford it.

Despite all these changes, however, the essential function of the working-class family remains the same: reproducing labor power for the capitalist system. The family's adults carry virtually the entire financial responsibility for maintaining its members, whether in single-parent or extended family households, and employed or unemployed. The day-to-day responsibilities of families still center on feeding, clothing, cleaning, and otherwise caring for their members, and that responsibility still falls mainly on women. Understanding how and why this is the case will not only theoretically address the source of women's oppression but also how it affects all women's status in society.

Women's unpaid domestic labor does not directly produce surplus value, yet it is vitally necessary to maintaining the capitalist system. Indeed, ruling-class ideology places primacy on women's reproductive lives, on the basis that women's nurturing capacity makes them "naturally" suited to prioritizing husband and children over all other pursuits.

The repercussions of this ideology extend far beyond family life and affect women of all classes: women's traditional role within the family defines them as subservient not only to their own male "head of the family" but to all men, politically and socially. Society's moral code views women's bodies and reproductive choices as subject to control by others. Opposition to abortion and contraception is aimed at restricting all women's right to limit childbirth. Medicaid policies that deny abortion funding but pay for sterilization for poor women combine racism and sexism, restricting the right of poor women of color to bear as many children as they want.

The fact that women's role as mothers inside the family is viewed as "primary" allows capitalists to pay women less when they are in the workforce, based on the assumption that their income is secondary to that of the male "breadwinner" of their family. These notions have in the past allowed capitalists to use women as part of the "reserve army of labor"—that section of the working class that can be brought into the labor force when needed and then pushed out again when not, thereby increasing competition between workers to the advantage of capital.

To be sure, all these assumptions have historically reflected ideology far more than reality for many working-class women, especially women of color—who have always held jobs outside the home in far greater numbers than their white, middle-class counterparts. These assumptions are even less realistic today: there are far fewer male "breadwinners" not only because so many women are single heads of their own households but also because men's wages have declined so dramatically in recent decades, narrowing the gap between men's and women's wages.

The 1970s Domestic-Labor Debate

Many of the activists and theorists involved in the 1970s domestic-labor debate looked to Marxist theory to discover the precise role of women's unpaid domestic labor for capitalism, which lays the basis for their oppression. Because Marx did not address this issue theoretically, however, those involved in the debate were not merely attempting to clarify Marxist theory but also to apply Marxist concepts in uncharted theoretical territory. This inevitably led to a certain degree of confusion at various points. But if it wasn't clear at the time, it is now apparent that even if the debate ended without a clear theoretical conclusion, it succeeded in advancing Marxist theory—with little guidance from Marx himself.

In hindsight, Lise Vogel observes of the domestic-labor debate that "with some justification, many in the women's movement regarded the debate as an obscure exercise in Marxist pedantry. Yet critical issues were at stake, even if they generally went unrecognized."[23] But just as Marx's *Capital* required a certain degree of abstraction in order to develop a theory of the workings of the capitalist system, so too does any attempt to use key elements of Marxist theory to advance a theory of women's oppression under capitalism.

It is true that some of those who participated in the domestic labor debate misinterpreted some of the concepts used by Marx—including the definitions of productive and unproductive labor—leading to theoretical errors and misguided conclusions. But even in those cases, the authors often offered insights, if only partial, which helped to clarify some issues and provoked useful responses that furthered the debate. The contributions described below should be assessed in this context, and also with the understanding that my aim is to describe the debate in its broadest strokes, which means that many valuable contributions do not appear here.[24]

1969: The Debate Begins

In 1969, an article entitled "The Political Economy of Women's Liberation," authored by Marxist feminist Margaret Benston, appeared in the left journal *Monthly Review*, touching off what would become the domestic-labor debate. She frames her analysis in economic terms, in contrast to the prevailing thought of many early women's liberationists:

> The status of women is clearly inferior to that of men, but analysis of this condition usually falls into discussing socialization, psychology, interpersonal relations, or the role of marriage as a social institution. Are these, however, the primary factors? In arguing that the roots of the secondary status of women are in fact economic, it can be shown that women as a group do indeed have a definite relation to the means of production and that this is different from that of men. The personal and psychological factors then follow from the special relation to production, and a change in the latter will be a necessary (but not sufficient) condition for changing the former. If this special relation of women to production is accepted, the analysis of the situation of women fits naturally into a class analysis of society.[25]

Benston goes on to distinguish the household labor performed by women by its *use value* versus the *exchange value* of commodities produced for the market, arguing that the "products in capitalist society which are not commodities but remain simple use-value consists of all things produced in the home. Despite the fact that considerable human labor goes into this type of household production, it still remains a production of use-values and not of commodities."[26]

Marx defined the use value of a labor product as satisfying a human need or want. Marx argued, in addition, "A use-value has value only in use, and is realized only in the process of consumption."[27] In contrast, exchange value at its most basic level requires labor that produces a commodity that is traded or sold on the market. All commodities have both use value and exchange value. Marx wrote, "Every commodity, however, has a twofold aspect—*use-value and exchange-value*. . . . Use-value as such, since it is independent of the determinate economic form, lies outside the sphere of investigation of political economy. It belongs in this sphere only when it is itself a determinate form. Use-value is the immediate physical entity in which a definite economic relationship—exchange-value—is expressed."[28]

On this basis Benston concludes, "In a society in which money determines value, women are a group who work outside the money economy. Their work is not worth money, is therefore valueless, is therefore not even real work. And women themselves, who do this valueless work, can hardly be expected to be worth as much as men, who work for money."[29]

Benston here points to the fact that women's household labor, because it is unpaid, is both undervalued by society and also "valueless" according to Marx. Marx defines *value* as specific to commodities: a commodity's value is roughly equivalent to the sum of the *socially necessary labor time* (the time needed according to the average rate of productivity) needed to produce it. Because domestic labor does not produce a commodity, it must technically be "valueless," as Benston notes. Benston did not develop this idea any further, but later contributions to the domestic-labor debate identified this "valueless" domestic labor as *socially necessary* for the continued existence of the capitalist system. This aspect of domestic labor will be examined in detail later in this chapter, for it provides a breakthrough in developing a Marxist analysis of women's oppression as a necessary component of the social reproduction of capital.

However, Benston veers well outside Marxist analysis in categorizing household labor as "preindustrial" in character, as if the family could be isolated from the rest of capitalist society, concluding that "most household labor in capitalist society (and in the existing socialist societies, for that matter) remains in the pre-market stage. This is the work which is reserved for women and it is in this fact that we can find the basis for a definition of women." She concludes, "In structural terms, the closest thing to the condition of women is the condition of others who are or were also outside of commodity production, i.e., serfs and peasants."[30]

While Benston's characterization of women's household labor within capitalist society as preindustrial is certainly incorrect, she was able to begin an analysis of the relationship between women's unpaid labor in the family with their second-class status throughout society, even when they participate in wage labor outside the home:

> We will tentatively define women, then, as that group of people who are responsible for the production for simple use-values in those activities associated with the home and family. Since men carry no responsibility for such production, the difference between the two groups lies here. Notice that women are not excluded from commodity production. Their

participation in wage labor occurs but, as a group, they have no structural responsibility in this area and such participation is ordinarily regarded as transient. Men, on the other hand, are responsible for commodity production; they are not, in principle, given any role in household labor.[31]

Finally, she argues insightfully, "The problem is not simply one of getting women into existing industrial production but the more complex one of converting private production of household work into public production."[32] In addition, she makes clear that such a conversion could only be meaningful in the aftermath of capitalism, in a socialist society: "To advocate the conversion of private domestic labor into a public industry under capitalism is quite a different thing from advocating such conversion in a socialist society. In the latter case the forces of production would operate for human welfare, not private profit, and the result should be liberation, not dehumanization. In this case we can speak of socialized forms of production."[33]

Benston's conclusions here are similar to those reached by Russian revolutionaries V. I. Lenin and Alexandra Kollontai in the context of building a socialist society: socializing household labor, so that the state takes on the responsibility for laundry, cooking, and housework, will not only free women from this drudgery but can also play a key role in raising women's status in society as a whole.

All told, Benston's contribution marked a useful departure from existing debates at the time over psychology and biology—instead focusing on the material roots of women's oppression in the nuclear family and its reverberations throughout society. While she advocates for women's participation in the workforce, she understands that eradicating the family as an institution for privatized reproduction is key to creating the material conditions for women's liberation: "Equal access to jobs outside the home, while one of the preconditions for women's liberation, will not in itself be sufficient to give equality for women; as long as work in the home remains a matter of private production and is the responsibility of women, they will simply carry a double work-load."[34]

In 1970, Peggy Morton published the article "Women's Work Is Never Done," in which she argued that the family is a unit "whose function is the maintenance of and reproduction of labor power." Specifically, the "task of the family is to maintain the present work force and provide the next generation of workers, fitted with the skills and values necessary for them to be productive members of the workforce."[35] Morton, unlike Benston, viewed both women's domestic labor and their role as workers as integral to the capitalist system, arguing, "This conception of the family allows us to look at women's public (work in the labor force) and private (work in the family) roles in an integrated way."[36]

Moreover, whereas Benston defines women as a class unto themselves, Morton argues that women's class locations lie squarely within the social relations of capitalism, whether they work outside the home or not: "Real contradictions exist for women as women. . . . Women are nevertheless objectively, socially, culturally and economically defined and subjectively define themselves through the class position of their husband or their family and/or the class position derived from work outside the home."[37]

Pat Armstrong and Hugh Armstrong argued in 1983,

> For Morton then, women do not simply produce use values; they produce something that connects them much more directly to capitalism—labor power. While she did not draw out the implications of this argument, and did not raise the question of value that was to become central to the later debate, she did develop a much more dynamic and dialectical approach to women's work, connecting women's domestic and wage labor, placing them within the contexts of capitalism and ideas about male supremacy, thus illustrating the contradictions that are inherent in this duality of domestic and wage labor. Recognizing the two workplaces of women and the class inequalities amongst women, she rejects the notion that women form a class. Not addressing directly women's shared procreative capacities, she raises, but does not explore, questions of women's control over their bodies and the class differences in access to birth control and abortion.[38]

Vogel notes that Benston's and Morton's contributions "established the material character of women's unpaid domestic labor in the family household. . . . Morton, in addition, formulated the issues in terms of a concept of the reproduction of labor power and emphasized the specific nature of contradictions within the working class. These theoretical insights . . . rooted the problem of women's oppression in the theoretical terrain of materialism."[39]

Does Household Labor Produce Surplus Value?

The domestic-labor debate fairly quickly entered a fork in the road, as theorists took their arguments in two different directions. As Vogel describes,

> Two general positions emerged. One claimed that the product of domestic labor is the commodity labor-power, bearing both use-value and exchange-value. This could be taken to imply that domestic labor is

productive of surplus-value and that those who do domestic labor—women—are exploited. In this way, sex contradictions acquire a clear material basis and housewives occupy the same strategic position in the class struggle as factory workers. The second position maintained that domestic labor produces only use-values for direct consumption by household members, including the worker, and thereby contributes to the overall maintenance and renewal of the working class. Neither productive nor unproductive, domestic labor had to be theorized as something else, an undertaking few attempted.[40]

The debate boiled down to whether or not domestic labor is "productive" (produces surplus value) or not. If it does not, the question remained: what role does the "reproduction of labor power" play in the capitalist system as a whole? As Vogel astutely observes, within the Marxist tradition, "The various notions associated with [the so-called woman question] actually conceal, as socialist feminists have pointed out, a theoretical problem of fundamental significance: the reproduction of labor power in the context of overall social reproduction. Socialist theorists have never sufficiently confronted this problem, yet the rudiments of a usable approach lie buried just below the surface of Marx's analysis of social reproduction in *Capital*."[41]

In 1972, Mariarosa Dalla Costa and Selma James introduced their own analysis of women's domestic labor in their pamphlet *The Power of Women and the Subversion of the Community*, published in Italy and the United States. They argued that household labor is productive—it produces surplus value—and sought to root this argument in Marxist theory.[42]

Like Benston, Dalla Costa and James refer to "the pre-capitalist relation of production in the home," but they reach the opposite conclusion. While Benston described women's domestic labor as lacking exchange value, Dalla Costa and James describe it as producing surplus value—that is, in Marxian terms, they argue that women are exploited within the family. As Dalla Costa and James argued,

> What we mean precisely is that housework as work is productive in the Marxian sense, that is, is producing surplus value. We speak immediately after about the productivity of the entire female role. . . . It is often asserted that, within the definition of wage labor, women in domestic labor are not productive. In fact precisely the opposite is true if one thinks of the enormous quantity of social services which capitalist organization transforms into privatized activity, putting them on the backs of housewives. Domestic labor is not essentially "feminine work"; a woman doesn't fulfill herself more or get less exhausted than a man from washing and cleaning. These are social services inasmuch as they serve

the reproduction of labor power. And capital, precisely by instituting its family structure, has "liberated" the man from these functions so that he is completely "free" for direct exploitation; so that he is free to "earn" enough for a woman to reproduce him as labor power.[43]

Here, Dalla Costa and James confuse the role of the reproduction of labor power with productive labor, implying that women's domestic labor produces the "commodity" of (men's) labor power, for capital. But as Engels makes clear, surplus value can only be produced if labor power is *first* sold for a wage: "The wage-worker sells to the capitalist his labor-power for a certain daily sum. After a few hours' work he has reproduced the value of that sum; but the substance of his contract is, that he has to work another series of hours to complete his working-day; and the value he produces during these additional hours of surplus labor is surplus value, which costs the capitalist nothing, but yet goes into his pocket."[44]

In addition, Marx makes a clear distinction between the laborer and labor power. Under capitalism, the laborer is not a commodity, but rather the *owner* of his or her labor power, which is *then* sold as a commodity to the capitalist, and even then only temporarily. However crucial domestic labor is in maintaining the laborer's ability to sell his or her labor power, by definition it cannot produce surplus value. As Marx writes in *Capital*, Volume 1:

> But in order that our owner of money may be able to find labor-power offered for sale as a commodity, various conditions must first be fulfilled. The exchange of commodities of itself implies no other relations of dependence than those which, result from its own nature [*sic*]. On this assumption, labor-power can appear upon the market as a commodity, only if, and so far as, its possessor, the individual whose labor-power it is, offers it for sale, or sells it, as a commodity. In order that he may be able to do this, he must have it at his disposal, must be the untrammelled owner of his capacity for labor, i.e., of his person. He and the owner of money meet in the market, and deal with each other as on the basis of equal rights, with this difference alone, that one is buyer, the other seller; both, therefore, equal in the eyes of the law. The continuance of this relation demands that the owner of the labor-power should sell it only for a definite period, for if he were to sell it rump and stump, once for all, he would be selling himself, converting himself from a free man into a slave, from an owner of a commodity into a commodity. He must constantly look upon his labor-power as his own property, his own commodity, and this he can only do by placing it at the disposal of the buyer temporarily, for a definite period of time. By this means alone can he avoid renouncing his rights of ownership over it.[45]

Armstrong and Armstrong clarify the distinction between productive and unproductive labor as follows: "For Marx, productive labor under capitalism is labor that is exchanged directly (that is, for a wage) with capital in order to provide surplus value. Since housework is not directly exchanged with capital to produce surplus value, it is not in strict Marxist terms productive, and those who do it are not exploited."[46] While domestic labor produces use value, it does not produce exchange value.

This conclusion does not minimize the importance of domestic labor to maintaining and reproducing labor power. Insisting on this theoretical distinction is crucial to understanding how the capitalist system works. Armstrong and Armstrong describe Dalla Costa and James's misuse of Marxist concepts as "confusing,"[47] arguing,

> [Dalla Costa and James] confuse productive and unproductive labor. . . . The significance of altered usage does not, however, lie in its being an act of disloyalty to the arcane jargon of a century-old revolutionary. At issue is neither dogmatism nor the claim to be true to Marx. Rather, what is of significance is the capacity of Marx's careful distinctions to expose how capitalism works. . . . Thus the social form termed "productive labor," and defined as labor exchanged directly with capital to produce surplus value, is specific to capitalism because it is central to the very definition of capitalism.[48]

Moreover, Dalla Costa and James conflate the role of the working-class housewife with that of women of all classes, thereby minimizing the class differences that exist between women. They refer at various points to women as a "caste"—implying a class system determined by heredity rather than the social relations between exploiters and exploited under capitalism:

> We assume that all women are housewives and even those who work outside the home continue to be housewives. That is, on a world level, it is precisely what is particular to domestic work, not only measured as number of hours and nature of work, but as quality of life and quality of relationships which it generates, that determines a woman's place wherever she is and to whichever class she belongs. We concentrate here on the position of the working-class woman, but this is not to imply that only working-class women are exploited. Rather it is to confirm that the role of the working-class housewife, which we believe has been indispensable to capitalist production, is the determinant for the position of all other women. Every analysis of women as a caste, then, must proceed from the analysis of the position of working-class housewives.[49]

"Wages for Housework"

In 1972 James helped to found the "Wages for Housework" campaign—demanding that women be financially compensated for their unpaid household duties—which resonated with a small but significant number of activists in that era. In the pamphlet, Dalla Costa and James explicitly reject strategies that emphasize the importance of women's participation in paid labor in order to maximize their social power as workers: "Those who advocate that the liberation of the working-class woman lies in her getting a job outside the home are part of the problem, not the solution."

At the same time, they denied that demanding wages for housework would further reinforce women's isolated role inside the family. On the contrary, they argue, the reasoning behind this strategy is "to smash the entire role of housewife." They conclude that the demand of wages for housework "is only a basis, a perspective, from which to start, whose merit is essentially to link immediately female oppression, subordination and isolation to their material foundation."[50] Thus, Dalla Costa and James envisioned the struggle to win wages for housework as a transitory phase to winning women's complete emancipation from the role of housewife.

This strategy proved shortsighted, however. Given the pivotal role of the traditional family (and women's role within it) for capitalism, nothing short of dismantling capitalist class relations can create the material conditions for its dissolution as an economic unit. Such an outcome requires a successful social revolution—a struggle to overturn the entire capitalist system utilizing the power of the organized working class, including women workers.

It is unfortunate that Dalla Costa and James tie their argument to a strategy to demand wages for housework because that strategy overshadows the important insights they offer. Like Benston and Morton before them, they seek to use a materialist framework to understand the relationship between the reproductive labor performed inside the family and the system of exploitation. Despite their misinterpretation of some key Marxist concepts, Dalla Costa and James convincingly describe working-class women's role in reproducing labor power as a service to capital, rather than merely to the male members of the household. In addition, they tie the (male) workers' wage to include the cost of the necessary domestic labor required for his continued ability to be exploited by capital:

> Since Marx, it has been clear that capital rules and develops through the wage, that is, that the foundation of capitalist society was the wage laborer

and his or her direct exploitation. . . . [But] the wage commanded a larger amount of labor than appeared in factory bargaining. Where women are concerned, their labor appears to be a personal service outside of capital. The woman seemed only to be suffering from male chauvinism, being pushed around because capitalism meant general "injustice" and "bad and unreasonable behavior." . . . The rule of capital through the wage compels every able-bodied person to function, under the law of division of labor, and to function in ways that are if not immediately, then ultimately profitable to the expansion and extension of the rule of capital.[51]

Dalla Costa and James also begin to develop what would become a crucial theoretical concept later in the domestic labor debate. While most theorists had focused on the reproduction of the current and future generations of labor—that of the father, mother, and children—Dalla Costa and James expand that view to include the maintenance of workers who are unable, due to disability or unemployment, to immediately participate in the labor force. They argue that women "always receive back into the home all those who are periodically expelled from their jobs by economic crisis. The family, this maternal cradle always ready to help and protect in time of need, has been in fact the best guarantee that the unemployed do not immediately become a horde of disruptive outsiders."[52]

The notion that women's domestic labor is productive in the Marxian sense was not limited to Dalla Costa and James's view in the debate. Even some of those theorists who disagreed that domestic labor produces surplus value attempted to show how domestic labor contributes value to the commodity of labor power that is sold to capital (and is included in the worker's wage)—based on the fact that a commodity's value is roughly equivalent to the sum of the labor time needed to produce it. As Armstrong and Armstrong remark, "The argument that women, in providing the care and feeding of men and children, are performing work that produces surplus value shifted the focus of the debate from questions of class to questions of value, sparking a theoretical struggle waged to a large extent on the pages of *New Left Review*."[53]

Wally Seccombe, one the key participants in the debate, argues, for example, "Where Marx subsumes the entire family's subsistence in the wage, I have broken it down, pitting the housewife's contribution to the reproduction of labor power sold to capital against the costs of her own subsistence. She creates value, embodied in the labor power sold to capital, equal to the value she consumes in her own upkeep. Note that the equation balances as before—value is neither created nor destroyed overall, but merely transferred."[54]

But this line of argument produced something of a theoretical cul-de-sac. As Armstrong and Armstrong conclude, "In struggling through the implications of applying the law of value to domestic labor, the participants in the debate have revealed the opposite of what was initially intended. They have shown how domestic labor *differs* from wage labor."[55] (Emphasis added.)

As Joan Smith argues,

> But the wage paid to each individual in the capitalist market is *not* paid to the family itself—it is paid whatever the individual's family circumstances. Therefore it is quite wrong to argue that the family "produces" workers and that the family can be seen as a unit of capitalism. It is also wrong to argue that housewives create value. The Capitalist family is a privatized system of reproduction which fits the Capitalist mode of production and is necessary to it—it is not part of the mode of Production in the sense of "producing" wage laborers.[56]

"Consumption" and the Necessary Role of Domestic Labor

Some domestic-labor theorists searched elsewhere in *Capital* to discover in what ways the reproduction of labor power is essential to the capitalist system. Marx's concept of *individual consumption* addressed this issue: put simply, all workers must consume food and other means of daily maintenance to survive. Marx discussed the need for consumption, however, without exploring the key role of domestic labor in making consumption possible.

Vogel makes the following observation about the missing elements from Marx's definition of individual consumption: "Individual consumption . . . happens when 'the laborer turns the money paid to him for his labor-power into means of subsistence.' . . . But he said little about the actual work involved in individual consumption. Here was a realm of economic activity essential to capitalist production yet missing from Marx's exposition."[57]

The laborer's means of subsistence is not something that can simply be purchased with wages but rather requires domestic labor for it to be consumed. Washing clothes and dishes, cooking, doing housework, performing the multitude of tasks involved in raising children—all of these require domestic labor. Without this labor, consumption could not take place.

Marx's concept of "consumption" also distinguishes between laborers' *individual consumption* and their *productive consumption*. The laborers' individual consumption involves the means of subsistence necessary for their daily survival. Productive consumption involves labor power that produces surplus value, in which laborers consume the means of production to produce a commodity—while at the same time their labor power is consumed by the capitalist who bought it.

> The laborer consumes in a two-fold way. While producing he[58] consumes by his labor the means of production, and converts them into products with a higher value than that of the capital advanced. This is his productive consumption. It is at the same time consumption of his labor-power by the capitalist who bought it. On the other hand, the laborer turns the money paid to him for his labor-power, into means of subsistence: this is his individual consumption. The laborer's productive consumption, and his individual consumption, are therefore totally distinct. In the former, he acts as the motive power of capital, and belongs to the capitalist. In the latter, he belongs to himself, and performs his necessary vital functions outside the process of production. The result of the one is, that the capitalist lives; of the other, that the laborer lives.[59]

In addition, Marx observed that the "means of subsistence" included in workers' individual consumption must also include the means of subsistence for their children because all workers are mortal and their labor power must be replaced by that of the next generation of laborers: "Hence the sum of the means of subsistence necessary for the production of labor-power must include the means necessary for the laborer's substitutes, i.e., his children, in order that this race of peculiar commodity-owners may perpetuate its appearance in the market."[60]

When domestic tasks are performed for the individual consumption of workers, they also play a central role in the reproduction of labor power—both in terms of the daily replenishment of labor power and also in preparing the next generation of workers to enter the workforce. When they are performed society-wide, they are part of the process of *social reproduction* described by Marx—in which the social relations of capitalism are continually reproduced.

Social Reproduction

As Marx argues in *Capital*, Volume 1, "Capitalist production . . . produces not only commodities, not only surplus-value, but it also produces and reproduces the capitalist relation; on the one side the capitalist, on the other the wage laborer."[61] He distinguishes between "individual capitals" (individual capitalist enterprises) and "social capital" (the sum total of all the individual capitals). He uses the term "social reproduction" to describe the means by which social capital is continually reproduced. This includes the physical reproduction of the means of production, which includes not only the machinery of production but also "the laborer himself."[62]

Marx explains in *Capital*, Volume 2:

> If we study the commodity-product furnished by society during the year, then it must become apparent how the process of reproduction of the social capital takes place, what characteristics distinguish this process of reproduction from the process of reproduction of an individual capital, and what characteristics are common to both. The annual product includes those portions of the social product which replace capital, namely social reproduction, as well as those which go to the consumption-fund, those which are consumed by laborers and capitalists, hence both productive and individual consumption. *It comprises also the reproduction (i.e., maintenance) of the capitalist class and the working-class, and thus the reproduction of the capitalist character of the entire process of production.*[63] (Emphasis added.)

As Vogel put it, "Some process that meets the ongoing personal needs of the bearers of labor power is therefore a condition of social reproduction, as is some process that replaces them over time. These processes of daily maintenance and long-run replacement are conflated in the term reproduction of labor power."[64]

In *Capital*, Volume 1, Marx defines "necessary labor" in terms of its cost to capital, hidden within the wage paid to workers. Marx first explains necessary labor with the individual laborer's workday in mind. He distinguishes between that part of the workday the laborer spends on *necessary labor*, or what is paid to the worker for his or her means of subsistence— the reproduction of his or her labor power. The rest of the day is made up of *surplus labor*, or labor that produces surplus value for the owner of the means of production, as the source of profit. Both necessary and surplus labor are hidden within the wage itself, so it is not apparent even to the worker where necessary labor ends and surplus labor begins. As Marx puts it, "The wage form thus extinguishes every trace of the division of the working-day into necessary labor and surplus-labor, into paid and unpaid labor. All labor appears as paid labor."[65]

Thus, Marx defines necessary labor in its relationship to the value of a given commodity: "The value of one commodity is to the value of any other, as the labor time necessary for the production of the one is to that necessary for the production of the other. As values, all commodities are only definite masses of congealed labor time."[66] Thus, necessary labor is roughly equivalent to the sum of the *socially necessary labor time* (the time needed according to the average rate of productivity) needed for laborers' means of subsistence—which includes the commodities for their individual consumption.

In *Marxism and the Oppression of Women*, Vogel argues, "Marx did not discuss a second component of necessary labor in capitalist society, one that we can call the domestic component of necessary labor—or domestic labor. Domestic labor is the portion of necessary labor that is performed outside the sphere of capitalist production."[67] Vogel later explains that her approach involved "reconceptualizing necessary labor to incorporate the processes of reproduction of labor power."[68] She breaks down the concept of necessary labor into two components:

> The first, discussed by Marx, is the necessary labor that produces value equivalent to wages. This component, which I called the *social component of necessary labor*, is indissolubly bound with surplus labor in the capitalist production process. The second component of necessary labor, deeply veiled in Marx's account, is the unwaged work that contributes to the daily and long-term renewal of bearers of the commodity labor power and of the working class as a whole. I called this the *domestic component of necessary labor*, or domestic labor.
>
> In other words, I argued that necessary labor is a more complicated conceptual category than previously thought. It has two components, one with value and the other without. Domestic labor, the previously missing second component, is sharply different from the social component yet similarly indispensable to capitalist social reproduction. It lacks value but nonetheless plays a key role in the process of surplus value appropriation. Locked together in the performance of necessary labor, social labor and its newfound mate, domestic labor, form an odd couple never before encountered in Marxist theory.[69]

Vogel further describes, "The social and domestic components of necessary labor are not directly comparable, for the latter does not have value. This means that the highly visible and very valuable social component of necessary labor is accompanied by a shadowy, unquantifiable, and (technically) valueless domestic labor component."[70]

Vogel is undoubtedly correct in asserting that domestic labor is indispensable to the process of capitalist social reproduction. At the same time, however, she misunderstands Marx's definition of *necessary labor* reflected in the worker's wage. In their introduction to the 2013 edition of *Marxism and the Oppression of Women*, Susan Ferguson and David McNally explain this theoretical distinction as follows:

> Vogel falls into the trap of arguing that domestic labor is a component of necessary labor in the sense in which Marx used the term in *Capital*. . . . Vogel was of course right that the labor of producing and reproducing current and future generations of wage-laborers is socially necessary to capital. But the term "necessary labor" has a much more restricted meaning for Marx in his theory of surplus value: it refers to the labor that comprises a *necessary cost* for capital, the labor that must be paid (in wages) out of capital's funds. This is why Marx refers to wages as variable capital. There is much more unwaged work—labor that does not have to be paid for by capital—that is necessary to the reproduction of a capitalist society. And capital is certainly greatly aided by the fact that children are birthed, nursed, nourished, loved, and educated in kin-based units, just as adults are physically, psychically, and socially reproduced there. But individual capitals here benefit from social practices that do not form any of their necessary costs. There is thus no rate of surplus value here both because these practices are not commodified (they produce use-values but not values), and because there is no direct cost structure for capital involved.[71]

In her 2000 *Science & Society* article "Domestic Labor Revisited," Vogel acknowledges the theoretical problem in her earlier assertion that domestic labor is a component of necessary labor. As she explains, "This analysis, which clarifies but does not alter my earlier argument, now seems to me less persuasive. What is clear, however, is that whether domestic labor is conceptualized as a component of necessary labor or not, the bottom line is that some way to theorize it within Marxist political economy must be found."[72] Vogel's "bottom line" is certainly correct.

Indeed, this correction does not diminish Vogel's enormous theoretical contribution. First, she situates women's unpaid domestic labor in the process of social reproduction essential to the continued functioning of the capitalist system. Second, she explains how the role of the working-class family in reproducing labor power is central to the oppression of all women under capitalism. Both of these will be examined later in this chapter.

Interestingly, by approaching Marx's concept of necessary labor from a different angle, Joan Smith was able to address the role of public workers within the broad category known as "caring labor" (teachers, health-care workers, and so on) in the reproduction of labor power. As more women have entered the labor force, the state has taken on many aspects of social reproduction once performed inside the family. As noted earlier, this process began with the advent of compulsory public education. Smith argues, "This State organization of reproduction takes two forms: on the one hand, I would argue, certain state activities become part of the *mode* of Reproduction of society—such as education, health etc.; on the other hand the state intervenes to organize and preserve the family."[73]

Smith also notes that Marx "argued throughout *Capital* and *Theories of Surplus Value* that the labor of teachers was unproductive." But she also observes that in *Capital*, Volume 3, Marx described a division of labor within the working class between those workers "who perform necessary labor and those who perform surplus labor." Just as the workday of an individual laborer can be divided between necessary and surplus labor, this method can be applied to the labor of the entire class.

As Marx puts it, "The aggregate labor of the working class may be so divided that the portion which produces the total means of subsistence for the working-class (including the means of production required for this purpose) performs the necessary labor for the whole of society." This necessary labor includes all the labor performed for the reproduction of labor power, or, in Marx's words, "the labor which produces all other products necessarily included in the average consumption of the laborer." Necessary and surplus labor are equally crucial in the capitalist production process. Marx argues, "From the social standpoint, some perform only necessary labor because others perform only surplus-labor and vice versa. It is but a division of labor between them."[74]

On this basis, Smith argues that the labor of teachers and other caring workers (who are overwhelmingly female) is "neither productive nor unproductive," but rather part of the "necessary reproduction of the working class":

> In the twentieth century the enormous development of productivity has given rise to a class of *public* servants. In the sphere of Education 67 per cent of these workers are women and in the sphere of Health, 75 per cent. I would argue that these workers should not be simply classified alongside of the other unproductive workers in the sphere of Production. Instead they should be seen as workers in the necessary base (Reproduction) of the Capitalist Mode of Production—engaged in the necessary reproduction of the working class.
>
> . . . I would not argue that teachers, nurses, school-cleaners are productive workers reproducing wage-laborers as commodities. Such public sector workers are service workers and not productive. But I would argue that we could extend the concept of the division of labor within the

working class and see these workers as being *necessary workers for the re-production of the working class as a whole.*[75] (Emphasis added.)

Women in the Workforce and the Persistence of Unpaid Domestic Labor

Both Smith and Vogel also addressed the capitalist class's tendency to draw women (and sometimes children) into the labor force—which, in turn, requires a reduction in domestic labor. The individual capitalist always seeks to increase surplus value in order to raise profits. This can be partially accomplished by forcing workers to work harder for lower wages—although this has built-in physical human and social limits.

"On the other hand," Vogel argues, "capitalists can reduce necessary labor by making the production process more productive. Greater productivity means the worker needs fewer working hours to complete necessary labor and more surplus value goes to the boss. Within limits, a wage increase could even be granted."[76] Thus, Vogel notes, "The drive for surplus value forces capitalists to constantly augment productivity, chiefly through the introduction of machinery," and the growing use of machinery "requires less and less human labor to be set in motion in the productive process."[77]

When the capitalist economy is growing, the use of machinery allows for expanding the number of workers because less labor power is required of each individual worker to produce the same amount of surplus value. The need for additional labor can be fulfilled through labor migration from the countryside to the cities, importing larger numbers of immigrant workers, and also employing additional family members. As Smith argues, "Because the wage already includes "the means necessary for the laborer's substitutes, i.e., his children," Marx concludes that this is the origin of the lower wages of men as well as women and youths under capitalism."[78] As he argues,

Machinery, by throwing every member of that family on to the labor-market, spreads the value of the man's labor-power over his whole family. It thus depreciates his labor-power. To purchase the labor-power of a family of four workers may, perhaps, cost more than it formerly did to purchase the labor-power of the head of the family, but, in return, four days' labor takes the place of one, and their price falls in proportion to the excess of the surplus-labor of four over the surplus-labor of one. In order that the family may live, four people must now, not only labor, but expend surplus-labor for the capitalist. Thus we see, that machinery, while augmenting the human material that forms the principal object of capital's exploiting power, at the same time raises the degree of exploitation.[79]

Vogel likewise remarks, "It is perfectly possible for the value of labor power expended by an entire household to rise substantially, accompanied by a real shift upward in its 'standard of life,' while at the same time the value of the labor power of the individuals comprising the household falls and the rate of exploitation increases."[80] This was certainly the experience of the US working class during the prolonged economic boom that followed World War II, when average wages rose substantially while productivity soared far beyond the wage rate.

When the business cycle goes from boom to bust, however, capital's need for labor decreases substantially. This cycle is built into the rising ratio of machinery to human labor in the production process, which eventually causes the rate of average profit to fall.

Thus, Marx regarded the "reserve army of labor" as essential to the capitalist system: "the greater this reserve army in proportion to the active labor army, the greater is the mass of a consolidated surplus population, whose misery is in inverse ratio to its torment of labor.... *This is the absolute general law of capitalist accumulation.*"[81] (Emphasis in original.) The reserve army is made up primarily of the chronically unemployed, who are willing to work for lower wages. Because they compete with employed workers, they exert a downward pressure on all wages.

Paid labor by necessity has been a constant feature of life for many working-class women, especially women of color, historically. These workers often are not counted in official labor statistics, especially those in jobs such as domestic servants, or those who perform industrial labor in cottage industries, take-in laundry, and the like. At the same time, the majority of women workers fit the classic definition of a reserve army of labor until the 1960s. No example demonstrates this more clearly than the massive entry of women into industrial jobs during World War II; they were driven out at the war's end to allow returning vets to reenter the industrial workforce.

But since the 1970s, a growing number of married women—now including a majority of women with children—hold jobs. To be sure, they are more likely to work part time to accommodate their family obligations and more likely to move out of the workforce temporarily after childbirth. Women are thus today a permanent and large part of the workforce, even if individual women tend to move in and out of paid labor or work fewer hours compared with male workers.

So women as a group no longer fit the precise definition of the reserve army of labor. Capitalism has come to rely upon women as a permanent, low-wage sector of the labor force, located in overwhelmingly female occupations. As a population, women earn substantially less than male workers, although it is important to note that their race and class also affect this wage comparison.

Over the last century, women's increasing participation in the workforce has been accompanied by a corresponding reduction in their time spent on domestic labor. As Vogel comments,

> When domestic labor is reduced, additional labor power is potentially released into the labor market. Reduction of domestic labor has been an ongoing process in the nineteenth and twentieth centuries. By the early 1900s, food preparation was less time-consuming, laundry was in some ways less onerous, and schools had taken over most of the task of teaching skills. More recently, frozen food, microwaves, laundromats, and the increased availability of day care, nursery, kindergarten, and after-school programs have decreased domestic labor even further. Reduction of domestic labor through technological and non-technological means does not inevitably make households send more of their members' labor power onto the market. It does, however, create a greater possibility that they might do so.[82]

There are, however, limits to the reduction of women's role in reproducing labor power. Capitalism has come to rely on the labor performed inside the family free of charge. No one capitalist society could abandon privatized reproduction in the family unless all do so because capitals compete with each other. As Smith comments, "The family system could not be abolished in Japan, with the substitution of baby farms and nurseries as profit-making enterprises or as part of a state capitalist system, without the reproduction of the Japanese work-force being either more costly or less efficient than its competitors."[83]

Lise Vogel: The Working-Class Family as the Root of *All* Women's Oppression

There is also a physical limit to reducing women's biological role in generational replacement, due to the nature of pregnancy and childbirth. By exploring this aspect of the reproduction of labor power under capitalism, Vogel is able to locate the precise reason women and not men are assigned to the domestic sphere.

She approaches the issue theoretically rather than empirically, beginning again with Marx's analysis of social reproduction: "Marx considered the reproduction of labor power to be central to social reproduction, but he never provided a thoroughgoing exposition of just what it entailed. At times he focused on renewal of the individual laborer; elsewhere, he underscored the importance of maintaining and replacing non-working members of the working class."[84]

While many theorists involved in the domestic-labor debate focus on the reproductive labor women perform for their husbands and children, Vogel incorporates the labor that maintains *all* nonworking members of the working class—including mothers while temporarily involved in the physical processes of childbirth and its immediate aftermath. She identifies the three key aspects involved in the reproduction of labor power in class societies as 1) the daily maintenance of the current generation of laborers so they are able to return to work every day; 2) the daily maintenance of the current generation of the working class who are "too young, old, sick, or who themselves are involved in maintenance activities or out of the work-force for other reasons"; 3) processes involved in replacing the laborers "who have died or no longer work."[85] As she remarked, "Defined this way, domestic labor became a concept specific to capitalism and without fixed gender assignment. This freed it from several common-sense assumptions that haunted the domestic labor debate, most especially the notion that domestic labor is universal and that it is necessarily women's work."[86]

The kin-based family unit known as the family has been the primary means of reproducing labor power in class societies, including capitalism. But Vogel observes that although "biological procreation in heterosexual family contexts" has been the most common form of reproduction, there are other ways that labor power could be replaced:

> Although the reproduction of labor power in actual societies has usually involved child-rearing within kin-based settings called families, it can in principle be organized in other ways, at least for a period of time. The present set of laborers could be housed in dormitories, maintained collectively, worked to death, and then replaced by new workers, brought from outside. This harsh regime has actually been approximated many times through history. Gold mines in Roman Egypt, rubber plantations in French Indochina, and Nazi Arbeitslager all come to mind.[87]

Vogel also poses the hypothetical example of "a slave system that imports laborers from outside its boundaries, and forces them to work at a literally killing pace. Under such conditions, generational replacement might become almost impossible, and the amount of necessary labor could be reduced to nearly zero."[88]

Therefore, if the labor force is not replaced by a new generation of workers, it must be replaced by "the entry of new workers into the labor force." Historically, this has included child labor, immigrant labor, seasonal labor—involving previously unemployed wives who enter the labor force, people who move from the countryside to take jobs in factories, and even people who are "forcibly kidnapped, transported far from home, and coerced into a new workforce, as was done for New World slave plantations."[89]

The fact that the kin-based family is by far the most common means of reproducing labor power under capitalism indicates its advantages not only for the capitalist class but also for the working class, given the alternatives on offer. While the family has changed in many ways over time, its essential function in social reproduction has not. All working-class families with children, even single-parent households or same-sex parents with children, perform the essential function of maintaining and reproducing labor power.

Either gender could technically perform the domestic labor inside the family. But the process of biological procreation—childbirth—is unique to women.* The working-class family bears most of the responsibility for reproducing labor power, and this responsibility includes support during the weeks or months immediately before and after childbirth. This may involve the assistance of an assortment of both parents' relatives, but typically the biological father assumes the primary responsibility for providing for women during this period when they are physically unable to fully partake in either productive or reproductive labor.

As Vogel argues, "Although in principle women's and men's differential roles need only last during those childbearing months," women's responsibilities tend to be identified with their role in childbearing in a kin-based family. The fact that women often give birth to more than one child reinforces this pattern. "The arrangements are ordinarily legitimated by male domination backed up by institutionalized structures of female oppression."[90] These institutionalized structures of female oppression include the restriction of women's legal rights, inscribed in laws regulating marriage, divorce, and reproductive rights described earlier.

To be sure, women's role inside the working-class family presents challenges for the capitalist class because of its contradictory interests in both maximizing surplus value (and therefore surplus labor) and also re-

---

* This passage is intended to explain the reason for gender norms within the traditional nuclear family. Many trans men and gender-nonconforming people are also capable of giving birth.

lying on women to reproduce labor power. As Vogel puts it,

> While pregnant and for a short time thereafter, subordinate-class women experience at least a brief period of somewhat reduced ability to work and/or to engage in the activities of daily maintenance. During such periods of lower activity, the women must themselves be maintained. In this way, childbearing can diminish the contribution subordinate-class women make as direct producers and as participants in maintenance activities. From the perspective of dominant classes, such childbearing is therefore potentially costly, for pregnant women's labor and that which provides for them might otherwise have formed part of surplus labor. At the same time, subordinate-class childbearing replenishes the work force and thereby benefits dominant classes. There is a latent contradiction, then, between dominant classes' need to appropriate surplus labor and their requirements for labor power to perform it.[91]

Nevertheless, the fact that the role of the working-class family endures is evidence that it remains the favored means of reproducing labor power by capitalists. And, as argued earlier, the system has managed to incorporate women into the labor force while continuing to maintain their essential role in domestic labor inside the family. Therefore, Vogel argues, "While they may also be workers, it is subordinate-class women's differential role in the maintenance and replacement of labor power that marks their particular situation."[92]

At the same time, it is the enduring role of women inside the working-class family that explains the oppression of women of all classes. "Lack of equality," Vogel argues, "represents a specific feature of women's (and other groups') oppression in capitalist societies. Only subordinate-class women perform domestic labor, as discussed above, but all women suffer from lack of equality in capitalist societies."[93]

Thus, the relations between working-class women and men are unequal inside the family, and also between all women and all men throughout society. As Vogel described, "On the one hand, subordinate-class women and men are differentially located with respect to important economic aspects of social reproduction. On the other, all women are denied equal rights. In actual societies, the dynamics of women's subordination respond to this dual positioning, among other factors."[94]

Oppression and Class

Sexism affects women of all classes in society—just as racism targets people of color of all classes and homophobia is a threat to all LGBT people. Special oppression is a cross-class phenomenon. One of the central tenets of the Marxist tradition is that the working-class movement for socialism must, as Lenin argued in 1902, "respond to *all* cases of, oppression, violence, and abuse, no matter *what class* is affected."[95] The working class can only create the material conditions for socialism by combating all forms of oppression throughout society, not merely those that affect the working class directly.

At the same time, women are also divided by class, as are all the oppressed. As Marxist feminist Martha Gimenez comments, while women of all classes share certain experiences of oppression, women of different classes are simultaneously locked into an antagonistic relationship. Thus, she notes, "Reproduction . . . entails important commonalities of experience, most of which cut across classes, establishing a material base for women's solidarity and shared interests (sexuality, childcare, reproductive rights, domestic responsibilities, problems and joys, etc.)."[96] At the same time, she wrote,

> There are, however, important class and socioeconomic status differences in women's experiences of biological reproduction, reflected in their attitudes towards abortion, desired family size, etc., as well as differences in the organization of social reproduction: the use of paid domestic workers not only by capitalist women but by women affluent enough to afford them highlights how oppression is not something that only men can inflict upon women. The real advances upper-middle-class professional and business women (those earning six-figure salaries) have made in the last 30 years presupposes the existence of a servant stratum, drawn from the less skilled layers of the working class, including a large proportion of women from racial and ethnic minorities, often undocumented immigrants.
>
> While the nature and number of divisions among women varies at the level of social formations, class divisions are common to all capitalist social formations and all social groups (e.g., immigrant populations, races, ethnicities, etc.) are themselves divided by class.[97]

Class differences between women help to explain the various strategies pursued by different wings of the women's movement of the 1970s and beyond. While class consciousness is not determined at birth, it is at least partially shaped by material reality. Since the rise of the modern women's movement, some white, middle-class women have chosen to champion the class viewpoint of working-class women, but most have not.

Since the 1970s, mainstream feminism has reflected the aims and concerns of middle-class professional women seeking to break through the glass ceiling of employment opportunity. This is a worthy cause, but it can be accomplished without challenging the class inequality that is fundamental to the oppression of working-class women. Even the radical wing of the women's liberation movement, which unapologetically demanded women's fundamental right to end an unwanted pregnancy, did not mount a similar challenge to the sterilization abuse targeting poor women of color that reached epidemic proportions during that era.

The domestic-labor theorists who used Marxist methodology located the root of women's oppression in their role in domestic labor for the social reproduction of capital. In so doing, they not only advanced the theory of women's oppression but also the implications for pursuing a strategy for women's liberation: The system of privatized reproduction cannot be eliminated without abolishing the capitalist system; women's liberation therefore requires eradicating both.

While Smith acknowledges that the family form has changed "from epoch to epoch and from class to class," she also argues, "In an oppressive Class society the privatized family system is the only way to organize reproduction and by its very nature gives rise to the oppression of women."[98] Later, Smith more explicitly connects women's subordinate role in the family to other facets of women's oppression in society at large: "The oppression of women in class societies quite clearly cannot be reduced to any economic analysis. . . . But the social oppression of women makes no sense without a Marxist analysis of the family. . . . It is the family system which creates the virgin, the prostitute, pornography and the oppression of women."[99] Engels's analysis of the monogamous family giving rise to prostitution and the sexual objectification of women remains relevant. His broad analysis helps to explain the contradictory expectations forced upon women—as nurturers and sex objects—which are in fact flip sides of the same coin.

Gimenez makes a similar point with regard to the political aspects of women's subordination, rooted in the nuclear family, that reinforce their subordinate role in the legal system:

> Under capitalist conditions . . . the relations between men and women . . . find their material basis in the private reproduction of physical and social life and their political, legal, and ideological expression in the concept of the nuclear family as the basic unit of society, and of the State, the marriage contract, inheritance laws, etc. Just as the relations of production imply a difference in power between capitalists and workers, the relations of reproduction imply the power of men and the oppres-

sion of women, independent of their actual consciousness about the existence of sexual discrimination and their actual willingness to do away with it.

This means that although some individual men and women may strive to achieve equality in their personal relations, sexual inequality, as a feature of the mode of reproduction which affects all men and women regardless of their private arrangements, remains unchanged as long as capitalism prevails.[100]

The Struggle for Women's Liberation and Socialism

The domestic-labor theorists who locate women's oppression in the processes of social reproduction do not leave their analyses at the level of theory but also advocate a strategy for women's liberation that includes struggles for reforms *alongside* a struggle for socialism. Thus, the struggles to advance women's political equality are not counterposed to but a part of the struggle to create the material conditions for women's liberation.

As Vogel argues, "Efforts to expand equality's scope make radical challenges on at least two fronts. First, they tend to reduce divisions within and among subordinate layers and sectors, by moving all persons towards a more equal footing."[101] This has certainly proven to be the case in the United States since the 1960s women's liberation movement. The struggles of 1960s-era women's liberationists for abortion rights and against the sexual objectification of women, however contested they are today, nevertheless advanced the overarching struggle for women's liberation over the long term. Likewise, women of color successfully exposed the atrocities of sterilization abuse in the 1970s, curbing most of the most blatantly racist programs.

Today's activists face many challenges, but not the same ones that faced women in the 1960s. While women remain oppressed in fundamental ways, their rising participation in the labor force has had long-lasting repercussions—from the decrease in time spent on domestic labor to greater control over fertility with the availability of contraception and abortion, while greater financial independence has allowed more women to leave unhappy marriages. All of these developments have materially challenged the sexist stereotype of women as destined to a life of nurturing inside the home.

In addition, struggles for equality, Vogel adds, "can reveal the fundamentally exploitative character of capitalism, for the further rights are extended, the more capitalism's economic and social character is exposed. Far from exercises in fruitless reformism or supposedly divisive identity politics, struggles for equality can contribute to building strategic alliances and even point beyond capitalism."[102]

At the same time, socialism is necessary to achieve equality. Vogel concludes, "So long as society is dominated by the capitalist mode of production, and opposition between surplus labor and necessary labor, and between wage labor and domestic labor, will exist. . . . Extension of democracy, no matter how wide, can never abolish capitalist exploitation, nor can it liberate women."[103]

Vogel envisions the possibilities for life beyond capitalism and the possibilities for women's liberation through achieving a socialist society. While she rightly acknowledges that socialist revolution does not automatically or immediately result in the elimination of domestic labor, she observes that while "domestic labor plays an important role during the socialist transition," it also "begins a long process of transformation into an integral component of social production in a communist society."[104]

She compares and contrasts the role of domestic labor between capitalist and socialist societies. In a socialist society, she argues, "as in capitalist society, a tendency exists to reduce the amount of domestic labor carried out in individual households. Rather than embodying the capitalist drive for accumulation, however, it represents the socialist tendency for all labor to become part of social production . . . in a planned and conscious manner, corresponding to the needs of the people as a whole."[105]

A socialist society, Vogel continues, tends to "undermine the foundation for the oppression of women within the individual household and in society. The extension of democracy, the drawing of women into public production, and the progressive transformation of domestic labor during the socialist transition open up the possibility for what Marx calls 'a higher form of the family and relations between the sexes.'"[106]

Chapter Seven

Black Feminism
and Intersectionality

Although we are in essential agreement with Marx's theory as it applied to the very specific economic relationships he analyzed, we know that his analysis must be extended further in order for us to understand our specific economic situation as Black women.

—Combahee River Collective Statement, 1977[1]

The concept of the simultaneity of oppression is still the crux of a Black feminist understanding of political reality and, I believe, one of the most significant ideological contributions of Black feminist thought.

—Barbara Smith, 1983[2]

Black legal scholar Kimberlé Crenshaw coined the term "intersectionality" in her insightful 1989 essay, "Demarginalizing the Intersection of Race and Sex: A Black Feminist Critique of Anti-discrimination Doctrine, Feminist Theory and Antiracist Politics."[3] Crenshaw argued that Black women are discriminated against in ways that often do not fit neatly within the legal categories of either "racism" *or* "sexism"—but rather as a combination of both racism *and* sexism, in which racism and sexism intersect. Thus, the concept of intersectionality is a description of the way multiple oppressions are concretely experienced, by Black women in particular. Indeed, Crenshaw used the following analogy, referring to a traffic intersection to concretize the concept:

> Consider an analogy to traffic in an intersection, coming and going in all four directions. Discrimination, like traffic through an intersection, may flow in one direction, and it may flow in another. If an accident happens in an intersection, it can be caused by cars traveling from any number of directions and, sometimes, from all of them. Similarly, if a Black woman is harmed because she is in an intersection, her injury could result from sex discrimination or race discrimination. . . . But it is

not always easy to reconstruct an accident: Sometimes the skidmarks and the injuries simply indicate that they occurred simultaneously, frustrating efforts to determine which driver caused the harm.[4]

The legal system's framework of "women" and "Blacks" frequently renders Black women legally "invisible" and without legal recourse. Crenshaw describes several employment discrimination lawsuits to illustrate how Black women's complaints often fall between the cracks precisely because they are discriminated against *both* as women and as Blacks. The ruling in one such case, *DeGraffenreid v. General Motors*, filed by five Black women in 1976, demonstrates this point vividly.

The General Motors Corporation had never hired a Black woman before the 1964 Civil Rights Act passed through Congress. All of the Black women hired after 1970 fairly quickly lost their jobs, however, in mass layoffs during the 1973–75 recession. Such a sweeping loss of jobs among Black women led the plaintiffs to argue that seniority-based layoffs, guided by the principle "last hired, first fired," discriminated against Black women workers at General Motors, extending past discriminatory practices by the company. Yet the court refused to allow the plaintiffs to combine sex-based and race-based discrimination into a single category of discrimination:

> The plaintiffs allege that they are suing on behalf of black women, and that therefore this lawsuit attempts to combine two causes of action into a new special sub-category, namely, a combination of racial and sex-based discrimination.... The plaintiffs are clearly entitled to a remedy if they have been discriminated against. However, they should not be allowed to combine statutory remedies to create a new "super-remedy" which would give them relief beyond what the drafters of the relevant statutes intended. Thus, this lawsuit must be examined to see if it states a cause of action for race discrimination, sex discrimination, or alternatively either, but not a combination of both.[5]

In its decision, the court soundly rejected the creation of "a new classification of 'black women' who would have greater standing than, for example, a black male. The prospect of the creation of new classes of protected minorities, governed only by the mathematical principles of permutation and combination, clearly raises the prospect of opening the hackneyed Pandora's box."[6] Crenshaw observed of this ruling, "providing legal relief only when Black women show that their claims are based on race or on sex is analogous to calling an ambulance for the victim only after the driver responsible for the injuries is identified."[7]

"Ain't *We* Women?"

After Crenshaw introduced the term *intersectionality* in 1989, it was widely adopted because it encompassed the simultaneous experience of the multiple oppressions faced by Black women. But the concept was not a new one. Since the times of slavery, Black women have articulately described the multiple oppressions of race, class, and gender—referring to this concept as "interlocking oppressions," "simultaneous oppressions," "double jeopardy," "triple jeopardy," or any number of similar descriptive terms.[8]

Like most other Black feminists, Crenshaw emphasizes the importance of Sojourner Truth's famous "Ain't *I* a Woman?" speech delivered to the Women's Convention in Akron, Ohio, in 1851:

> That man over there says that women need to be helped into carriages and lifted over ditches, and to have the best place everywhere. Nobody ever helps me into carriages, or over mud-puddles, or gives me any best place! And ain't I a woman? Look at me! Look at my arm! I could have ploughed and planted, and gathered into barns, and no man could head me! And ain't I a woman? I could work as much and eat as much as a man—when I could get it—and bear the lash as well! And ain't I a woman? I have borne thirteen children, and seen them most all sold off to slavery, and when I cried out with my mother's grief, none but Jesus heard me! And ain't I a woman?[9]

Truth's words vividly contrast the character of the oppression faced by white and Black women. While white, middle-class women have traditionally been treated as delicate and overly emotional—destined to subordinate themselves to white men—Black women have been denigrated and subject to the racist abuse that is a foundational element of US society. Yet, as Crenshaw notes, "When Sojourner Truth rose to speak, many white women urged that she be silenced, fearing that she would divert attention from women's suffrage to emancipation," invoking a clear illustration of the degree of racism within the suffrage movement.[10]

Crenshaw draws a parallel between Truth's experience with the white suffrage movement and Black women's experience with modern feminism, arguing, "When feminist theory and politics that claim to reflect *women's* experiences and *women's* aspirations do not include or speak to Black women, Black women must ask, "Ain't *we* women?"

Intersectionality as a Fusion of Racial and Gender Oppressions

Thus, Crenshaw's political aims reached further than addressing flaws in the legal system. She argued that Black women are frequently absent from analyses of either gender oppression or racism, since the former focuses primarily on the experiences of white women and the latter on Black men. She sought to challenge both feminist and antiracist theory and practice that neglected to "accurately reflect the interaction of race and gender," arguing that "because the intersectional experience is greater than the sum of racism and sexism, any analysis that does not take intersectionality into account cannot sufficiently address the particular manner in which Black women are subordinated."[11] Crenshaw argued that a key aspect of intersectionality lies in its recognition that multiple oppressions are not each suffered separately but rather as a single, synthesized experience. This has enormous significance at the very practical level of movement building.

In *Black Feminist Thought: Knowledge, Consciousness and the Politics of Empowerment*, published in 1990, Black feminist Patricia Hill Collins extends and updates the social contradictions raised by Sojourner Truth, while crediting collective struggles waged historically with establishing a "collective wisdom" among Black women:

> If women are allegedly passive and fragile, then why are Black women treated as "mules" and assigned heavy cleaning chores? If good mothers are supposed to stay at home with their children, then why are U.S. Black women on public assistance forced to find jobs and leave their children in day care? If women's highest calling is to become mothers, then why are Black teen mothers pressured to use Norplant and Depo Provera? In the absence of a viable Black feminism that investigates how intersecting oppressions of race, gender, and class foster these contradictions, the angle of vision created by being deemed devalued workers and failed mothers could easily be turned inward, leading to internalized oppression. But the legacy of struggle among U.S. Black women suggests that a collectively shared, Black women's oppositional knowledge has long existed. This collective wisdom in turn has spurred U.S. Black women to generate a more specialized knowledge, namely, Black feminist thought as critical social theory.[12]

Like Crenshaw, Collins uses the concept of intersectionality to analyze how "oppressions [such as 'race and gender' or 'sexuality and nation'] work together in producing injustice." But Collins adds the concept "matrix of dominations" to this formulation, which "refers to how these intersecting oppressions are actually organized. Regardless of the particular intersections involved, structural, disciplinary, hegemonic, and interpersonal domains of power reappear across quite different forms of oppression."[13]

Elsewhere, Collins acknowledges the crucial component of social class among Black women in shaping political perceptions. As she argued in "Beyond the Margins" in 1995, "While a Black woman's standpoint and its accompanying epistemology stem from Black women's consciousness of race and gender oppression, they are not simply the result of combining Afrocentric and female values—*standpoints are rooted in real material conditions structured by social class.*"[14] (Emphasis added.)

Left-Wing Black Feminism of the 1960s and 1970s

Frances Beal's 1970 essay "Double Jeopardy: To Be Black & Female"[15] was one of the first analyses of the interlocking oppressions of race, gender, and class in the modern Black feminist movement. Beal had worked within SNCC and was a founding member of the SNCC Black Women's Liberation Caucus, followed by membership in the Third World Women's Alliance between 1970 and 1978. Her essay combines a powerful indictment of the capitalist system with a clear critique of nationalist movements' and the predominantly white feminist movement's approaches to Black women.

"Double Jeopardy" begins by arguing, "The system of capitalism (and its after birth . . . racism) under which we all live, has attempted by many devious ways and means to destroy the humanity of all people, and particularly the humanity of black people. This has meant an outrageous assault on every black man, woman and child who reside in the United States."[16]

Of the Black movement, Beal remarks, "Since the advent of black power, the black male has exerted a more prominent leadership role in our struggle for justice in this country. He sees the system for what it really is for the most part. But where he rejects its values and mores on many issues, when it comes to women, he seems to take his guidelines from the pages of the *Ladies' Home Journal.*"[17]

Beal also criticizes the failure of many white feminists to address racism, arguing, "Any white group that does not have an anti-imperialist and anti-racist ideology has absolutely nothing in common with the black women's struggle. What assurances have black women that white women will be any less racist and exploitative if they had the power and were in a position to do so? These are serious questions that the white women's liberation movement has failed to address itself to."[18] Later in the essay, Beal develops her understanding of the contradictions of capitalism, making the insightful observation:

> The economic system of capitalism finds it expedient to reduce women to a state of enslavement. They oftentimes serve as a scapegoat for the evils of this system. Much in the same way that the poor white cracker of the South who is equally victimized, looks down upon blacks and contributes to the oppression of blacks. So by giving to men a false feeling of superiority (at least in their own home or in their relationships with women), the oppression of women acts as an escape valve for capitalism. Men may be cruelly exploited and subjected to all sorts of dehumanizing tactics on the part of the ruling class, but they have someone who is below them—at least they're not women.[19]

Finally, Beal raises the issue of racist sterilization abuse, which became a defining issue for women of color in the 1970s. She noted that "perhaps the most outlandish act of oppression in modern times is the current campaign to promote sterilization of nonwhite women in an attempt to maintain the population and power imbalance between the white haves and the non-white have nots. . . . However, what the authorities in charge of these programs refer to as "birth control" is in fact nothing but a method of outright surgical genocide."[20]

The Racial Divide in "Women's Rights" Issues

Black feminist Angela Davis[21] also contested the theory and practice of white feminists of the 1960s and 1970s who failed to address the centrality of racism. Davis's pioneering book *Women, Race and Class* examines the history of Black women in the United States from a Marxist perspective, beginning with the system of slavery and continuing through to modern capitalism. Her book also examines the ways in which the issues of reproductive rights and rape in particular represent profoundly different experiences for Black and white women because of racism. Each of these is examined in turn below.

Reproductive Rights and Racist Sterilization Abuse

Mainstream feminists of the 1960s and 1970s regarded the issue of reproductive rights as exclusively one of winning legal abortion, despite widespread racist sterilization abuse at that time.

Davis argues that the history of the birth-control movement and its racist sterilization programs necessarily make the issue of reproductive rights far more complicated for Black women and other women of color, who have historically been the targets of this abuse. Davis traces the path of twentieth-century birth-control pioneer Margaret Sanger from her early days as a socialist to her conversion to the eugenics movement, which espoused an openly racist approach to population control based on the slogan "[More] children from the fit, less from the unfit."

Those "unfit" to bear children, according to the eugenicists, included the mentally and physically disabled, prisoners, and the nonwhite poor. As Davis noted, "By 1932, the Eugenics Society could boast that at least twenty-six states had passed compulsory sterilization laws, and that thousands of 'unfit' persons had been surgically prevented from reproducing."

In launching the "Negro Project" in 1939, Sanger's American Birth Control League argued, "The mass of Negroes, particularly in the South, still breed carelessly and disastrously." In a personal letter, Sanger confided, "We do not want word to get out that we want to exterminate the Negro population and the minister is the man who can straighten out that idea if it ever occurs to their more rebellious members."[22]

Racist population-control policies left large numbers of Black women, Latinas, and Native American women sterilized against their will or without their knowledge. In 1974, an Alabama court found that between 100,000 and 150,000 poor Black teenagers had been sterilized each year in Alabama.[23]

The 1960s and 1970s witnessed rampant sterilization abuse and other forms of coercion aimed at Black women, Native American women, and Latinas—alongside a sharp rise in struggles against this mistreatment. A 1970s study showed 25 percent of Native American women had been sterilized, and that Black and Latina married women had been sterilized in much greater proportions than married women in the population at large. By 1970, 35 percent of women of childbearing age in Puerto Rico—still a US colony—had been permanently sterilized.[24] Yet mainstream white feminists not only ignored these struggles but also added to the problem. Many embraced the goals of population control, with all its racist implications, as an ostensibly "liberal" cause.

In 1972, for example, a time when Native American women and other women of color were struggling against coercive adoption policies that targeted their communities, *Ms.* magazine asked its predominantly white and middle-class readership, "'What do you do if you're a conscientious citizen, concerned about the population explosion and ecological problems, love children, want to see what one of your own would look like, and want more than one?'" *Ms.* offered as a solution: "Have One, Adopt One."[25] *Ms.* thus encouraged white, middle-class couples to fulfill their "natural" desire for their own [white] child and then to combat overpopulation by adopting a second child [of color], for the betterment of humanity. *Ms.* seemed unaware of the racist implications of this advice, despite the fact that the children on offer for adoption were overwhelmingly Native American, Black, Latino, and Asian.

To be sure, the legalization of abortion in the US Supreme Court's 1973 *Roe v. Wade* decision was of paramount importance to all women and was the direct result of grassroots struggle. Because of both the economic and social consequences of racism, the lives of Black women, Latinas, and other women of color were most at risk when abortion was illegal. In the years before abortion was made legal in New York City in 1970, for example, Black women and Puerto Rican women made up 80 percent of all women who died after an illegal abortion.[26]

The legalization of abortion in 1973 is usually regarded as the most important success of the modern women's movement. That victory, however, was accompanied by the end of the 1970s decade by the far less heralded but *equally important victories against sterilization abuse*, the result of grassroots struggles waged primarily by women of color. In 1978, the federal government conceded to demands by Native American, Black, and Latina activists by finally establishing regulations for sterilization. These included required waiting periods and authorization forms in the same language spoken by the woman agreeing to be sterilized.[27]

Davis notes that women of color "were far more familiar than their white sisters with the murderously clumsy scalpels of inept abortionists seeking profit in illegality,"[28] yet were virtually absent from abortion-rights campaigns. She concludes, "The abortion rights activists of the early 1970s should have examined the history of their movement. Had they done so, they might have understood why so many of their Black sisters adopted a posture of suspicion toward their cause."[29]

The Racial Component of Rape

Rape is one of the most damaging manifestations of women's oppression the world over. But rape also has had a toxic racial component in the

United States since the time of slavery as a key weapon in maintaining the system of white supremacy. Davis argues that rape is "an essential dimension of the social relations between slave master and slave," involving the routine rape of enslaved Black women by their white masters.[30]

She describes rape as "a weapon of domination, a weapon of repression, whose covert goal was to extinguish slave women's will to resist and, in the process, to demoralize their men."[31] The institutionalized rape of Black women survived the abolition of slavery and took on its modern form: "Group rape, perpetrated by the Ku Klux Klan and other terrorist organizations of the post–Civil War period, became an uncamouflaged political weapon in the drive to thwart the movement for Black equality."[32]

The caricature of the virtuous white Southern belle as constant prey for Black male rapists had its opposite in that of the promiscuous Black woman seeking the sexual attention of white men. As Davis argued, "The fictional image of the Black man as rapist has always strengthened its inseparable companion: the image of the Black woman as chronically promiscuous. . . . Viewed as 'loose women' and whores, Black women's cries of rape would necessarily lack legitimacy."[33] Lerner likewise described, "The myth of the Black rapist of white women is the twin of the myth of the bad Black woman—both designed to apologize for and facilitate the continued exploitation of Black men and women."[34]

Davis strongly criticized 1970s-era white feminists for neglecting to integrate an analysis of racism with the theory and practice of combating rape: "During the contemporary anti-rape movement, few feminist theorists seriously analyzed the special circumstances surrounding the Black woman as rape victim. The historical knot binding Black women—systematically abused and violated by white men—to Black men—maimed and murdered because of the racist manipulation of the rape charge—has just begun to be acknowledged to any significant extent."[35]

It is rarely acknowledged in mainstream feminist narratives that, decades before the rise of the modern women's liberation movement, Black women were organizing against their systematic rape at the hands of white racist men. Women civil rights activists, including Rosa Parks, were part of a vocal grassroots movement to defend Black women subject to racist sexual assaults—in an intersection of oppression historically unique to Black women in the United States.

Danielle L. McGuire, author of *At the Dark End of the Street: Black Women, Rape, and Resistance—a New History of the Civil Rights Movement from Rosa Parks to the Rise of Black Power*, argues:

Throughout the twentieth century . . . Black women regularly denounced their sexual misuse. By deploying their voices as weapons in the
wars against white supremacy, whether in the church, the courtroom, or
in congressional hearings, African-American women loudly resisted
what Martin Luther King, Jr., called the "thingification" of their humanity. Decades before radical feminists in the women's movement urged
rape survivors to "speak out," African-American women's public protests
galvanized local, national, and even international outrage and sparked
larger campaigns for racial justice and human dignity.[36]

In 1974, twenty-year-old Joan Little, imprisoned at the Beaufort
County Jail in Washington, North Carolina, killed white jailer Clarence
Alligood after he tried to sexually assault her—and then she escaped.
After she surrendered a grand jury indicted her, with the possibility of
death by gas chamber if convicted. The local newspaper claimed Alligood "gave his life in service of his country," although he was found
naked from the waist down with semen on his thighs and had likely
died at the moment of orgasm.[37]

As McGuire describes, by then, "decades of black women's organizing
and personal testimony" had "altered the political and legal landscape for
black women raped or sexually abused by white men."[38] She adds, "In
1974 Joan Little became the symbol of a campaign to defend black womanhood and to call attention to the sexualized racial violence that still existed ten years after Congress passed the 1965 Voting Rights Act."[39]

Civil rights and Black Power activists, including Rosa Parks and Angela Davis, launched the Free Joan Little Campaign, which soon gained
the involvement of feminists and leftists around the country. Davis argued in a *Ms.* magazine article, "All people who see themselves as members of the existing community of struggle for justice, equality, and
progress have a responsibility to fulfill toward Joan Little."[40] At rallies
and fundraisers, these activists also raised the right of *all* women to defend themselves against sexual assault. In a 1975 press release, the De-
troit branch of the Joan Little Legal Defense Committee argued that it
aimed for Little's acquittal, "but also, that the question, 'should a woman
defend herself against a rapist?' will be decided in the affirmative."[41]

During the trial, Little's attorneys, Jerry Paul and Karen Galloway,
based their arguments on the Southern police's history of racism, brutality,
and sexual harassment of Black women, while documenting these practices at Beaufort County Jail. As McGuire described, Little testified that
"when she wanted to take a shower, she 'had to call the jailer and have him
turn the water on.' Then he would stand outside her cell and watch."[42] The

twelve-person jury, made up of six who were Black and nine who were women, deliberated for just seventy-eight minutes before voting unanimously to acquit Joan Little. When she emerged from the courthouse, the crowd of supporters chanted, "Freedom! Freedom! Freedom!"[43]

Black Feminism as a Politics of Inclusion

The Combahee River Collective's defining statement, issued in 1977, describes its vision of Black feminism as opposing *all* forms of oppression—including sexuality, gender identity, disability, and age oppression—later embedded in the concept of intersectionality.

> The most general statement of our politics at the present time would be that we are actively committed to struggling against racial, sexual, heterosexual, and class oppression, and see as our particular task the development of integrated analysis and practice based upon the fact that the major systems of oppression are interlocking. The synthesis of these oppressions creates the conditions of our lives. As Black women we see Black feminism as the logical political movement to combat the manifold and simultaneous oppressions that all women of color face.[44]

They add, "We know that there is such a thing as racial-sexual oppression which is neither solely racial nor solely sexual, e.g., the history of rape of Black women by white men as a weapon of political repression."[45]

The Combahee River Collective built upon the Black feminist political tradition, basing its analysis on the interlocking oppressions of race, gender, sexuality, and class and developing an approach that provides an explicit strategy for combating all forms of oppression within a common struggle.

The Combahee River Collective was made up of women who were veterans of the Black Panther Party and other antiracist organizations. These Black feminists established a tradition that rejects prioritizing women's oppression over racism and vice versa. This tradition assumes the connection between racism and poverty in capitalist society, thereby rejecting middle-class strategies for women's liberation that disregard the centrality of class in poor and working-class women's lives. When they rightfully asserted the racial and class differences between women, they did so because these differences were largely ignored and neglected by much of the women's movement at that time, thereby rendering Black women and other women of color invisible in theory and in practice.

While many women of color were strongly critical of mainstream feminism's refusal to challenge racism and other forms of oppression, the end goal for most 1970s-era Black feminists and other feminists of color was not permanent racial separation. Barbara Smith conceived of an *inclusive* approach to combating multiple oppressions, beginning with coalition-building around particular struggles.

As Smith argued, "The most progressive sectors of the women's movement, including radical white women, have taken [issues of racism], and many more, quite seriously."[46] Asian American feminist Merle Woo argued explicitly, "Today . . . I feel even more deeply hurt when I realize how many people, how so many people, because of racism and sexism, fail to see what power we sacrifice by not joining hands." But, she added, "not all white women are racist, and not all Asian-American men are sexist. And there are visible changes. Real, tangible, positive changes."[47]

In an interview between sisters Barbara and Beverly Smith (also a cofounder of the Combahee River Collective) and the editors of *This Bridge Called My Back*, Barbara Smith argues for a strategy of "coalition building" rather than "racial separatism." Arguing that "any kind of separatism is a dead end," she continues, "I do feel that the strongest politics are coalition politics that cover a broad range of issues. There is no way that one oppressed group is going to topple a system by itself. Forming principled coalitions around specific issues is very important." She adds, "That is why Third World women are forming the leadership in the feminist movement because we are not one-dimensional, one-issued in our political understanding. Just by virtue of our identities we certainly define race and usually define class as being fundamental issues that we have to address. The more wide-ranged your politics, the more potentially profound and transformative they are."[48]

The aim of the Black feminist tradition has been toward building a stronger movement for women's liberation that represents the interests of *all* women. Smith described her own vision of feminism in 1983: "I have often wished I could spread the word that a movement committed to fighting sexual, racial, economic and heterosexist oppression, not to mention one which opposes imperialism, anti-Semitism, the oppressions visited upon the physically disabled, the old and the young, at the same time that it challenges militarism and imminent nuclear destruction, is the very opposite of narrow."[49]

This approach to fighting oppression does not merely complement but also strengthens Marxist theory and practice—which seeks to unite not only all those who are exploited but also all those who are oppressed by capitalism into a single movement that fights for the liberation of all humanity. The Combahee River Collective, which was perhaps the most self-consciously left-wing organization of Black feminists in the 1970s, acknowledged its adherence to socialism and anti-imperialism, while rightfully also arguing for greater attention to oppression:

> We realize that the liberation of all oppressed peoples necessitates the destruction of the political-economic systems of capitalism and imperialism as well as patriarchy. We are socialists because we believe that work must be organized for the collective benefit of those who do the work and create the products, and not for the profit of the bosses. Material resources must be equally distributed among those who create these resources. We are not convinced, however, that a socialist revolution that is not also a feminist and anti-racist revolution will guarantee our liberation. . . . Although we are in essential agreement with Marx's theory as it applied to the very specific economic relationships he analyzed, we know that his analysis must be extended further in order for us to understand our specific economic situation as Black women.[50]

Intersectionality: A Concept, Not a Theory

Intersectionality is a concept describing the experience of oppression, not a theory explaining its cause(s). It can therefore be applied to a variety of theories—from those informed by Marxism to those influenced by postmodernism. Below I explore the ways in which Marxist theory and practice can benefit by incorporating the concept of intersectionality, while chapter 8 examines intersectionality's contrasting interpretation by some postmodernists, post-Marxists in particular.

Marxism provides a framework for understanding the relationship between oppression and exploitation (that is, oppression as a byproduct of the system of class exploitation), and also identifies the strategy for creating the material and social conditions that will make it possible to end both oppression and exploitation. Marxism's critics have disparaged this framework as an aspect of Marx's "economic reductionism."

But, as Marxist feminist Martha Gimenez responds, "To argue, then, that class is fundamental is not to 'reduce' gender or racial oppression to class, but to acknowledge that the underlying basic and 'nameless' power at the root of what happens in social interactions grounded in 'intersectionality' is class power."[51] The working class holds the potential to lead a struggle in the interests of all those who suffer injustice and oppression. This is because both exploitation and oppression are rooted in capitalism.

Exploitation is the method by which the ruling class robs workers of surplus value; the various forms of oppression play a primary role in maintaining the rule of a tiny minority over the vast majority. In each case, the enemy is one and the same.

The class struggle helps to educate workers—sometimes very rapidly—by challenging the reactionary ideas and prejudices that keep workers divided. When workers go on strike, confronting capital and its agents of repression (the police), the class nature of society becomes suddenly clarified. Racist, sexist, or homophobic ideas cultivated over a lifetime can disappear within a matter of days in a mass strike wave. The sight of hundreds of police lined up to protect the boss's property or to usher in a bunch of scabs speaks volumes about the class nature of the state within capitalism.

The process of struggle also exposes another truth hidden beneath layers of ruling-class ideology: as the producers of the goods and services that keep capitalism running, workers have the ability to shut down the system through a mass strike. And workers not only have the power to shut down the system but also to replace it with a socialist society, based upon collective ownership of the means of production. Although other groups in society suffer oppression, only the working class possesses this objective power.

These are the basic reasons why Marx argued that capitalism created its own gravediggers in the working class. But when Marx defined the working class as the agent for revolutionary change, he was describing its historical potential, rather than a foregone conclusion. This is the key to understanding Lenin's argument that workers must respond to all cases of oppression, described above. The whole Leninist conception of the vanguard party rests on the understanding that a battle of ideas must be fought *inside* the working-class movement. A section of workers, won to a socialist alternative and organized into a revolutionary party, can win other workers away from ruling-class ideologies and provide an alternative worldview. For Lenin, the notion of political consciousness entailed workers' willingness to champion the interests of all the oppressed in society as an integral part of the struggle for socialism.

The concept of intersectionality leads the way toward a much higher level of understanding of how multiple oppressions are experienced than that developed by classical Marxists, enabling the further development of the ways in which *solidarity* can be built between all those who suffer oppression and exploitation under capitalism to forge a unified movement.

Imperialism and Global Feminist Solidarity

It is well beyond the scope of this book to address the potential of inter-sectionality to combat women's oppression on a global scale. My analysis, however, would be lacking if it did not focus attention on how, in contrast to mainstream feminism's embrace of imperialism, left-wing feminists have developed a distinct and forthright anti-imperialist method for understanding and battling women's oppression globally. Below I will briefly summarize the contributions of Argentine-born Marxist feminist Martha Gimenez, Egyptian feminist Leila Ahmed, and Indian postcolonial feminist Chandra Mohanty.

In 1975, Gimenez began to pursue an analysis of the global effects of imperialism in a postcolonial world. In particular she integrated the role played by imperialism historically in perpetuating women's oppression worldwide. "The separation between the family and the economy," she argues, "can be understood, in the context of western countries, as a product of the process of capitalist development which eroded the feudal forms of agriculture and of domestic industries."[52] But imperialist nations then imposed these same gender relations on "nonwestern countries through the penetration of capitalist forms of socioeconomic organization brought about by the colonial and neo-colonial policies of the advanced capitalist countries."[53] Colonial policies advanced imperial, not women's, interests over their conquered populations, all in the name of promoting the "superior" values of "Western civilization."[54]

More often than not, colonial policies diminished rather than advanced women's rights. Before the British occupied Egypt in 1882, for example, Egyptian women were offered medical training alongside men. British Consul General Lord Cromer, however, banned women doctors, emulating women's inferior position in his home country.[55]

Indeed, as Ahmed argues, "This champion of the unveiling of women was, in England, the founding member and sometime president of the Men's League for Opposing Women's Suffrage. Feminism on the home front and feminism directed against white men was to be resisted and suppressed; but taken abroad and directed against the culture of colonized peoples, it could be promoted in ways that admirably served the project of the dominance of the white man."[56]

Gimenez also argues that while "the same capitalist processes operate in advanced capitalist countries and in Third World countries," appearances can be deceiving. In advanced capitalist economies, women's laborforce participation is greater and "in terms of sex stratification, relations between the sexes may appear to be more egalitarian." But "because of the coexistence in Third World countries of capitalist forms of production, domestic industries, and subsistence agriculture, it could be shown that the extent of women's productive activity may be even greater in those countries."[57] Gimenez describes the variations of "sex stratification and sex differentiation" as "linked to a) the stage of capitalist development characterizing a given country, b) the dominant or subordinate place which a given country has within the world-wide network of imperialism, and c) the extent of uneven development within the country."[58]

More recently, Mohanty makes the following observation in her book *Feminism Without Borders*:

> When the category of "sexually oppressed women" is located within particular systems in the Third World that are defined on a scale that is normed through Eurocentric assumptions . . . the assumption is reinforced that the Third World just has not evolved to the extent that the West has. This mode of feminist analysis, by homogenizing and systematizing the experiences of different groups of women in these countries, erases all marginal and resistant modes and experiences."[59]

Mohanty adds that such an approach results in a "colonialist discourse" based on "feminist analyses that perpetuate and sustain the hegemony of the idea of the superiority of the West produce a corresponding set of universal images of the Third World woman, images such as the veiled woman, the powerful mother, the chaste virgin, the obedient wife, and so on."[60]

Those struggling for women's liberation in the heart of world imperialism therefore must consider the impact of their own demands on the societies of historically oppressed nations. Gimenez warns, "The interdependence created by imperialism cannot be overlooked as an important structural determinant of the position of women. The course of feminist struggles in a given country, the gains as well as the setbacks, cannot be properly understood without a careful investigation of their relationship to the fate of women in other countries." In individual societies, in addition to variations in the capitalist processes, women's oppression is further shaped "by the political, legal, and ideological structures peculiar to each country, as well as by national and international circumstances."[61]

Feminists in imperialist countries, therefore, have a responsibility to women in oppressed nations. This point has been affirmed in the negative in the current endless "war on terror," launched in 2001. In the aftermath of the September 11 attacks, as noted earlier, mainstream feminists' endorsement of the war on Afghanistan helped the Bush administration to promote the fiction that the war aimed to "liberate" Afghan women, while in reality it only advanced the imperialist aims of the United States.

At the same time, Gimenez also appreciates the degree of similarity in the struggles of working-class women globally, however different their immediate circumstances. "Under capitalist conditions, whether in advanced or in Third World countries, all working-class women, employed or unemployed and regardless of socioeconomic status, are subject to oppression and economic exploitation. These women must wage an unceasing struggle for their existence and their selfhood."[62]

Mohanty emphasizes the importance of promoting appreciation of global culture, arguing, "Rather than formulating activism and agency in terms of disconnected cultures and nations, it allows us to frame agency and resistance across the borders of nation and culture."[63] She describes her aim, through her analysis of the consequences of neoliberal capitalist globalization, as promoting international "feminist solidarity," showing

> the interconnectedness of the histories, experiences and struggles of U.S. women of color, white women, and women of the Third World/South. . . . Thus, the focus is not just on the intersection of race, class, gender, nation and sexuality in different communities of women but on mutuality and complication, which suggest attentiveness to the interweaving of these communities. In addition the focus is simultaneously on individual and collective experiences of oppression and exploitation and of struggle and resistance.[64]

Chapter Eight

Feminism and Radicalism in the Age of Neoliberalism

The postmodern rubric of decentering seemingly supports Black women's long-standing efforts to challenge false universal knowledge that privileged Whiteness, maleness and wealth. However . . . current meanings attached to decentering as a construct illustrate how terms can continue to be used yet can be stripped of their oppositional intent.

—Patricia Hill Collins, 1998[1]

The decline of mass struggle, including feminist struggle, during the second half of the 1970s was coupled with a sharp shift rightward in mainstream politics. The 1980s were inaugurated with the election of President Ronald Reagan, followed by the rapid ascendancy of the Christian right.

This rightward shift in mainstream politics represented a sustained bipartisan project that began in the mid-1970s in response to the upheavals of the late 1960s and early 1970s that continues today—uniting the various wings of the capitalist class to shift the balance of class and social forces back in favor of the ruling order. One of this project's central aims has been economic: to lower working-class living standards by attacking unions, which have historically fought to raise workers' wages. The success of this economic attack can be measured in straightforward statistics: whereas 24.2 percent of private-sector workers belonged to a union in 1973, the percentage dropped to 6.6 percent in 2014, while economic inequality in the United States has returned to levels not seen since the Gilded Age a century ago.[2]

This ruling-class enterprise, which has since become known as neoliberalism, defined itself by its stated worship of the free market, but is actually based upon imposing the twin policies of government-sponsored welfare for the rich and austerity for all those who rely on selling their labor power to survive. Beginning in the 1980s, neoliberal policy aggressively swept the globe via organizations such as the International Monetary Fund, the World Trade Organization, and the World Bank. After four decades of neoliberalism, its results are on full display today in the impoverishment of the global working class.

The Backlash against Women

This anti–working class onslaught attacked all the gains of the 1960s-era social movements, utilizing open racism, misogyny, and homophobia as acceptable mainstream discourse, gaining traction in the late 1970s, and continuing ever since.

The racist image of the Black "welfare queen" promoted by Ronald Reagan became entrenched in mainstream politics in the 1980s—and then provided the unspoken justification for Bill Clinton to end "welfare as we know it" in the 1990s. In this context, the ideological backlash against feminism came to dominate the political mainstream in the 1980s, documented brilliantly by journalist Susan Faludi in her 1991 book *Backlash: The Undeclared War Against American Women*.[3] As Faludi showed, the mass media played a key role in hyping the anti-feminist themes of self-proclaimed "experts" who lacked convincing evidence and conducted "research" with suspicious methodology. Through sheer repetition, however, these themes became absorbed into popular culture. The backlash has not only continued but has accelerated since the 1980s.

The "Man Shortage" of the 1980s

Career women were early targets in the war on feminism, when the mass media advanced the theory that women professionals who postponed marriage or having children until they reached their thirties or beyond, as their biological clocks ticked, looked back with regret. Using faulty evidence from a Harvard-Yale study on marriage, the media declared a "man shortage" crisis in the 1980s. *Newsweek* went so far as to claim in 1986 that a single woman in her forties was more likely to be "killed by a terrorist" than ever marry. Although it was subsequently proven that the study was complete nonsense—it turned out there were actually substantially more unmarried men than women in this age group—the damage had been done: the myth of the "man shortage" became embedded in popular culture.[4]

The "Rape Crisis Melodrama" of the 1990s

The issue of rape—and date rape in particular—has been central to the right-wing backlash since the 1990s. Conservative pundits repeatedly accused feminists of creating a "victim" consciousness among women, causing college-aged women to falsely accuse men of date rape. Harvard graduate Katie Roiphe made a big splash with her 1993 book, *The Morning After: Sex, Fear and Feminism*, blaming feminists for creating an atmosphere of "rape crisis melodrama" that greatly exaggerated the problem of date rape on college campuses.[5]

Newsweek ran a ten-page spread on the evils of "sexual correctness" in 1994, with the headline "Stop Whining" and a feature story by Republican consultant Mary Matalin admonishing women for filing "frivolous" date-rape and sexual-harassment claims that "clog the system."[6] Right-wing syndicated columnist Kathleen Parker regularly ridiculed the problem of date rape with comments such as: "The biggest myth that won't die is that one of four college women is raped on campuses each year. . . . If 25 percent of Daddy's little girls were being sexually assaulted at college, there wouldn't be any girls on campus."[7]

The figures Parker held in such contempt are based on an extensive study sponsored by *Ms.*, directed by psychologist Mary P. Kos, surveying 6,100 undergraduate students from thirty-two college campuses across the United States. The *Ms.* study, published in the 1988 book *I Never Called It Rape* finally provided the evidence: one in four women students surveyed "had an experience that met the legal definition of rape or attempted rape."[8] In a separate survey, 43 percent of college-aged men admitted to having used coercive behavior to obtain sex, including ignoring a woman's protest, using physical aggression, and forcing intercourse, but did not consider it to be "rape."[9] Date rape is not a figment of the imaginations of "hysterical" feminists, but an indisputable reality for young women.

The "Opt-Out Revolution" of the 2000s

But the right-wing backlash was not limited to the archetypal "single woman." Working mothers have been fed a steady diet of guilt for the last several decades for leaving their children in day care. Although the majority of women with young children work outside the home, this line of attack has not abated. One notable installment in the 2000s was *Home-Alone America: The Hidden Toll of Day Care, Behavioral Drugs and*

Other Parent Substitutes, by Mary Eberstadt, research fellow for Stanford's Hoover Institution. The book's front cover depicts a woman dressed in a business suit leaving for work as her small child desperately clings to her.[10]

Eberstadt blames working mothers, single mothers, and divorced parents for such wide-ranging social problems as child obesity, teen pregnancy, and sexually transmitted diseases. "Over the past few decades, more and more children have spent considerably less time in the company of their parents or other relatives, and numerous fundamental measures of their well-being have simultaneously gone into what once would have been judged scandalous decline," Eberstadt argues.[11]

Around the same time, the backlash incorporated the claim that women professionals were quitting their jobs in droves to embrace stay-at-home motherhood. In October 2003, the *New York Times Magazine* featured a cover story, "The Opt-Out Revolution," describing a small group of white, middle-class Yale and Princeton graduates who decided to quit their careers because they were more fulfilled by full-time motherhood.[12]

One of the women interviewed argues, "I think some of us are swinging to a place where we enjoy, and can admit we enjoy, the stereotypical role of female/mother/caregiver. I think we were born with those feelings." Although the article describes the experience of a mere handful of privileged women, its conclusion is sweeping: "Why don't women run the world? Maybe it's because they don't want to."[13]

Ten years later, however, a follow-up article with a very different title, "The Opt-Out Generation Wants Back In," appeared in the *New York Times Magazine*.[14] Things had not worked out quite as well as most of these women expected, and most were either back in the workforce or seeking to return. The effects of the recession made their earnings more essential to their family's survival in some cases; in others, domestic tensions had led to divorce or deterioration in marital life.

Moreover, as the article describes, attitudes toward working mothers had changed substantially in the previous decade, primarily due to economic necessity: "By 2010, with recovery from the 'mancession' slow and a record 40 percent of mothers functioning as family breadwinners, fully 75 percent of Americans agreed with the statement that 'a working mother can establish just as warm and secure a relationship with her children as a mother who does not work.'"[15] In 2012, 75.1 percent of mothers whose youngest child was between the age of six and seventeen years old was either working or seeking work; the figure for women with children under the age of six was 64.8 percent.[16]

The Rise of Postmodernism

Radical activists and theorists were rapidly forced to absorb the dramatic transformation in US politics described above. Whereas in the early 1970s, many radicals believed revolution would soon be on the agenda, by the end of that decade the political trajectory was moving in the opposite direction. Because the neoliberal project has been bipartisan from the beginning, Democrats followed Republicans rightward in the late 1970s, dragging liberal organizations—including those of mainstream feminists—with them.

Lise Vogel describes the impact on left-wing feminists forced to grapple with the 1980s shift rightward in mainstream politics: "Feminist intellectual work managed to advance, even prosper," but it had "far fewer links than earlier to women's movement activism. Surviving on college and university campuses, its practitioners encountered a range of disciplinary constraints and professional pressures. Younger generations of feminist scholars had missed, moreover, the chance to participate in a radical women's movement rooted in the upheavals of the 1960s."[17]

The world of academia, which functioned as a center for ideas and debates about living movements in the 1960s and early 1970s, became increasingly absorbed in debates over ideas that were irrelevant to the lives of ordinary people. In this context, Marxism was widely dismissed as "reductionist," as radical social theorists turned toward a variety of alternative viewpoints within the practice of postmodernism. Some of the academics involved were veteran 1960s radicals who had lost faith in the possibility for revolution. They were joined by a new generation of radicals too young to have experienced the tumult of the 1960s but influenced by the pessimism of the period.

A variety of postmodern theories flourished in the 1980s and 1990s. While postmodernism defies easy definition, Helene A. Shugart, Catherine Egley Waggoner, and D. Lynn O'Brien Hallstein summarize, "Postmodernism, positioned in contrast to modernist assumptions of absolute, knowable truths, is premised instead on the understanding that all knowledge is relative and multiple; it is thus characterized by paradox and inconsistency."[18] For both better and for worse, postmodernism indicated a fairly decisive theoretical break with the past among radicals.

One aspect of this break marked an enormous advance: championing the fight against *all* forms of oppression as a political priority for radicals. British literary theorist Terry Eagleton describes postmodernism's "single most enduring achievement" as "the fact that it has helped to place questions of sexuality, gender and ethnicity so firmly on the political agenda that it is impossible to imagine them being erased without an almighty struggle."[19]

In activist circles, this process was first set in motion by the social movements of the late 1960s and early 1970s, but its progress stalled until queer activists, initially organizing around the AIDS epidemic, began to struggle militantly around the slogan "We're here; we're queer; get used to it" in the 1980s. Likewise, beginning in the 1990s, so-called "third-wave feminists" thoroughly embraced the struggles of all those facing racial, sexual, and gender discrimination, including transgender people.[20]

Postmodernism both informed and was informed by queer and third-wave feminist activism, and its importance should not be underestimated. In this way, postmodernism helped to transform the character of activism in a myriad of ways—most importantly toward an *inclusive* approach to fighting oppression on every front. This includes the oppression experienced by trans people, those who suffer from disabilities or face age discrimination, and many other forms of oppression that had been neglected on the left.

A Retreat from Marxism and Class Politics

Other aspects of postmodernism marked more of a retreat than an advance, however. Postmodernists stressed that a transformed social reality—termed *postindustrial* or *post-Fordist*—required a new and different set of politics. In this context, Marxism was widely disparaged as "reductionist" and "essentialist" by academics calling themselves postmodernists, poststructuralists, and post-Marxists. These theorists rejected political generalization, categories of social structures, and material realities (referred to as "truths," "totalities," and "universalities")—in the name of "anti-essentialism." Postmodernists instead placed an overriding emphasis on subjective, individual, and cultural relations as centers of struggle—as the importance of class struggle receded. As feminist theorist Teresa Ebert explained in 2005,

> [The] canonical feminist understandings of gender and sexuality institutionalized by "post" theories (as in poststructuralism, postcolonialism, postmodernism, postmarxism) are—after one allows for all their local differences and family quarrels (e.g., Benhabib, et al., 1995; Butler, et al., 2000)—strategies for bypassing questions of labor (as in the labor theory

of value) and capital (the social relation grounded in turning the labor power of the other into profit) and instead dwell on matters of cultural differences (as in lifestyles).[21]

While it flourished in the 1970s and 1980s, the fragmented and subjective focus of postmodernism effectively marginalized historical materialism. Within the broad theoretical category of postmodernism, post-Marxism provided a new theoretical framework. Two of its key theorists, Ernesto Laclau and Chantal Mouffe, published the book *Hegemony and Socialist Strategy: Towards a Radical Democratic Politics* in 1985, which contains many of the themes underpinning a new concept that has since become known as "identity politics."[22] Laclau and Mouffe explain their theory as a negation of socialist "totality":

> The classic conception of socialism supposed that the disappearance of private ownership of the means of production would set up a chain of effects which, over a whole historical epoch, would lead to the extinction of all forms of subordination. Today we know that this is not so. There are not, for example, necessary links between anti-sexism and anti-capitalism, and a unity between the two can only be the result of a hegemonic articulation. It follows that it is only possible to construct this articulation on the basis of separate struggles. . . . This requires the autonomization of the spheres of struggle.[23]

Such "free-floating" struggles should thus be conducted entirely within what Marxists describe as the superstructure of society, with no relationship to its economic base.

To be sure, Laclau and Mouffe are correct that the "disappearance of private ownership of the means of production" does not automatically "set up a chain of effects" that would "lead to the extinction of all forms of subordination."[24] But only the crudest of economic determinists would make such a claim—which removes human agency from the equation. Marx himself, as shown earlier, takes a much more nuanced approach. Dismantling capitalist social relations will not automatically liberate women but will create the material *possibility* for achieving women's liberation, which requires *further struggle*. This is certainly the lesson of the postrevolutionary struggles against women's oppression undertaken by the leaders of the Russian Revolution.

Perhaps what is most remarkable about Laclau and Mouffe's concept of the "autonomization of the spheres of struggle" is not only that each struggle is limited to combating only a particular form of subordination within a particular social domain, but that *it does not even need to involve more than one person.* They state this explicitly: "Many of these forms of resistance are made manifest not in the form of collective struggles, but through an increasingly armed individualism."[25] In this way, interpersonal relationships can be key sites of struggle, based on subjective perceptions of which individual is in a position of "dominance" and which is in a position of "subordination" in any particular situation.

In a 1985 article, queer theorist Jeffrey Escoffier summarized his own view of identity politics as follows: "The politics of identity must also be a politics of difference. . . . The politics of difference affirms limited, partial being."[26] For Escoffier, arriving at this conclusion involves a conscious repudiation of working-class agency and an accompanying sense of demoralization at the "flawed vision" of socialism: "We are now in a period of decline and discouragement. We have no objective guarantee that the working class recognizes capitalism as the cause of the injustice and inequalities of American life. The recent history of the American working class clearly shows that it lacks the organizational and political capacity to struggle effectively for the fundamental transformation of society."[27]

One of the products of this pessimistic approach to fighting oppression is the notion of reclaiming or reappropriating oppressive language as a tool to combat oppression. As gender historian Joan W. Scott notes, "Post-structuralists insist that words and texts have no fixed or intrinsic meanings, that there is no transparent or self-evident relationship between them and either ideas or things, no basic or ultimate correspondence between language and the world."[28]

As Eagleton writes of postmodernism, "For all its talk of difference, plurality, heterogeneity, postmodern theory often operates with quite rigid binary oppositions, with 'difference,' 'plurality' and allied terms lined up bravely on one side of the theoretical fence as unequivocally positive, and whatever their antitheses might be (unity, identity, totality, universality) ranged balefully on the other."[29] Teresa Ebert described the wing of poststructuralists that she calls "ludic" (playful or ironic) feminists as "caught in the contradictions between the political necessity of materialism and its displacement by the ludic priority given to discourse. They end up substituting discursive determinism for what they reject as an economic determinism in classical Marxism."[30]

Social Identity versus Individual Identity

In this way, poststructuralists appropriated the meanings of terms such as "identity politics" and "difference" that originated in 1970s-era Black feminism. When the Combahee River Collective referred to the need for "identity politics," for example, they were describing the group identity of Black women; when they emphasized the importance of recognizing "differences" among women, they were referring to Black women's collective invisibility within predominantly white feminism at the time. But there is a world of difference between *social* identity—identifying as part of a social group—and *individual* identity. The poststructural conception of "identity" is based on that of individuals, while "difference" likewise can refer to any characteristic that sets an individual apart from others.

Black feminist Kimberlé Williams Crenshaw, writing in the 1990s, takes issue with the "version of anti-essentialism, embodying what might be called the vulgarized social construction thesis, [which] is that since all categories are socially constructed, there is no such thing as, say, 'Blacks' or 'women,' and thus it makes little sense to continue reproducing those categories by organizing around them."[31] In contrast, she argues,

> Intersectionality might be more broadly useful as a way of mediating the tension between assertions of multiple identity and the ongoing necessity of *group politics*. It is helpful in this regard to distinguish intersectionality from the closely related perspective of anti-essentialism, from which women of color have critically engaged white feminism for the absence of women of color on the one hand, and for speaking for women of color on the other. . . . While the descriptive project of postmodernism of questioning the ways in which meaning is socially constructed is generally sound, this critique sometimes misreads the meaning of social construction and distorts its political relevance.[32] (Emphasis added.)

She adds, "A beginning response to these questions requires that we first recognize that the organized identity groups in which we find ourselves are in fact coalitions, or at least potential coalitions waiting to be formed." She concludes, "At this point in history, a strong case can be made that the most critical resistance strategy for disempowered groups is to occupy and defend a politics of social location rather than to vacate and destroy it."[33]

Black feminist Patricia Hill Collins likewise formulates a strong challenge to postmodern assumptions. As she writes in *Black Feminist Thought*, "Postmodernism . . . has been forwarded as the antithesis and inevitable outcome of rejecting a positivist science. Within postmodern logic, groups themselves become suspect as well as any specialized thought. In extreme postmodern discourse, each group's thought is equally valid. No group can claim to have a better interpretation of the 'truth' than another."[34]

In *Fighting Words*, Collins writes, "The postmodern rubric of decentering seemingly supports Black women's long-standing efforts to challenge false universal knowledge that privileged Whiteness, maleness and wealth. However ... current meanings attached to decentering as a construct illustrate how terms can continue to be used yet can be stripped of their oppositional intent."[35]

Thus, the concept of intersectionality first developed within the Black feminist tradition but more recently emerged in the context of postmodernism. Although Black feminism and some currents of postmodernist theory share some common assumptions and some common language, these are overshadowed by key theoretical differences that make them two distinct approaches to combating oppression. Thus the concept of intersectionality has two different political foundations, one informed primarily by Black feminism and the other by postmodernism.

As feminist scholar Susan Archer Mann argues,

> Both [Black feminist] intersectionality theorists and poststructuralists speak of "marginalized" peoples. Yet the former anchor this concept in hierarchically structured, group-based inequalities, while poststructuralists often are referring to people whose behaviors lie outside of or transgress social norms. This latter conception of "margins" includes a much broader swath of people where the normative structure rather than structural relations of oppression is determinate. Indeed, not all countercultural lifestyles and politics reflect the historical, institutionalized oppressions highlighted by [Black feminist] intersectionality theorists.[36]

Third-Wave Feminism and Personal Empowerment

Recent generations of activists have embraced the poststructuralist approach to identity politics and intersectionality as common sense, without awareness of the deeper theoretical implications described above. After all, every human being is profoundly affected by a set of unique personal experiences that together help to shape their personal identity. Furthermore, in the neoliberal era, changing individual behavior has often seemed the most effective way to combat oppression, giving rise to the notion of "empowerment" as a personal act.

In the 1990s, a younger generation of feminists sought to distance themselves from their 1960s predecessors, labeling their contribution as a new, "third wave" of feminism. Adherents of third-wave feminism are typically described in generational terms, as post–Baby Boomers who grew up in the shadows of second-wave feminism and, upon reaching adulthood in the 1990s, realized that the social conditions they faced required a different set of priorities than those of the 1960s women's movement. There is no doubt that third-wavers grew up in starkly different conditions than those the 1960s-era generation faced. The consciousness of the post-1960s generation was shaped both by the retreat of the political left and the ascendancy of the political right. But it is also clear that self-defined third-wave feminists were reacting not simply to perceived inadequacies of second-wave feminism but at least as strongly to the backlash against feminism (posturing as "post-feminism") that rose to prominence in the 1980s.

As third-waver Melissa Klein described at the time, her generation was producing "a new feminism, a new kind of activism emphasizing our generation's cynical and disenfranchised temperament, born of distaste for the reactionary politics and rat-race economics of the 1980s."[37] Rebecca Walker, daughter of Alice Walker, played a key role in both organizing and popularizing third-wave feminism, and her contributions highlight some of the generational differences described above. In 1992, Rebecca Walker wrote a *Ms.* article, "Becoming the Third Wave," in response to the scathing attacks on Anita Hill after Hill accused Supreme Court justice Clarence Thomas of sexual harassment—and this article quickly propelled her into the national spotlight.[38]

In her introduction to the 1995 book *To Be Real: Telling the Truth and Changing the Face of Feminism*, Walker emphasizes the enormous contrast between the two generations, describing her own generation as having grown up "transgender, bisexual, interracial, and knowing and loving people who are racist, sexist, and otherwise afflicted." She concludes that "as a result we find ourselves seeking to create identities that accommodate ambiguity and our multiple positionalities: including more than excluding, exploring more than defining, searching more than arriving."[39]

Margrit Shildrick writes in *Third Wave Feminism: A Critical Exploration*, "The critique of sex and gender—only as an absent presence—remains, then, one central mode of enquiry, but those concepts no longer occupy the position of primacy afforded to them, both theoretically and empirically, in earlier feminist outings." Other central issues include "global concerns," "non-normative sexualities," "discourses of race and ethnicity," "postcoloniality," and the "cultural imaginary more broadly."[40] The break between the two generations of feminists was also substantial in defining notions of struggle and political power. Women's liberationists of the 1960s aimed to forge a collective struggle to achieve a clear set of political goals on behalf of all women. In contrast, the 1990s generation, heavily influenced by postmodernism, sought to achieve the goal of individual fulfillment and personal empowerment.

As Lise Shapiro Sanders describes in *Third Wave Feminism: A Critical Exploration*, "This sense of a feminism that is constructed by—indeed, animated through—contradiction and difference is fundamental to many conceptions of Third Wave and contemporary feminisms. . . . Drawing upon the critiques of universalism and essentialism from within and outside of the movement, Third Wave feminists have come to emphasize the diversity of women's experience over the similarities amongst women."[41] In this process, third-wave feminism inverted the 1960s slogan "The personal is political." That slogan originated through early attempts by women in a rising movement for women's liberation to acknowledge that their individual experiences with sexism were symptoms of their *collective* oppression. In contrast, Walker's *Ms.* article tellingly concludes with the words, "I am the Third Wave," utilizing the singular rather than the plural.[42]

Journalists Jennifer Baumgardner and Amy Richards also quickly became spokespeople for feminism's third wave with the publication of their book, *Manifesta: Young Women, Feminism and the Future*, in 2000.[43] Richards, along with Rebecca Walker, was a founder in 1992 of the Third Wave Direct Action Corporation (later the Third Wave Foundation) "as a multiracial, multicultural, multi-issue organization to support young activists."[44] Like Walker, Baumgardner and Richards stressed the role of individual choice in defining feminism. In an *Alternet* interview, Baumgardner argues, "People always ask us what the most important issue is, and my response is, name an issue. If that's what you're interested in, then it's the most important, whether it's eating disorders, sexual harassment, child care, etc. This insistence on definitions is really frustrating because feminism gets backed into a corner. . . . Feminism is something individual to each feminist."[45]

Third-wavers defined themselves through their own contradictions, asserting feminist principles largely within the confines of prevailing culture—which remained overrun by sexism. Some third-wavers adopted "girlie" culture in defining their generation's new approach to feminism. "We, and others, call this intersection of culture and feminism 'Girlie,'" Baumgardner and Richards explain in *Manifesta*. "Girlies say we're not broken, and our desires aren't simply booby traps set by the patriarchy. Girlie encompasses the tabooed symbols of women's feminine enculturation—Barbie dolls, makeup, fashion magazines, high heels—and says using them isn't shorthand for 'we've been duped.'"[46]

As Stacy Gillis and Rebecca Munford describe it,

> "Girl" culture is an extremely eclectic phenomenon which includes the Riot Grrrls of the punk movement, the Hello Kitty-accessorised and lipglossed Girlies exemplified by the writers of zines such as *Bitch* and *BUST*, as well as the more anodyne mainstream proponents of 'girl power' identified with the Spice Girls. Although these various groups are not always politically aligned, they do have in common a vigorous reclamation and recuperation of the word 'girl' as no longer a simply derogatory and disrespectful term but one that captures the contradictions shaping female identity for young women whose world has been informed by the struggles and gains of Second Wave feminism.[47]

Girlie culture also contained a distinct satirical component: embracing and exaggerating the language and cultural symbols from the political mainstream as an act of resistance. Klein emphasizes how this approach was informed by postmodernism: "Our politics reflect a postmodern focus on contradiction and duality, on the reclamation of terms. S-M, pornography, the words *cunt* and *queer* and *pussy* and *girl*—are all things to be re-examined or reclaimed. In terms of gender, our rebellion is to make it camp."[48]

Gillis and Munford add, "Marcelle Karp and Debbie Stoller, the editors of *BUST* . . . claim that the zine captures 'the voice of a brave new girl: one that is raw and real, straightforward and sarcastic, smart and silly, and liberally sprinkled with references to our own Girl Culture—that shared set of female experiences that includes Barbies and blowjobs, sexism and shoplifting, *Vogue* and vaginas.'"[49] But despite attempts at irony, appropriations of derogatory terms often echoed the very insults they were meant to parody to those not already in on the joke. In the editor's letter in the inaugural issue of *Bitch* in 1995, Lisa Jervis explained the name choice: "So why Bitch? Because—regardless of those who still think it's an insult—it's an action. . . . This magazine is about thinking critically about every message the mass media sends; it's about loudly articulating what's wrong and what's right with what we see. This magazine is about speaking up. Will that make us bitchy? Yeah."[50]

When interviewer Tamara Straus asks Baumgardner and Richards in the *Alternet* interview, "You embrace several new, and for some, outrageous feminist epithets: girl, bitch, slut, and cunt. What does the use of these words by Third Wave feminists mean?" Richards replies,

> Well, I think it stems from the perception that the discussion of sex was shut off to feminists, except if it involved violent or invasive sex. But I think there's also a question of who is in control of those words. For so long those words were used against women. Now using them is women's attempt to reclaim them and to say, "Yes, I am difficult. I am a bitch. Call me a bitch. I'm going to reclaim bitch and make it my own word, because the word has more hostility when it's being used against me than when it's being used by me. Slut, too. Slut is just a girl with a libido, whereas a boy with a libido is just a boy."[51]

In their 1999 book *The BUST Guide to the New Girl Order*, Marcelle Karp and Debbie Stoller reveal a distinct sense of resignation in their embrace of "porn culture." As they argue, "We realize that American porn culture is here to stay. So rather than trying to rid the world of sexual images we think are negative, as some of our sisters have done, we're far more interested in encouraging women to explore porn, to find out whether it gets them hot or merely bothered."[52]

Defining feminism as "something individual to each feminist" thus denied the third wave a cohesive political framework, the consequences of which became more apparent with the passage of time. Activism often took a back seat to cultural pursuits, but far from forming a distinct "counterculture" in opposition to the mainstream, third-wave feminism appropriated some of mainstream culture's most retrograde icons (Barbie dolls) and language ("bitch"). Many third-wavers, like the "ludic" feminists Ebert describes above, utilized this appropriation in irony. But Barbie dolls (with their anatomically impossible measurements) and words like "bitch" (as a term of female degradation) never left the sexist world of mainstream culture—begging the question of how this could be accomplished without challenging mainstream society.

Marx: Relevant Once Again?

Postmodernism, in both theory and practice, effectively sidelined socialist feminism and Marxist feminism throughout the 1990s. As socialist feminist Susan Ferguson argued in 2000, "Socialist feminism as a vibrant intellectual and political current has come and gone.... A few erstwhile socialist feminists retreated into an economic reductionism while others moved increasingly toward a purely cultural explanation of women's oppression that has culminated in feminist postmodernism." She added, "In fact, over the course of this past decade, the work of theorizing has too frequently been turned over to feminist Foucauldians and Derridians; the domination of academic postmodernism, and its insistence on the fragmented, fictional nature of experience, has led many materially inclined socialist feminists to shy away from developing a broad, unifying perspective."[53]

But the world has also changed dramatically since the rise of postmodernism. Writing at the height of the global justice movement, Ferguson observes, "In the late 1990s, however, with globalization foisting upon us a host of unwelcome economic realities, even many postmodern feminists have begun to search for a materialist explanation."[54]

Beginning in 2008, class inequality took center stage against the background of an economic crisis that has transformed US society through plunging median incomes and skyrocketing poverty. It would be difficult today to attract large numbers of activists by claiming, as many in the 1960s New Left did, that the US working class is an impediment to the struggle to transform society. When so many young radicals are struggling members of the working class who have watched their opportunities for higher education and job opportunities be snatched away, a class analysis provides an obvious framework for understanding social injustice. The rise of the Occupy movement in autumn 2011, expressing the anger of the 99 percent against the 1 percent, marked the first sign of a nationwide resistance against the dramatic decline of working-class living standards while the superrich became yet richer. Marx's ideas can no longer be summarily dismissed as reductionist when economic disparity looms so large. Likewise, the fight against the New Jim Crow—so poignantly described by legal scholar Michelle Alexander in her 2010 book *The New Jim Crow: Mass Incarceration in the Age of Colorblindness*—has brought the racist epidemic of mass incarceration to the forefront of the struggle against racism.[55] It is no longer possible to envision a successful struggle against women's or LGBT oppression without placing the struggle against racism at the center of movements for social change. Moreover, the scale of sexism—and outright misogyny—in the political mainstream cannot be combated effectively on an individual level. It will require renewed collective struggle.

In 2012, right-wing radio host Rush Limbaugh called Georgetown University law student Sandra Fluke a "slut" and a "prostitute" after she testified in favor of access to contraception. During the media uproar that followed, Limbaugh escalated his attacks on Fluke, arguing, "She's having so much sex it's amazing she can still walk."[56] But such sexual crudities are not limited to conservative hypocrites like the pill-popping Limbaugh. Comedian Bill Maher—widely regarded as a liberal—made calling right-winger Sarah Palin a "cunt" and a "dumb twat" a fixture of his stand-up routine throughout 2011. Maher is, however, an equal-opportunity misogynist, and every woman is fair game. In February 2008, while discussing media censorship on his talk show *Real Time with Bill Maher*, he quipped, "Now they fined CBS a million dollars, a million dollars for Janet Jackson's nipple. Think what they could get for Hillary Clinton's cunt."[57]

Meanwhile, Republicans jousting for "family values" votes have taken aim at attacking all aspects of women's sexual and reproductive freedom. Debates over not only abortion but also contraception that seemed settled in the early 1970s are raging once again, degrading women at every juncture. US mainstream discourse has reached such an extreme level of sexism because four decades of attacks on women's rights have *already* taken such a severe toll.

In 2012, when Republican presidential candidate Mitt Romney pledged, "Planned Parenthood, we're going to get rid of that,"[58] the state of Texas had already done so. Its state legislature refused federal funding for its Medicaid Women's Health Program solely to prevent Planned Parenthood from receiving Medicaid money. While legislators claimed their goal was to "defund the abortion industry," none of the dozens of clinics forced to shut down actually provided abortions. They did, however, provide basic health care, contraception, and cancer screenings to more than a hundred thousand poor women, most from rural areas of Texas.[59]

The Return of Struggle

Indeed, some of these escalating attacks on women have begun to produce resistance. In January 2011, Toronto police officer Michael Sanguinetti was addressing an Osgoode Hall Law School campus-safety seminar when he unexpectedly made the following suggestion to women wishing to avoid sexual assault: "I've been told I'm not supposed to say this—however, women should avoid dressing like sluts in order not to be victimized."[60] While there were only ten students in the audience, word of Sanguinetti's comments spread rapidly, outraging women far beyond Toronto who were fed up with being routinely blamed for rape. Toronto organizers held the first "Slutwalk" in response in April, expecting a hundred protesters to attend. Instead three thousand showed up, chanting. Many carried sarcastic signs such as, "Met a slut today? Don't assault her." Others carried signs expressing their own trauma, including one that read, "It was Christmas Day. I was 14 and raped in a stairwell wearing snowshoes and layers. Did I deserve it too?"[61]

Toronto's Slutwalk touched off a rapid-fire movement that spread as far away as Argentina and New Zealand. Slutwalks took place in cities across the United States, often organized via Facebook and Twitter. Whether large or small, the protests carried a clear message: rape is not caused by victims, but by rapists. Women who are raped deserve no blame, no matter what clothing they choose to wear or whether they enjoy consensual sex.

In June 2012, Texas Republican governor Rick Perry called a special thirty-day legislative session to address, among other things, a bill requiring that abortion clinics be certified as "ambulatory surgical centers" and that all abortion providers hold admitting privileges at a hospital within thirty miles of where they perform their procedures. The bill would allow only five clinics to remain open, all located in urban areas—out of reach for rural and poor women spread throughout an enormous geographic area.

During the week of legislative debate—at the end of which the special session would expire—activists began mobilizing by the hundreds to the state capitol building in Austin to protest the bill, through testimony and protest. On the final day of debate, as the clock ticked toward midnight and the end of the special session, Democratic senator Wendy Davis conducted a one-woman filibuster of the bill, speaking for eleven hours straight before senate Republicans orchestrated a parliamentary maneuver to end it at 10 p.m.

Meanwhile, thousands of abortion-rights protesters crowded into the capitol, inside and outside the Senate chambers. By 11 p.m., when it became clear that Republicans might succeed in passing the bill, protesters began clapping and chanting, "Kill the bill!" and "Wendy! Wendy!" As midnight approached the chanting and clapping grew louder as thousands of people began shouting in unison, successfully drowning out the Senate procedures altogether. As a result, the Senate was unable to complete its vote until 12:03 a.m. and the bill was pronounced dead at 3 a.m.

The pro-choice mass action at the Austin capitol was quickly dubbed the "people's filibuster." Mainstream media outlets also took note that the coalition of activists involved not only pro-choice organizations but also LBGT activists, socialists, and other radicals. As the *New York Times* describes it,

> The remarkable moment had not been planned by the established groups like Planned Parenthood, NARAL Pro-Choice Texas and the Texas Democratic Party that had organized protests against the Senate vote on the measure. Instead, it grew with the help of a smaller coalition—including local chapters of the Occupy movement and the International Socialist Organization, or I.S.O.—that helped goad the crowd to a level of civil disobedience not seen in the Texas Capitol in decades.[62]

To be sure, this victory was short-lived. The Texas Senate approved the bill intact on July 12. When protesters returned to the capitol for the second round of debate, security police confiscated not only their leaflets but also their tampons in the name of tightened safety measures. In early November the new law went into effect; most clinics were shuttered, while the few remaining open were forced to turn away hundreds of women. Nevertheless, the Texas people's filibuster in June 2013 showed the potential for a unified women's movement to combat women's oppression successfully by relying on mass mobilization and a commitment to a set of clear principles.

The Centrality of Class

While postmodernism impacted feminist theory, socialist feminists and Marxist feminists did not disappear but continued their own theoretical pursuits from the margins. Even in 1995, for example, Ebert argued for a "red feminism" that would reintegrate Marxism into its analysis:

> For a red feminism this means that issues about the "nature of individuals"—gender, sexuality, pleasure, desire, needs—cannot be separated from the conditions producing individuals: not just the discursive and ideological conditions but most important the material conditions, the relations of production, which shape discourses and ideologies. Thus the struggle to end the exploitation and oppression of all women, and in particular of people of colour, lesbians and gays, within the metropole as well as the periphery, is not simply a matter of discursive or semiotic liberation or a question of the resisting "matter of the body," but a global social relation:

it thus requires the transformation of the material conditions—the relations of production—producing these forms of oppression.[63]

The current economic and political climate is ripe for reclaiming the genuine Marxist tradition, with the theoretical advances contributed by generations of feminists since the time of classical Marxism. Gimenez, whose
Marxist application to theorizing women's oppression has spanned
decades, deserves a new hearing among socialists and feminists today. She
made the following case against accusations of "reductionism" in 2005:

> The notion that under capitalism the mode of production determines
> the mode of reproduction and, consequently, observable unequal rela-
> tions between men and women is not a form of "economism" or "class
> reductionism," but the recognition of the complex network of macro-
> level effects, upon male-female relationships, of a mode of production
> driven by capital accumulation rather than by the goal of satisfying peo-
> ple's needs. To argue otherwise, postulating the "mutual interaction" be-
> tween the organization of production and the organization of
> reproduction, or giving causal primacy to the latter, is to overlook the
> theoretical significance of the overwhelming evidence documenting the
> capitalist subordination of reproduction to production.[64]

Gimenez concludes the defense of Marxism above by noting the political challenges facing feminists in the neoliberal era:

> As the world capitalist economy grows in strength and the unprece-
> dented mobility of capital can overnight devastate national and regional
> economies, the vulnerability of workers increases exponentially. In this
> context, there is bound to be a resurgence of labor organizing within and
> across national boundaries. Feminism cannot afford to be absent from
> the process, but this would require the recognition of the relevance of
> Marx's work for the emancipation of women and acknowledgment of
> the significance of class divisions among women, thus raising the issue
> whether feminist theory can ignore class and remain politically relevant
> for the vast majority of women.[65]

Four decades of neoliberalism have taken a severe toll on the working
class, resulting in deep and permanent cuts in living standards. In the
United States, the gap between the rich and poor has reached levels not
seen in a century, with the percentage of income going to the top 10
percent of the US population now exceeding that of the bottom 90 percent. As Berkeley economist Emmanuel Saez observes, "The top decile
share in 2012 is equal to 50.4 percent, a level higher than any other year
since 1917 and even surpasses 1928, the peak of the stock market bub-
ble in the 'roaring' 1920s."[66]

Although neoliberal policies were responsible for the 2008 global financial meltdown neoliberalism survived virtually intact—with austerity remaining the centerpiece of ruling-class policy worldwide. In the years after the Great Recession, the capitalist class accelerated its offensive around a shared agenda of restoring profitability. During the economic recovery between 2009 and 2012, the incomes of the top 1 percent of the US population soared by more than 31 percent, compared with 0.4 percent for the bottom 99 percent of the population.[67]

Despite longstanding and widespread working-class anger, however, the class struggle remained largely subdued throughout this period. Strike levels fell to a historic low in 2009, when only five major work stoppages involving a thousand or more workers took place—the lowest number since 1947, when the Bureau of Labor Statistics began tracking strike statistics. In 2014, there were just eleven major work stoppages involving a thousand or more workers (equal to the number in 2010), the second lowest annual total since 1947.[68] Union membership stood at just 11.1 percent in 2014, while only 6.6 percent of private-sector workers belonged to unions.[69] There were, however, a few important exceptions to this bleak situation. The most important was the Chicago Teachers Union (CTU) strike of 2012. The CTU strike provided a glimpse of how working-class struggle can begin to redefine the political landscape—and the role that women workers can play.

The Chicago Teachers' Strike: Social-Justice Unionism in Practice

In September 2012, the twenty-six thousand members of the Chicago Teachers Union (CTU) went on strike for nine days. This was the first strike in twenty-five years for the CTU, the nation's third-largest teachers' union. The majority of Chicago Public Schools teachers are women; as of 2010, 29 percent were Black, and 15 percent were Hispanic.[70]

The CTU leadership had been elected as a reform slate from the Caucus of Rank and File Educators (CORE), a caucus of progressive teachers, including a small but significant number of socialists, committed to fighting the privatization of public schools and to democratizing the union from below. This group of reformers had formed fairly recently, in 2008. But two years after winning the union leadership, they led a strike against Chicago mayor Rahm Emanuel—a cold-blooded champion of school privatization who made no secret of his plan to fight the union tooth and nail. Emanuel had left his job as chief of staff in Obama's White House to run for mayor of Chicago in 2011, with the aim of showcasing his ability to run a major urban city in order to further his long-term political ambitions.

Emanuel's program for education "reform" included a plan to close public schools en masse, on the grounds that they were "failing children." The second part of the plan involved replacing them with for-profit and nonunion "charter" schools, along with competitive "magnet" schools that choose their students through lotteries or scholastic requirements. The schools targeted for closure were almost exclusively located in working-class Black and Latino neighborhoods, while new magnet schools catered primarily to "high achieving" (disproportionately white and middle-class) students. New charter schools often took over the buildings of the public schools they replaced.

Meanwhile wealthy Chicagoans, including Mayor Emanuel, sent their children to expensive private schools. Upon taking office, Emanuel immediately set his sights on preventing a teachers' strike, successfully convincing state lawmakers to pass a law requiring 75 percent of all union members (not just voting members) to authorize a strike. Emanuel thought the CTU would never be able to meet this preposterous threshold, thereby preempting even the possibility of a teachers' strike in the foreseeable future. Meanwhile, Emanuel floated his intention to impose merit pay on teachers, which would base teachers' wage increases on how well their students performed on standardized tests.

The future looked grim for the CTU in the spring of 2012, when it became clear that Emanuel was preparing to close an unprecedented number of schools.[71] Although CORE members were inexperienced as union leaders, these activists already had plenty of experience in grassroots organizing in Chicago, forging links between teachers, parents, and community organizations while fighting together against the (unelected) Chicago Board of Education's relentless assault on so-called underperforming schools. These included not only school closures but also "turnarounds"—which entailed firing the entire school staff while blaming teachers for the school's problems. These attacks made teachers threatened with job losses the natural allies of the parents and students whose schools were facing closure and turnaround. As Robert Barlett describes in *Monthly Review*,

> People who wanted to fight back against the encroaching privatization
> began to be attracted to CORE, which started a series of audacious ac-

tions against school closings. When a school was targeted for closing or turnaround, CORE members went to the school and met the teachers and parents who wanted to fight the closings and did whatever they could to help build a resistance in that community. This ranged from leafleting at the school to camping out overnight in front of the Board of Education in January or in front of schools with parents. . . .

Most teachers threatened with losing their jobs do not automatically respond by trying to fight back, but a critical layer started going to school board meetings, bringing with them parents and teachers from the affected schools, as well as community organizations that were also opposed to board policies, to testify at board meetings and become a public opposition to privatization.[72]

The CTU continued this method of community activism against school closures while preparing for a possible strike as soon as they took office. The union's Black president, Karen Lewis, sparred publicly with Emanuel on a regular basis—to the delight of CTU members and the disdain of corporate media outlets (which labeled her "confrontational").[73] When Emanuel blamed teachers for the low quality of education in the city schools, the CTU retorted that the problem was the city's *underfunding* of public schools due to its *undertaxing* of corporations. In February 2012, the CTU released a well-researched report, *The Schools Chicago's Children Deserve*, highlighting the racism that led to a system of "educational apartheid" in Chicago.[74]

The CORE union leadership, unlike its predecessors, cut their own pay and put financial resources into its organizing department, whose members spent more time at the schools than in the union's offices. Perhaps most importantly, the CTU leadership recognized that a union is no stronger than the commitment of its rank and file. As Lee Sustar notes in the *International Socialist Review*, "Training for delegates and other CTU members went well beyond the usual network of activists to create an organizational backbone of 1,000–3,000 teachers and paraprofessionals who led discussion about contract demands and made the argument that a strike would be necessary."[75] When the strike authorization vote took place in June, it not only met but vastly exceeded Emanuel's required 75 percent authorization threshold—when nearly *90 percent of eligible union members voted to authorize a strike.* The CTU spent the summer preparing members through strike training to lead the picketing and organizing at every school. As Sustar described, when the CTU finally declared a strike on September 10, "tens of thousands of red-shirted members of the Chicago Teachers Union (CTU) and supporters swarmed downtown, shutting down traffic around the Board of Education headquarters and City Hall in what a local radio news reporter aptly called 'an older and more polite version of Occupy Chicago.'"[76]

Every day during the nine-day strike, parent, student, and community supporters joined striking teachers at school pickets across the city. Teachers organized marches through their schools' neighborhoods and repeatedly marched by the thousands through downtown Chicago, circling the school board headquarters and City Hall. The strikers enjoyed widespread popularity among bus drivers, truckers, and other passers-by, who honked their horns in solidarity whenever they saw a red CTU shirt on the street. Opinion polls showed that 66 percent of parents sided with the union in the strike, a remarkably high number since working parents were largely left to scramble for child care as long as the walkout continued.

The CTU leadership's commitment to rank-and-file democracy meant that, even after union negotiators reached a tentative contract agreement with the city, they brought the details of the contract for a vote by the union's eight hundred delegates. At that meeting, the delegates voted to extend the strike by two extra days in order to take the agreement to the picket lines for discussion by the entire membership. For the next two days, members took part in meetings that lasted for hours on sidewalks in front of schools across the city while they debated the terms of the contract. On September 18, the CTU House of Delegates voted to end their strike and resume work the next morning. The new contract defeated merit pay in favor of continuing seniority-pay increases, in a major setback for the centerpiece of the mayor's plan. But the contract also contained a number of important teacher concessions—most importantly, it left open the possibility of more school closures.

The strike's success must be measured by its context, however. Taking place in the midst of the staggering assault on public sector unions, Chicago teachers scored a significant advance not only for public sector unions but for all unions. With all the chips stacked against them, they stood up as a united force and forced Emanuel, a Democratic Party power broker, to face a major strike in Obama's home city. This was a far cry from the mayor's expectations when he took office. In this context, the CTU scored a rare victory for organized labor using a strategy of social-justice unionism. In so doing, they pointed the way forward for a revival of the entire labor movement.

To be sure, Emanuel struck back in the spring of 2013, closing fifty-four public schools and laying off thousands of teachers and staff, the largest numbers in Chicago history—while agreeing to finance the construction of a ten-thousand-seat local basketball stadium for private DePaul University. Thousands of teachers, parents, and students again took to the streets in protest, to no avail.

While not a struggle explicitly for women's liberation, the lessons of this important strike—and its ramifications for working-class struggle involving women workers who also fight against racism and poverty—point to future possibilities for integrating class and social struggle.

Combating Gender and National Oppression in Revolutionary Russia

> *But there is no doubt that in the accomplished Communist society, love, "winged Eros," will be transformed into something completely unfamiliar to us. . . . What will this new transformed Eros be? The boldest fantasy is unable to capture its form.*
>
> —Alexandra Kollontai, 1923[1]

The Bolshevik-led Russian Revolution in 1917 did not take place in an advanced capitalist economy but in a country that remained economically undeveloped—as Leon Trotsky argued, Russia was an example of "uneven and combined development." Its factories were among the largest in the world, but as a whole the country was economically underdeveloped. Its population was still some 80 percent peasant, spread across vast rural areas. Furthermore, its economy had been devastated by World War I, and was soon to be further devastated by a Western economic blockade and civil war. Fourteen counterrevolutionary armies backed by the Western powers invaded Russia in 1918, with the aim of overthrowing the newly established workers' state. For the next three years, the Bolsheviks were forced to use most of the country's declining resources to fight that civil war, setting back its ability to implement a socialist agenda.[2]

But tsarist Russia had also been an imperialist power in its own right. In 1917, just 43 percent of the Russian empire's population was Russian; the majority of its population was made up of the formerly colonized peoples living in surrounding nations. If most of Russia itself was economically backward, Russian imperialism had ensured that the vast Muslim regions of Central Asia were yet more so. As Trotsky described, "Hierarchically organized exploitation, combining the barbarity of capitalism with the barbarity of patriarchal life, successfully held down the Asiatic peoples in extreme national abasement."[3]

From 1903, the Bolshevik platform of the Russian Social Democratic Labor Party (RSDLP) incorporated the principle of the "right of self-determination for all nations included within the bounds of a state."[4] This principle has guided the revolutionary Marxist tradition ever since that time. Lenin emphasized that the "self-determination of nations today *hinges* on the conduct of socialists in the oppressor nations. A socialist of any of the oppressor nations . . . who does not recognize and does not struggle for the right of oppressed nations to self-determination (i.e., the right to secession) is in reality a chauvinist, not a socialist."[5]

On November 2, 1917, one of the first acts of the revolutionary government was to decree the right of Russia's oppressed nations to self-determination, up to secession and the formation of an independent state.[6] Ending women's oppression was also central to the Bolshevik project. But while one-third of Petrograd's factory workers in 1917 were women, the vast majority of women lived far from cities, thoroughly oppressed and isolated in peasant communities heavily influenced by doctrines of Christianity in Russia, and in some cases communities dominated by Islam in the oppressed nations of Central Asia.[7]

Marxism and Religion

The Bolsheviks' analysis of the role of religion, informed by Marx, was a key element in their approach both to women's and national oppression. Lenin argues in detail on this subject, emphasizing that "Marxism has always regarded all modern religions and churches, and each and every religious organization, as instruments of bourgeois reaction that serve to defend exploitation and to befuddle the working class."[8] But he also adds, "Those who toil and live in want all their lives are taught by religion to be submissive and patient while here on earth, and to take comfort in the hope of a heavenly reward."[9]

The revolutionary government did not seek to outlaw Christianity, Islam, Judaism, or any other religion. If religion is a product of the inequalities of class society, then ultimately its function should fade away in the absence of inequality, in a classless society. The Bolsheviks did not condemn those who practiced religion, but rather regarded religion to be a purely personal matter. The point was not to persecute religious worshippers, but in the first instance, to enact a firm separation between religious doctrine and civil law. Lenin emphasized, "Religion must be of no concern to the state. . . . Everyone must be absolutely free to profess any

religion he pleases, or no religion whatever. . . . Discrimination among citizens on account of their religious convictions is wholly intolerable. Even
the bare mention of a citizen's religion in official documents should un-
questionably be eliminated."[10] But Lenin also foresaw a future in which
"in this political system, cleansed of medieval mildew, the proletariat will
wage a broad and open struggle for the elimination of economic slavery,
the true source of the religious humbugging of mankind."[11]

The Comintern, the international movement of revolutionary parties
set up by the Bolsheviks in 1919, understood the oppressive character of
both Christianity and Islam and these religions' complex relationships to
imperialist projects. Thus, it adopted two statements as part of its "Theses
on the National and Colonial Question" in 1920. The first statement read,
"A struggle absolutely must be waged against the reactionary and medieval
influences of the clergy, the Christian missions, and similar elements." The
second read, "It is necessary to struggle against the Pan-Islamic and Pan-
Asian movements and similar currents that try to link the liberation struggle against European and American imperialism with strengthening the
power of Turkish and Japanese imperialism and of the nobles, large
landowners, clergy, and so forth."[12]

In 1922, Lenin advanced the following polemic against Joseph Stalin
over the rights of the oppressed republic of Georgia:

> Internationalism on the part of oppressors or "great" nations, as they are
> called (though they are great only in their violence, only great as bul-
> lies), must consist not only in the observance of the formal equality of
> nations but even in an inequality of the oppressor nation, the great na-
> tion, that must make up for the inequality which obtains in actual prac-
> tice. . . . What is needed to ensure this? Not merely formal equality. In
> one way or another, by one's attitude or by concessions, it is necessary to
> compensate the non-Russian for the lack of trust, for the suspicion and
> the insults to which the government of the "dominant" nation subjected
> them in the past.[13]

But the need to rectify the colonial injustices of tsarist Russia also con-
flicted with the goal of combating women's oppression in Islam in Central
Asia. In many respects, the Bolshevik approach to Islam was the same as
toward the Russian Orthodox Church—recognizing that women's liberation cannot be imposed from above but that women themselves are the
agents of their own emancipation. Whereas Christianity was the religion
favored in Russia, the oppressor nation, Islam was the religion of many of
those in former colonies oppressed by tsarist Russia.

Russian imperialism had not merely prevented entire colonial populations from advancing economically and politically, but suppressed their rights to speak their own languages or practice their own religions and cultures. As Leon Trotsky described, "The peoples and tribes along the Volga, in the northern Caucasus, in Central Asia . . . the struggle here was about matters like having their own alphabet, their own teachers— even at times their own priests."[14]

Russian colonialists, like their European counterparts, were openly racist toward Muslims and hostile to Islamic culture. But Islam was, in turn, oppressive to women. By the end of 1922, seven of the Soviet Union's eight autonomous republics were populated mainly by Muslims.[15] Bolshevik leaders forcefully argued that revolutionaries had a duty both to struggle against sexist attitudes that continued to oppress women *and also* against Russian chauvinism in Russia's former colonies. If autonomy was to be meaningful, Russian laws granting women's equality could not be imposed from Russia. Public opinion had to be shifted from below, through struggle and patient argument.

Women's Self-Organization

As noted in chapter 1, the Bolsheviks understood that removing household drudgery would be key to achieving women's liberation. Lenin argued,

> The real emancipation of women, real communism, will begin only where and when an all-out struggle begins (led by the proletariat wielding state power) against this petty housekeeping, or rather when its wholesale transformation into a large-scale socialist economy begins. . . . Public catering establishments, nurseries, kindergartens—here we have examples of these shoots, here we have the simple, everyday means, involving nothing pompous, grandiloquent, or ceremonial, which can really emancipate women, really lessen and abolish their inequality with men as regards their role in social production and public life.[16]

In 1919, the Bolsheviks created a party women's bureau, Zhenotdel, under the direction of Inessa Armand and, after Armand's death in 1920, headed by Alexandra Kollontai. Zhenotdel—whose motto, coined by Kollontai, came to be "agitation by deed"—mobilized teams of organizers, traveling on "agit" boats and trains throughout the vast countryside. They produced a newspaper of their own, *Kommunistika*. In addition, developing an idea of Armand's, Zhenotdel agitators organized "delegates' assemblies," in which women were elected from factories and villages to work in apprenticeships running factories or hospitals, to serve in the soviets and unions, or even to function as administrators and judges.[17]

In Zhenotdel's second year, 853 conferences of working and peasant women were held throughout Russia. By the mid-1920s, more than five hundred thousand women had attended as conference delegates.[18] In the revolution's early years, Zhenotdel took up a variety of campaigns, from support for the Red Army in the civil war to the promotion of education and literacy for women, with the aim of involving ever larger numbers of women. Zhenotdel was also responsible for organizing communal kitchens, nurseries, and laundries to begin to free working and peasant women from the burdens of housework—which met with some success. Some of the reason for this success related to the civil war's hardships. For many, the choice was between eating in a communal restaurant or not eating at all. Nevertheless, it is estimated that during 1919 and 1920, almost 90 percent of the Petrograd population was fed communally, and in 1920, 40 percent of Moscow housing was communal. Furthermore, at the Ninth Party Congress in 1920, the Women's Bureau reported that it had organized thirty-eight day-care nurseries in a province where "women had feared nurseries like the plague."[19]

Kollontai had played a prominent leadership role throughout 1917, both within the workers' councils, or soviets, and as a leader of the Bolshevik Party. After the revolution, the Second All-Russian Congress of Soviets elected Kollontai commissar of social welfare. In *Communism and the Family*, published in 1920, she outlined how the new socialist society would take over responsibility for the domestic labor previously performed by women in the family:

> The individual household is dying. It is giving way in our society to collective housekeeping. Instead of the working woman cleaning her flat, the communist society can arrange for men and women whose job it is to go round in the morning cleaning rooms. The wives of the rich have long since been freed from these irritating and tiring domestic duties. Why should the working woman continue to be burdened with them? In Soviet Russia the working woman should be surrounded by the same ease and light, hygiene and beauty that previously only the very rich could afford. Instead of the working woman having to struggle with the cooking and spend her last free hours in the kitchen preparing dinner and supper, communist society will organize public restaurants and communal kitchens.
>
> . . . The working woman will not have to slave over the washtub any longer, or ruin her eyes in darning her stockings and mending her linen;

she will simply take these things to the central laundries each week and collect the washed and ironed garments later. That will be another job less to do. Special clothes-mending centers will free the working woman from the hours spent on mending and give her the opportunity to devote her evenings to reading, attending meetings and concerts.[20]

It is also clear that the Bolsheviks did not seek to "abolish" family living units, but rather envisioned a time when they would be able to provide the material basis for reorganizing families into "group communities" different than any model yet experienced.

In 1923, Trotsky acknowledged, "It is true that the state cannot as yet undertake either the education of children or the establishment of public kitchens that would be an improvement on the family kitchen, or the establishment of public laundries where the clothes would not be torn or stolen."[21] But he also described the hopes for a socialist future:

> The building of houses—and, after all, we are going to build houses!— must be regulated by the requirements of the family group communities. . . . At a given moment, the state will be able, with the help of local soviets, cooperative units, and so on, to socialize the work done, to widen and deepen it. In this way, the human family, in the words of Engels, will "jump from the realm of necessity to the realm of freedom."[22]

But this vision was never realized. The years of civil war took their toll on postrevolutionary Russia. Disease, famine, and poverty resulted in an epidemic of homeless children, widespread unsafe abortions resulting in illness or death, and desperate, unemployed women turning to prostitution.

Nevertheless, the revolutionary government sought to attack the root causes of prostitution—rather than penalize its victims. Although widespread poverty prevented prostitution's eradication, Kollontai's approach is clear in the following passage from a speech in 1921 on the persistence of prostitution in postrevolutionary Russia:

> Prostitution arose with the first states as the inevitable shadow of the official institution of marriage, which was designed to preserve the rights of private property and to guarantee property inheritance through a line of lawful heirs. The institution of marriage made it possible to prevent the wealth that had been accumulated from being scattered amongst a vast number of "heirs.". . .
>
> This is the horror and hopelessness that results from the exploitation of labor by capital. When a woman's wages are insufficient to keep her alive, the sale of favors seems a possible subsidiary occupation. The hypocritical morality of bourgeois society encourages prostitution by the structure of its exploitative economy, while at the same time merci-

lessly covering with contempt any girl or woman who is forced to take this path. . . .

Even though the main sources of prostitution—private property and the policy of strengthening the family—have been eliminated, other factors are still in force. Homelessness, neglect, bad housing conditions, loneliness, and low wages for women are still with us. Our productive apparatus is still in a state of collapse, and the dislocation of the national economy continues. These and other economic and social conditions lead women to prostitute their bodies.[23]

As Kollontai noted above, eradicating widespread poverty was key to combating prostitution. But the economic devastation of the civil war years left the revolutionary government, despite its best intentions, without the resources to realize its goals for women. While its intention had been to continue to expand public nurseries, laundries, and restaurants to eliminate household drudgery for women, this could not take place as long as the economy was in near-complete collapse. Trotsky observed years later,

> It proved impossible to take the old family by storm—not because the will was lacking, and not because the family was so firmly rooted in men's hearts. On the contrary, after a short period of distrust of the government and its crèches, kindergartens and like institutions, the working women, and after them the more advanced peasants, appreciated the immeasurable advantages of the collective care of children as well as the socialization of the whole family economy.
>
> Unfortunately society proved too poor and little cultured. The real resources of the state did not correspond to the plans and intentions of the Communist Party. You cannot "abolish" the family; you have to replace it. The actual liberation of women is unrealizable on a basis of "generalized want." Experience soon proved this austere truth which Marx had formulated eighty years before.[24]

Yet more hurdles confronted the revolutionary government—and Zhenotdel—in realizing their goals for women's liberation in Central Asia.

Combating Women's Oppression in Central Asia

If the precondition for women's equality in Russia was to address its economic backwardness, this was yet more the case in Russia's former colonies, where imperialism had prevented the development of the forces of production. The Bolsheviks who led the 1917 revolution understood this. Within Central Asia, Islamic customs varied from region to region. For example, in the regions that today are called

Uzbekistan and Tajikistan—where the economies were based on set-tled agriculture—women were veiled and secluded within the home and prohibited from speaking to men other than relatives. But women in Turkmenistan—and numerous other nomadic societies of Central Asia—were neither forcibly secluded nor veiled.[25]

Lacking local Bolsheviks to begin working among Muslim women, teams of Zhenotdel organizers quietly began to meet with women in these nationally oppressed regions to discuss women's rights and social-ism, make crafts, and offer literacy instruction. When necessary, Zhenot-del organizers wore veils to avoid attracting attention because they frequently encountered hostility. On occasion, Zhenotdel workers and Muslim women members were attacked or killed by men hostile to changing women's status. (It should be noted, however, that a similar de-gree of hostility also existed in remote Christian areas, such as Ukraine.)

Through this process, in some Central Asian localities, the Zhenotdel was able to build up local organizations of Muslim women.[26] But there were also enormous obstacles to overcome before the ground could be prepared socially and economically for genuine reform. This process would undoubtedly have taken many years. As Trotsky asserts, "The fate of the colonial possessions, especially in central Asia, would change to-gether with the industrial evolution of the center."[27]

The Comintern's "Theses on the National and Colonial Question" states:

> It follows from these principles that the entire policy of the Communist International on the national and colonial questions must be based pri-marily upon uniting the proletarians and toiling masses of all nations and countries in common revolutionary struggle to overthrow the landowners and the bourgeoisie. Only such a unification will guarantee victory over capitalism, *without which it is impossible to abolish national oppression and inequality.*[28] (Emphasis added.)

Nevertheless, the early years of the Russian Revolution offer a glimpse, albeit a rudimentary one, of the potential for a socialist society to liberate all of humanity. Trotsky writes, "Political practice remained, of course, far more primitive than political theory. For things are harder to change than ideas."[29] This would have been true in any case, but any honest assessment of the Bolsheviks' accomplishments must also take into account that the revolution was hamstrung by the conditions of civil war, while disease and famine plagued all parts of society. In this context, the revolution succeeded remarkably in combating oppression in all its forms. The Bolsheviks, as leaders of the world revolutionary movement in the years immediately after 1917, built a struggle that truly was, in Lenin's words, a "tribune of the people."[30] A speech given by Nadzhiya, a Turkish woman representative at the Baku Congress of the Peoples of the East in 1920, summarizing the demands of women in Muslim societies in the fight against their own oppression, offers a glimpse of the process that had begun among women of oppressed nations:

> The women's movement beginning in the East must not be looked at from the standpoint of those frivolous feminists who are content to see woman's place in social life as that of a delicate plant or an elegant doll. This movement must be seen as a serious and necessary consequence of the revolutionary movement which is taking place throughout the world. The women of the East are not merely fighting for the right to walk in the street without wearing the *chadra* [veil], as many people suppose. For the women of the East, with their high moral ideals, the question of the chadra, it can be said, is of the least importance. . . .
>
> The women Communists of the East have an even harder battle to wage because, in addition, they have to fight against the despotism of their menfolk. If you, men of the East, continue now, as in the past, to be indifferent to the fate of women, you can be sure that our countries will perish, and you and us together with them: the alternative is for us to begin, together with all the oppressed, a bloody life-and-death struggle to win our rights by force. I will briefly set forth the women's demands. If you want to bring about your own emancipation, listen to our demands and render us real help and co-operation.
>
> Complete equality of rights.
>
> Ensuring for women unconditional opportunity to make use of the educational and vocational-training institutions established for men.
>
> Equality of rights of both parties to marriage. Unconditional abolition of polygamy.
>
> Unconditional admission of women to employment in legislative and administrative institutions.
>
> Everywhere, in cities, towns and villages, committees for the rights and protection of women to be established.
>
> Undoubtedly we can ask for all of this. The Communists, recognizing that we have equal rights, have reached out their hand to us, and we women will prove their most loyal comrades. True, we may be stumbling in pathless darkness, we may be standing on the brink of yawning chasms, but we are not afraid, because we know that in order to see the dawn one has to pass through the dark night.[31]

Although the possibilities of the revolutionary Marxist tradition have yet to be realized, its potential to oppose both national and women's oppression can be seen in embryonic form in the Russian Revolution. These revolutionaries did not counterpose the need to combat women's oppression to the fight against national oppression. Moreover, they never veered from the basic Marxist principle of self-emancipation, understanding that the fight against oppression must be organized from below rather than imposed from above.

Their approach coupled with a clear understanding of the role of Islam as a religious doctrine that both sanctions the inequalities produced by class society—notably, women's oppression—*and* as an aspect of national culture brutally suppressed by imperialism in oppressed nations, offers lasting theoretical clarity.

This history makes clear that in practice the Bolsheviks employed the concept of what is today known as intersectionality in its efforts to *simultaneously* combat both gender and national oppression. While they ultimately did not succeed in realizing either women's or national liberation in their brief existence, the lessons of these revolutionaries should not be lost.

Bolshevism versus Stalinism

During the second half of the 1920s, after Lenin's death, Stalin consolidated his authority within the state's growing bureaucracy—and began to outlaw so-called "crimes of custom" throughout Central Asia. One such crime of custom was the practice of paying "bride wealth" (*galing*)—payment from the groom's family to the bride's parents in marriage, often when the bride was very young.

To be sure, this practice is a form of "selling" women. But bride wealth was central to an elaborate kinship network on which social structures were based. In Turkmenistan, for example, banning this custom was widely opposed by the population. Bride wealth could not be simply "outlawed" from above. Most importantly, the Russian state had no right to impose its rule on any issue in Russia's former colonies. New forms of social organization could only be built up over time from below, not via the sudden issue of a political edict from the former Russian colonizers. In so doing, Stalin betrayed the very principles of national liberation that were a hallmark of the Bolshevik tradition.

Too many historians blur the crucial distinction between Lenin and Stalin—and note without comment, for example, that Zhenotdel developed a campaign in which Muslim women ceremoniously tore off their veils on International Women's Day and May Day in Central Asia. That campaign reached its peak from 1927 to 1929—Stalin's ultraleft "third period" that accompanied the forced collectivization of agriculture. The unveilings were followed by the slaughter of many of the Muslim women who had participated, by their enraged husbands and brothers. In one quarter of 1929 alone, some three hundred women were murdered in Central Asia.[32] Moreover, the notion that the veiling of women is the hallmark of Muslim women's oppression reflects thoroughly imperialist prejudices against Muslim women, well established by the 1920s. Many choose to wear headscarves and other Islamic covering as a religious and cultural expression, not because they are forced to do so. The issue is one of choice, not custom.

No woman should be forced to dress in any particular way, a principle applying equally to all societies, including those of the West, which have objectified women's bodies from the time of the Victorian-era bustle to the present day. As Nadzhiya argued above, "the question of the chadra, it can be said, is of the least importance." Like the ban on "crimes of custom," the campaign against the veil was a product of Stalin's increasing control, solidified in 1928, with a devastating impact on oppressed nations, women, and Russia's peasantry and working class generally.

As the revolution disintegrated, the Stalinist bureaucracy seized the reins, erasing any distinction between the Bolshevik Party and the state. The consolidation of Stalinist rule marked the beginning of a period of massive industrialization in Russia and the brutal onset of a bureaucratic regime bent on competing with the West. Under the weight of this state bureaucracy, not just women but the entire working class once again returned to an existence of ruthless exploitation and oppression by the system.

Far from promoting women's equality, Stalin upended the theoretical foundations of the Bolshevik Revolution. In 1930, not long after outlawing "crimes of custom" in the name of women's "equality," Stalin's regime dissolved Zhenotdel. During the 1930s, abortion was outlawed, divorce became much more difficult, and Stalin proclaimed the "New Soviet Family," which meant the old "bourgeois family" with a new name.

In the process, this bureaucratic ruling class reversed the revolutionary socialist principles of the Bolsheviks—of revolutionary, democratic workers' power—into state control and repression. Stalinism became a tragic example of "socialism from above" that dismantled not only workers' power but also women's liberation. Millions of people were killed in this process—peasants, workers, and many Bolsheviks who had participated in the October Revolution.

This regressive course was personified by the transformation of Kollontai herself—from a key architect of the Bolshevik Party's strategy for women's liberation to a diplomat under Stalin's dictatorship, silent about the enormous betrayal of Stalinism until her death in 1952. Lenin's widow, Nadezhda Krupskaya, also stayed silent as Stalin cut ties to the Bolsheviks who led the 1917 revolution, which included labor camps and mass executions by death squad in the 1930s. These women should not, however, be judged by the choices they made under the horror of Stalinism, but by their contributions to the revolutionary movement in the years before and after 1917.

Kollontai's Vision of Sexual Relations in a Classless Society

Kollontai devoted considerable attention in the 1920s to sexual relations in communist societies. In that decade, she wrote a number of short stories, including *A Great Love* and *Love of Worker Bees*, that have been republished in recent decades. These stories are far from utopian romances, but rather describe the heartwrenching challenges women faced as sexual relationships changed in the early stages of the Russian Revolution while women remained oppressed. Kollontai began to describe her vision of the potential for transforming sexual relations in a future socialist society in *Communism and the Family*:

> In place of the old relationship between men and women, a new one is developing: a union of affection and comradeship, a union of two equal members of communist society, both of them free, both of them independent and both of them workers. No more domestic bondage for women. No more inequality within the family. No need for women to fear being left without support and with children to bring up. . . . Marriage will lose all the elements of material calculation which cripple family life. Marriage will be a union of two persons who love and trust each other. . . .
> Once the conditions of labor have been transformed and the material security of the working women has increased, and once marriage such as the church used to perform it, this so-called indissoluble marriage, which was at bottom merely a fraud—has given place to the free and honest union of men and women who are lovers and comrades, prostitution will disappear. This evil, which is a stain on humanity and the scourge of hungry working women, has its roots in commodity production and the institution of private property. Once these economic forms

are superseded, the trade in women will automatically disappear. The women of the working class, therefore, need not worry over the fact that the family is doomed to disappear. They should, on the contrary, welcome the dawn of a new society, which will liberate women from domestic servitude, lighten the burden of motherhood and finally put an end to the terrible curse of prostitution.[33]

In 1923, Kollontai delved further into the subject of human sexuality, expounding on her view that relationships could evolve far beyond the limitations imposed by capitalism, in her poignant essay "Make Way for Winged Eros."[34] Like Engels's conclusion to *Origin of the Family*, Kollontai does not venture beyond a heterosexual framework, but speculates that future generations in a society without oppressive property relations will create their own kinds of sexual relations. In Kollontai's words: "But there is no doubt that in the accomplished Communist society, love, 'winged Eros,' will be transformed into something completely unfamiliar to us. . . . What will this new transformed Eros be? The boldest fantasy is unable to capture its form."[35] Unlike Engels, however, Kollontai does not assume that the present norms of monogamy will continue beyond class society. As she describes, "It makes absolutely no difference whether love takes the form of a long-term and documented union or is expressed in the form of a transitory tie."[36]

Kollontai contrasts the collective identity of a future working class, after the achievement of full communism, to the individualism fitting the needs of a class society. She argues that this collective identity will supplant the "'conjugal pair marriage' and the 'all embracing love' of two spouses with the sense of 'love-comradeship.'"[37] She concludes, "The striving to express love not only in kisses and embraces, but in togetherness in action, in unity of will, in joint creation, will grow."[38]

Conclusion

Where Do We Go from Here?

More than four decades after the rise of the 1960s women's liberation movement, women's oppression remains firmly embedded in everyday life under capitalism. Each decade that has passed without a fighting movement for women's rights has seen an increase in blatant sexism in mainstream US discourse. Since the 1980s, the neoliberal political establishment has echoed the "family values" refrains of Christian conservatives while organizing an unrelenting assault on all the gains that the women's liberation movement won. Yet mainstream feminist organizations followed the Democratic Party even as it continually tacked rightward, courting socially conservative "swing voters" and funding sources. The result has been disastrous for women.

It is not a coincidence that the same neoliberal policies that have produced a return to Gilded Age–era heights of class inequality have also produced vile levels of misogyny, racism, and anti-LGBT bigotry in the political mainstream. A sustained ideological backlash against women has been integral to the neoliberal agenda over the last four decades—directed at feminism and everything it stands for. The women's liberation movement won the right to legal abortion based on the understanding that women cannot hope to become the equals of men without the right to control their own reproductive lives—shifting mass consciousness in favor of efforts to fight for women's equality. Since that time, the political establishment and the mainstream media have successfully promoted the falsehood that women choose abortion for "frivolous reasons" and "selfishly" delay abortions for the sake of convenience. This ideological attack has been tied to an unrelenting legislative assault on women's right to choose abortion—and more recently, on their right to contraception. The unstated assumption of this legislative assault is that women cannot be trusted to control their own reproductive destinies.

This antifeminist backlash has also further fueled the illusion that women who are raped have no one to blame but themselves. The women's liberation movement of the 1960s strongly challenged such sexist assumptions about rape. Yet the legal system, college administrations, and the mainstream media continue to advance the same myths from a century ago: that "real" rape occurs only when a stranger jumps out of the bushes, not on dates or between acquaintances or family members; that women's sexual-assault claims should be distrusted because women often "ask for it" by dressing certain ways or flirting, sending nonverbal signals that mean "yes" even if they say "no"; that women cannot be believed unless they can provide convincing evidence that they physically "resisted"; that women whose sexual histories show they have had previous sexual intercourse must be considered "promiscuous"—and therefore not trustworthy.

It is tempting to explain the revolting attitudes described above as a product of the rise of "porn culture" or "rape culture." But while cultural images and attitudes reinforce the material reality of women's oppression, they do not produce them. The sexual objectification of women and their dehumanization into collections of body parts long predate the widespread commercialization of pornography.

Moreover, "porn culture" or "rape culture" alone cannot explain the competing ideals simultaneously foisted upon women. For every cultural image that sexually objectifies women's bodies, there is another that sanctifies motherhood—depicting women as most fulfilled when they're tending to all aspects of their families' needs, from providing healthy, home-cooked meals to ensuring that clothes are washed and toilets cleaned with only the highest-quality products. These images reflect the dueling ideals imposed upon girls from childhood: to achieve a prescribed standard of sexual attractiveness (to men) *and* to become a devoted wife and mother. These ideals are less contradictory than they might appear: both are intended to channel women toward heterosexuality and, ultimately, marriage and motherhood.

To be sure, women's lives have changed in many ways over the last century. Most women—including mothers with small children—hold jobs outside the home and this has been the case for decades. Access to a paycheck affords some degree of financial independence, offering more women the possibility of leaving unhappy domestic situations. "Motherhood" no longer takes place primarily in the traditional heterosexual nuclear family, with a rise in single-parent families and increasing numbers of same-sex parents. Domestic labor takes less time, thanks to vacuum cleaners, washers, dryers, microwaves, and store-bought prepared foods.

But however much the configuration of families has changed, the capitalist class remains as dependent as ever on the role of the family in reproducing labor power for the system. Individual working-class families still shoulder virtually the entire responsibility for bearing and raising children and otherwise caring for family members. And this responsibility still falls disproportionately on women. Most working-class mothers struggle on a daily basis to keep up with the competing demands of home and work.

The capitalist class could, of course, choose to provide government assistance to working-class families to ease the burdens of housework and childrearing—there is certainly ample wealth to do so. At the very minimum, paid parental leave would make it much easier to take time off from a job after the birth of a child and subsidized daycare centers would make childcare more affordable. But, for the same reasons that individual employers aim to keep their workers' wages as low as possible, the ruling class also seeks to reproduce labor power at as little cost to itself as it can get away with. In addition, the neoliberal project has thus far produced only cuts in social welfare spending, with no end in sight. Winning substantial reforms will require a fighting movement from below.

It can be difficult today to imagine the emergence of a movement on a scale comparable to those of the 1960s. If anything, today's ideological onslaught resembles that of the 1950s, when sexist, racist, and homophobic stereotypes informed acceptable mainstream discourse. Today's younger generations have thus far in their lives experienced only rising bigotry in the world around them, facing futures of high debt and low-wage jobs. Older generations have witnessed their own living standards fall drastically over the last four decades, along with the erosion of their expectations for anything resembling a comfortable retirement.

The dramatic growth of class and social inequality in recent decades has led to widespread anger at the injustices of the system, but this has not yet been accompanied by the growth of the kind of sustained movements that can force through change from below. While the misery caused by the system is obvious to all those who suffer from it, the potential power of the working class to transform society is not. This is entirely understandable, given the near absence of strikes and mass class struggle in recent decades.

But silence should not be mistaken for consent. Voting for the "lesser evil" on Election Day—guessing which is the less harmful candidate from one of the two corporate parties on offer—does not constitute endorsement of the political status quo. The most important political decisions are not open to public referendum but made behind closed doors by a tiny ruling elite, without input or accountability. Once the big policy decisions have already been made, the details become open for debate. This was the way the entire neoliberal agenda was launched in the mid-1970s. Since then, debates have been allowed only over the details: How much should be cut from the budgets for food stamps, Medicare, and Medicaid? How much should taxpayers be obligated to pay to bail out the banks? What is the appropriate level of legal restriction that should be imposed upon women seeking abortions? Given an actual choice, the overwhelming majority of working-class people would surely not decide to lower their own wages for the sake of the wealthiest few. Women would not choose to suffer humiliation when they attempt to report their rapists. Black mothers would not wish to sacrifice their children to racist police murderers. But most of those who are oppressed and exploited by the system are given no voice in shaping economic and social policies, much less to express their discontent with the neoliberal agenda overall.

The ruling class is not unassailable, however, as difficult as it might be to envision otherwise. The Marxist understanding of historical materialism is that the very contradictions of class society ultimately produce resistance from below—and the opportunity for change. That is how the enormous racial, sexual, and political repression of the 1950s gave way to the rise of radical social movements in the 1960s. Likewise, the appalling levels of class inequality throughout the early decades of the twentieth century eventually produced the working-class strike waves of the Great Depression that finally won workers the right to form unions.

Social upheavals on this scale do not happen very often, but when they do, they not only make it possible to demand reforms that were previously unthinkable but also to build lasting social movements and working-class organizations that can fight to transform the class and social status quo. The excesses of capitalism do not automatically produce resistance and can even continue to worsen for quite long periods, as we have witnessed over recent decades. Opposition movements can neither be wished into being nor predicted with a precise timeline. Nevertheless, economic and ideological extremes such as exist today have proven historically to portend opposition from below. Indeed, the flashpoints of struggle in recent years—Occupy Wall Street, the LGBT movement for equal marriage, low-wage workers' struggles, and the Black Lives Matter movement—indicate that the contradictions of the present social order are becoming untenable for many who suffer because of them.

◆ ◆ ◆

Having become politically aware in the late 1960s and early 1970s in a blue-collar household, I can attest to the significance of the 1960s social movements in shaping my own worldview. Mom and Dad had dropped out of high school and entered the workforce as teens. Their greatest hope was for their daughters to attend secretarial school upon graduating from high school, which in their view would be a big step up for us. My sister, who was several years ahead of me in school, fought with my parents to be allowed to enroll in the "college prep" curriculum in high school instead of the secretarial courses. I remain indebted to my sister for fighting and winning this battle, which paved the way for both of us to attend college. But I doubt very much that she would have aimed this high a decade earlier, when higher education was out of reach for most women, particularly those without financial means. The women's liberation movement not only fought to open doors of opportunity that had previously been slammed shut to most women but also gave my generation the confidence to raise our hopes and expectations for ourselves.

Although both my parents were proud when my sister and I graduated from college, Dad was reluctant to embrace the goals of the women's movement—at least not those that might affect his "royal" status within his own household. But so too was Mom averse to change, despite her frequently mumbled expressions of resentment toward him. She continued to butter his bread and await his verdict on the quality of her cooking at every meal until they entered a nursing home together. Mom was unable to disentangle her self-esteem from his approval, despite my and my sister's best attempts to coax her.

At the same time, I also witnessed in the 1960s and early 1970s how the ideas of Black liberation and gay liberation influenced my parents—who by all outward appearances seemed to fit the stereotype of "backward" white workers. But they were not actually cut from that mold. Mom was the child of Southern Italian immigrants and told us stories of being ridiculed as a "spaghetti bender" and a "greaseball" in childhood. From my earliest memories, Dad was not only against racism but a passionate antiracist. At the age of five I said the N-word, having heard it thrown around in the neighborhood but having no idea what it meant. Dad was within earshot and rushed over to whack me across the face. "Never say that word again," he told me. I never did, and eventually began to understand why he hated that word so much.

From his parlor chair, Dad supported the Black Power movement. In 1969, we were engaged in our nightly ritual of watching the six o'clock news when the announcement came that Chicago police had killed Black Panthers Mark Clark and Fred Hampton while they slept in their beds. I asked Dad how such a thing could have happened. He explained in a few words: "When Black people fight back, the government kills them." I later understood why he was so incensed by racism. He explained to me that his family, like so many others impoverished during the Depression, was evicted roughly every three months for nonpayment of rent and moved to different neighborhoods around the city. His Irish American family had relocated multiple times to predominantly African American areas of Providence, and he identified with the friends he had made there.

Likewise, the rise of the gay liberation movement affected our entire household. The only thing I remember from watching Providence's first Gay Pride march in the early 1970s was that almost all the marchers had paper bags over their heads to avoid being identified. No other image could have more powerfully conveyed the enormous risks these protesters took to make a public demand for gay liberation—and also how unreachable that goal seemed at the time. I felt ashamed to live in a society that could inflict such humiliation on other human beings on a daily basis for no other reason than their chosen sexuality. Mom and Dad were similarly moved, although I didn't fully realize how much at the time. A few years later, Mom and Dad eagerly recounted to me how Dad had defended a gay teen being bullied at the school where they worked. Dad had shouted at the harassers, "He isn't hurting anybody! Leave him alone!" I found it amusing to imagine the surprise and fear those bullies must have felt when my macho, burly father chased them away.

I don't believe that my parents were all that different from most other working-class people, past or present. Like most people, they were of "mixed consciousness," with a variety of contradictory ideas in their heads, some of which changed over time because of the 1960s-era social movements. Neither of them ever walked a picket line or took part in a protest, which undoubtedly would have affected them deeply. I would even guess that Dad might have been quite a rabble-rouser if he had been given the opportunity.

I am fortunate to have grown up in the midst of the social up-heavals of the late 1960s and early 1970s, even if I experienced them primarily through a television screen. I was able to witness with my own eyes how rapidly mass movements can change the world. I was also able to observe the power of the strike weapon during that era, when militant strikes of rank-and-file workers swept the nation, often without union authorization. Postal workers, autoworkers, truckers, miners, teachers, and UPS workers all went on strike in the short pe-riod between 1968 and 1975. Judging from the alarm with which commentators on TV reported the disastrous effects these strikes were having on the US economy, it was clear to me that the working class could be a force to be reckoned with. I instinctively sided with the striking workers, having already identified our common class enemies as the perpetrators of war, racism, sexism, and homophobia.

So many years later, these still-vivid memories continue to inform my understanding of Marxist and feminist theory and the prospects for fu-ture struggle. I remain optimistic about the future because, as a Marxist, I recognize that just as surely as economic booms create the conditions that lead to the next economic crisis, the very excesses of capitalism ulti-mately generate opposition from below. However much neoliberalism has damaged working-class organizations, it can never take away the po-tential power of workers to paralyze production—and, in the case of public-sector workers, crucial aspects of social reproduction—by disrupt-ing "business as usual" through mass strike action.

Moreover, the composition of the US working class has change dra-matically over the last forty years. White, male, heterosexual workers are a proportional minority within the working class today. Women, includ-ing women of color, make up a large and permanent part of the labor force. The working class includes people of many races and nationalities, a variety of sexual and gender identities, and workers with disabilities and urgent special needs that go unaddressed within capitalist society. Today's working class holds the potential to propel issues of racism and other forms of oppression to the center of the class struggle in ways that would have been unimaginable in the past. The 2012 Chicago Teachers Union strike, for example, with a majority female workforce, was waged not only over teachers' compensation and working conditions but also as a social-justice struggle against racism and school closures, involving not only teachers but also parents and students. This strike provides a mere glimpse of the possibilities that lie ahead.

This book is an attempt to theorize and historicize women's oppression in the hopes of strengthening a future movement that can effectively fight for and win women's liberation. While understanding the lessons from the past is an invaluable part of preparing for the future, history never repeats itself exactly—because human progress intervenes. The struggles of the 1930s produced not only unions and Social Security but also the broad expectation that workers deserve certain basic civil rights, including the right to human dignity and some share of the wealth they produce in the form of profits. The late-1960s social movements fought against racism and the war in Vietnam, and later struggled for Black Power and women's and gay liberation. These movements have influenced generations of activists ever since. There is no way to erase this past and its lasting implications. The revolutionary potential of the working class as it is currently composed has yet to be seen, but it can most certainly be anticipated. When that time comes, working-class women will no doubt take center stage.

Acknowledgments

First and foremost, I would like to thank Anthony Arnove, Julie Fain, and Ahmed Shawki from Haymarket Books for their support and patience throughout this project. What began as a quick update for a second edition of *Women and Socialism: Essays on Women's Liberation* soon grew in scope and became a new (and much longer) book, taking two years instead of two months to complete. Anthony, Julie, and Ahmed offered only encouragement, despite the need to drastically change the editing and production schedules, because they believe as strongly as I do in the importance of women's liberation. They are my comrades, in every sense of the word.

I would also like to thank the entire staff at Haymarket Books: Nisha Bolsey, Rachel Cohen, Rory Fanning, Jason Farbman, Eric Kerl, Jon Kurinsky, Daphne Jackson, John McDonald, Jim Plank, Bill Roberts, Dao X. Tran, and Jesus Vega. Their hard work and dedication to social justice make Haymarket Books unique among publishers in today's market-driven world, and I am grateful to all of them.

There are also numerous people whose ideas—written, spoken, and/or acted upon—have inspired, challenged, and thereby helped to guide my own thinking over a period of many years, in ways they might not have realized at the time. I thank them all, and fully understand that they may not agree with the conclusions I have drawn. They include Mick Armstrong, Anthony Arnove, Abbie Bakan, brian bean, Tithi Bhattacharya, Madeline Burrows, Charlotte Bence, Todd Chretien, Rachel Cohen, Nicole Colson, Brenda Coughlin, Paul D'Amato, Antonis Davanellos, Susan Dwyer, Julie Fain, Phil Gasper, Cindy Kaffen, Dennis Kosuth, Susan Ferguson, Joel Geier, Ragina Johnson, Paul Kellogg, Brian Kelly, Deepa Kumar, Alan Maass, Marlene Martin, David McNally, Scott McLemee, Bill Mullen, Alpana Mehta, Celia Petty, John Riddell, Bill

Roberts, Deborah Roberts, Kirstin Roberts, Eric Ruder, Jennifer Roesch, Elizabeth Schulte, Lance Selfa, Ahmed Shawki, Ashley Smith, Lee Sustar, Keeanga-Yamahtta Taylor, David Whitehouse, Sherry Wolf, and Annie Zirin. I especially thank Abbie Bakan for taking the time to review the manuscript. In addition, I would like to express my great appreciation to Paul D'Amato, who managed to convert most of the Marx and Engels citations from a variety of sources to reference one unitary source: Marx and Engels's *Collected Works*.

Finally, I want to express my tremendous gratitude to Dao X. Tran, who was an amazing editor. Her political feedback was invaluable to me, and she deserves abundant credit for forcing me to clarify a number of points that had been muddled in the original manuscript, while suggesting alternative phrases and viewpoints that would strengthen the arguments made here. I feel very fortunate to have had the opportunity to work with Dao for a second time. Any remaining errors in this volume are, of course, my own.

I am excited to see what the next generation of fighters for women's liberation will achieve, but I also know that the history and theory created by past generations can play a crucial role in helping to shape future struggles.

Sharon Smith
June 2015

Notes

Preface

1. Jewelry manufacturing has since declined in Rhode Island, making up just 18 percent of the state's manufacturing base in 2013. See Flo Jonic, "Made in Rhode Island: Jewelry Making, an Industry on the Move," Rhode Island Public Radio, August 13, 2013, http://ripr.org/post/made-rhode-island-jewelry-making-industry-move.
2. Susan Ferguson and David McNally, "Capital, Labor Power, and Gender Relations," introduction in Lise Vogel, *Marxism and the Oppression of Women: Toward a Unitary Theory* (Leiden, Netherlands: Brill, 2013), xvii–xl.
3. Any analysis of LGBT oppression is entirely absent from both Marx's and Engels's analysis, even though more recent Marxist scholarship has pinpointed the roots of gay oppression, like that of women's oppression, in the rise of the nuclear family. See, for example, Sherry Wolf, *Sexuality and Socialism* (Chicago: Haymarket Books, 2009).
4. Neither did their feminist contemporaries challenge certain Victorian assumptions about women's roles.
5. John Riddell, "The Communist Women's Movement, 1921–26," *International Socialist Review* 87 (2013): 37.
6. Lise Vogel, "Domestic Labor Revisited," *Science & Society* 64, no. 2 (2000): 165.

Chapter One

1. Quoted in Barbara Evans Clements, *Bolshevik Feminist: The Life of Aleksandra Kollontai* (Bloomington: University of Indiana Press, 1979), 155.
2. See chapter 6 in this volume.
3. Vladimir Ilyich Lenin, *What Is to Be Done? Burning Questions of Our Movement*, in *Collected Works*, vol. 5 (Moscow: Foreign Languages Publishing House, 1961), 347–530, https://www.marxists.org/archive/lenin/works/1901/witbd/index.htm.
4. Karl Marx and Frederick Engels, *Manifesto of the Communist Party*, chapter 1 (1848), http://www.marxists.org/archive/marx/works/1848/communist-manifesto/ch01.htm.
5. Hal Draper, "The Principle of Self-Emancipation in Marx and Engels," *Socialist Register* (1971): 81–109, http://www.marxists.org/archive/draper/1971/xx/emancipation.html#f6.
6. Leon Trotsky, "Against Bureaucracy, Progressive and Unprogressive," *Problems of Everyday Life* (York: Methuen, 1924), 65, http://www.marxists.org/archive/trotsky/1924/xx/bureaucracy.htm.
7. Richard Stites, *The Women's Liberation Movement in Russia: Feminism, Nihilism and Bol-*

shevism 1860–1930 (Princeton, NJ: Princeton University Press, 1978), 282.

8.   Hal Draper and Anne G. Lipow, "Marxist Women versus Bourgeois Feminism," *Socialist Register*, 1976, 179–226, http://www.marxists.org/archive/draper/1976/women/women.html.

9.   August Bebel, *Woman and Socialism*, chapter 15, http://www.marxists.org/archive/bebel/1879/woman-socialism/ch15.htm.

10. Draper and Lipow, "Marxist Women versus Bourgeois Feminism."

11. Clara Zetkin, "Social-Democracy & Woman Suffrage" (1906), http://www.marxists.org/archive/zetkin/1906/xx/womansuffrage.htm.

12. Alix Holt, *Selected Writings of Alexandra Kollontai* (Westport, CT: Lawrence Hill & Co., 1977), 59.

13. Ibid., 126.

14. Clara Zetkin, "Only in Conjunction with the Proletarian Woman Will Socialism Be Victorious," Speech at the Party Congress of the Social Democratic Party of Germany, Gotha, October 16, 1896, Berlin, in Clara Zetkin: Selected Writings, ed. Philip Foner (New York: International Publishers, 1984), http://www.marxists.org/archive/zetkin/1896/10/women.htm.

15. Ibid.

16. Ibid.

17. Ibid.

18. Tiffany K. Wayne, ed., *Women's Rights in the United States: A Comprehensive Encyclopedia of Issues, Events, and People*, vol. 1 (Santa Barbara, CA: ABC-CLIO, LLC, 2014), 280.

19. Linda O. McMurry, *To Keep the Waters Troubled: The Life of Ida B. Wells* (New York: Oxford University Press, 1998), 305.

20. Ann Schofield, "Rebel Girls and Union Maids: The Woman Question in the Journals of the AFL and IWW, 1905–1920," *Feminist Studies* 9, no. 2 (1983): 338.

21. Ibid.

22. Meredith Tax, *The Rising of the Women: Feminist Solidarity and Class Conflict, 1880–1917* (Champaign: University of Illinois Press, 1980), 256.

23. Robin Blackburn, ed., *An Unfinished Revolution: Karl Marx and Abraham Lincoln* (London: Verso Books, 2011), 251–52.

24. Ira Kipnis, *The American Socialist Movement 1897–1912* (Chicago: Haymarket Books, 2005), 278–79.

25. Kate Richards O'Hare, "'Nigger' Equality," first published in National Ripsaw [St. Louis, MO]. Reprinted by the Ripsaw as a pamphlet in an edition of 30,000 copies on March 25, 1912. Available online at http://www.marxisthistory.org/history/usa/parties/spusa/1912/0325-ohare-niggerequality.pdf.

26. Kipnis, *American Socialist Movement*, 268.

27. Ibid., 265.

28. Diane Feeley, "Antoinette Konikow: Marxist and Feminist," *International Socialist Review* 33 (January 1972), 19–23.

29. Ibid.

30. Ibid.

31. See Tax, *Rising of the Women*.

32. Ibid., 232.

33. Quoted in John Lauritson and David Norsad, *The Early Homosexual Rights Movement 1864–1935* (New York: Times Change Press, 1974); cited in Noel Halifax, *Out, Proud*

and Fighting (London: Socialist Workers Party, 1988), 17.

34. V. I. Lenin, Speech at the Working Women's Congress, Moscow, 1919, Lenin's *Collected Works*, vol. 3, 4th English ed. (Moscow: Progress Publishers, 1965), 40–46, https://www.marxists.org/archive/lenin/works/1919/sep/23a.htm.

35. Clara Zetkin, *Lenin on the Woman Question*, 2nd English ed. (New York: International Publishers, 1934), 21.

36. Leon Trotsky, "From the Old Family to the New," *Pravda* (July 1923), http://www.marxists.org/archive/trotsky/women/life/23_07_13.htm.

37. See Kipnis, *American Socialist Movement*.

38. Janice Hassett, "Never Again Just a Woman: Women of the Auxiliary and Emergency Brigade in the General Motors Sit-Down Strike of 1937," American Socialist Collection of Sol Dollinger, March 11, 1994, http://www.marxists.org/history/etol/newspape /amersocialist/neveragain.htm#53n.

39. Ibid.

40. Ibid.

41. Ibid.

42. Erik S. McDuffie, *Sojourning for Freedom: Black Women, American Communism, and the Making of Black Left Feminism* (Durham, NC: Duke University Press, 2011), 1.

43. Ibid.

44. Ibid., 79.

45. Hassett, "Never Again Just a Woman."

46. Kate Weigand, *Red Feminism: American Communism and the Making of Women's Liberation* (Baltimore: Johns Hopkins University Press, 2002), 87.

47. Ibid., 87–88.

48. Ibid., 88.

49. Ibid., 89.

50. Ibid., 89–90.

51. Ibid., 128.

52. Beverly Guy-Sheftall, ed., *Words of Fire: An Anthology of African-American Feminist Thought* (New York: New Press, 1995), 109.

53. Ibid., 115.

54. Ibid., 117.

55. Ibid., 119–20.

56. Ibid., 120.

57. Weigand, *Red Feminism*, 74.

58. Selma James was part of the Workers Party and then the Socialist Workers Party between 1940 and 1950. After that, she was part of the break-off organization Correspondence.

59. Selma James, *Sex, Race and Class—the Perspective of Winning: A Selection of Writings, 1952–2011* (Oakland, CA: PM Press, 2012), 16–17.

60. Ibid., 35.

61. Ibid.

62   Evelyn Reed, "The Myth of Women's Inferiority," *Fourth International* 15, no. 2 (Spring 1954), https://www.marxists.org/archive/reed-evelyn/1954/myth-inferiority.htm.

63. Weigand, *Red Feminism*, 7.

64. Quoted in Barbara Smith, ed., *Home Girls: A Black Feminist Anthology* (New York: Kitchen Table: Women of Color Press, 1983), xxxii.

65. Ibid.
66. Evelyn Reed, "Women: Caste, Class or Oppressed Sex," *International Socialist Review* 31, no. 3 (September 1970): 15–17 and 40–41, http://www.marxists.org/archive /reed-evelyn/1970/caste-class-sex.htm.
67. Ibid.

Chapter Two

1. Frederick Engels, *The Origin of the Family, Private Property and the State* (New York: International Publishers, 1972), 139.
2. Gerda Lerner, *The Creation of Patriarchy* (New York: Oxford University Press, 1986), 16.
3. Stephanie Coontz and Peta Henderson, eds., *Women's Work, Men's Property: The Origins of Gender and Class* (New York and London: Verso, 1986), 23.
4. Eleanor Burke Leacock, *Myths of Male Dominance: Collected Articles on Women Cross-Culturally* (New York: Monthly Review Press, 1981), 17.
5. Quoted in ibid., 215–31. Leacock goes on to comment, "The terminology of woman exchange distorts the structure of egalitarian societies, where it is a gross contradiction of reality to talk of women as in any sense 'things' that are exchanged. Women are 'exchangers' in such societies, autonomous beings who, in accord with the sexual division of labor exchange their work and their produce with men and with other women." (241)
6. Eleanor Burke Leacock, "Introduction," in *Origin of the Family*, Engels, 31.
7. Marvin Harris, *Cannibals and Kings* (New York: Vintage Books, 1991), 71–72.
8. See Leacock, *Myths of Male Dominance*, 198, Coontz and Henderson, *Women's Work, Men's Property*, 17–18.
9. R. Brian Ferguson,, *Yanomami Warfare: A Political History* (Santa Fe, NM: School of American Research Press, 1995), 6.
10. Coontz and Henderson, *Women's Work, Men's Property*, 19.
11. Sherry B. Ortner, "Is Female to Male as Nature Is to Culture?," in *Woman, Culture, and Society*, eds. Michelle Zimbalist Rosaldo and Louise Lamphere (Stanford, CA: Stanford University Press, 1974), 69–70.
12. Lerner, *Creation of Patriarchy*, 25.
13. Coontz and Henderson, *Women's Work, Men's Property*, 12–13.
14. Maria Alexandra Lepowsky, *Fruit of the Motherland: Gender in an Egalitarian Society* (New York: Columbia University Press, 1993), 42.
15. Ibid., 288–89.
16. Karl Marx and Frederick Engels, *The Communist Manifesto* (New York: International Publishers, 1948), 27.
17. Karl Marx and Frederick Engels, *The German Ideology* (New York: International Publishers, 2004), 49.
18. Ibid., 52.
19. Ibid., 50.
20. Kevin Anderson, *Marx at the Margins: On Nationalism, Ethnicity, and Non-Western Societies* (Chicago: University of Chicago Press, 2010), 197.
21. Ibid., 201.
22. Quoted in Heather A. Brown, *Marx on Gender and the Family: A Critical Study* (Chicago: Haymarket Books, 2013), 150.
23. Lawrence Krader, ed., *The Ethnographical Notebooks of Karl Marx* (Assen: Van Gorcum, 1972). [Note: When the second edition appeared in 1974, the title was changed to *The*

Ethnological Notebooks of Karl Marx.] It is worth noting that Krader transcribed Marx's notes in the languages Marx used: a combination of English, German, Greek, and Latin. An English edition is forthcoming. Chapter 3 of the 1972 edition of *The Ethnographical Notebooks of Karl Marx* is available at the Marxist Internet Archive: http://www.marxists.org/archive/marx/works/1881/ethnographical-notebooks/ch03.htm.

24. Franklin Rosemont, "Karl Marx and the Iroquois," in *Arsenal/Surrealist Subversion*, no. 4 (Chicago: Black Swan Press, 1989), 201.

25. Frederick Engels, T*he Origin of the Family, Private Property and the State* (New York: International Publishers, 1972), 71.

26. The classic patriarchal family is a specific family form that existed among ancient Greeks and Romans, of absolute rule by the male head of the household over its male and female dependent members.

27. Hal Draper, "Marx and Engels on Women's Liberation," *International Socialism* 44 (July/August 1970), http://www.marxists.org/archive/draper/1970/07/women.htm#f35.

28. Quoted in Eleanor Burke-Leacock's introduction to Engels, *Origin of the Family*, 10.

29. Bachoven's theory is described in Lerner, *Creation of Patriarchy*, 21–29.

30. Engels, *Origin of the Family*, 98.

31. Ibid., 126.

32. Ibid., 138.

33. Ibid., 128.

34. Ibid., 131.

35. Ibid., 129.

36. Ibid., 130.

37. Ibid., 139.

38. Ibid., 120–21, 122.

39. "The Power to Make a Difference," *Office for the Prevention of Domestic Violence* bulletin, Spring 2000. See R. Barri Flowers, *Domestic Crimes, Family Violence and Child Abuse: A Study of Contemporary American Society* (Jefferson, NC: McFarland & Company, 2000), 83–84.

40. Brown, *Marx on Gender*, 134.

41. Ibid,. 160.

42. Ibid., 150.

43. Ibid., 154.

44. Ibid., 154–55.

45. Ibid., 155.

46. Ibid., 157–58.

47. Engels's concept of "individual sex love" is discussed at length in Draper, "Marx and Engels on Women's Liberation."

48. Quoted in Brown, *Marx on Gender*, 171.

49. Ibid., 154.

50. Ibid., 175.

51. Engels, *Origin of the Family*, 71.

52. Lise Vogel, *Marxism and the Oppression of Women* (Chicago: Haymarket Books, 2014), 128.

53. Chris Harman, "Engels and the Origins of Human Society," *International Socialism* 65 (Winter 1994): 84.

54. Harman, "Engels and the Origins," 88.

55. Frederick Engels, "The Part Played by Labour in the Transition from Ape to Man" (Moscow: Progress Publishers, 1934). Unfinished article, available at https://www.marxists.org/archive/marx/works/1876/part-played-labour/.

56. Ibid.

57. Leacock, *Myths of Male Dominance*, 38.

58. Ibid., 35.

59. Judith Brown, "Iroquois Women: An Ethnohistoric Note," in *Toward an Anthropology of Women*, ed. Rayna Reiter (New York: Monthly Review Press, 1975), 237.

60. Lerner, *Creation of Patriarchy*, 18.

61. Patricia Draper, "!Kung Women: Contrasts in Sexual Egalitarianism in Foraging and Sedentary Contexts," in *Toward an Anthropology of Women*, Reiter, 91.

62. Lepowsky, *Fruit of the Motherland*, 32.

63. Harman, "Engels and the Origins," 96–98.

64. Engels, *Origin of the Family*, 92.

65. Harman, "Engels and the Origins," 120–21.

66. See, for example, Karen Sachs, "Engels Revisited: Women, the Organization of Production, and Private Property," in *Toward an Anthropology of Women*, Reiter, 211–12.

67. Lerner, *Creation of Patriarchy*, 52.

68. Engels, *Origin of the Family*, 118.

69. Leacock, introduction to *Origin of the Family*, 16–17.

70. Harman, "Engels and the Origins," 125.

71. Coontz and Henderson, *Women's Work, Men's Property*, 125.

72. Ibid., 127–28.

73. Sachs, "Engels Revisited," 216–17.

74. Engels, *Origin of the Family*, 134.

75. Ibid., 121.

76. Ibid., 121–22.

77. Leacock, introduction to Engels, *Origin of the Family*, 41.

78. Engels, *Origin of the Family*, 119–20.

79. Lerner, *Creation of Patriarchy*, 30.

80. Coontz and Henderson, *Women's Work, Men's Property*, 124–25.

81. Lerner, *Creation of Patriarchy*, 52–53.

82. Engels, *Origin of the Family*, 137.

83. Ibid., 135.

84. Lise Vogel, *Marxism and the Oppression of Women*, 137.

85. Martha Gimenez, "Marxist and Non-Marxist Elements on Engels' Views," in *Engels Revisited: New Feminist Essays*, eds. Janet Sayers, Mary Evans, and Nanneke Redclift (London: Tavistock, 1987), 48.

86. Engels, *Origin of the Family*, 139.

87. See, for example, Sherry Wolf, *Sexuality and Socialism: History, Politics, and Theory of LGBT Liberation* (Chicago: Haymarket Books, 2009).

88. Engels, *Origin of the Family*, 145.

Chapter Three

1. Cherríe Moraga, Gloria Anzaldúa, et al., eds., *This Bridge Called My Back: Writings by*

Women of Color (New York: Kitchen Table: Women of Color Press, 1983), 99.

2. Stephanie Coontz, *A Strange Stirring: The Feminine Mystique and American Women at the Dawn of the 1960s* (New York: Basic Books, 2011), 5.

3. Ibid., 7.

4. Ibid., 9–10.

5. Quoted in Susan Estrich, *Real Rape* (Cambridge, MA: Harvard University Press, 1987), 39.

6. Ibid., 38.

7. Marian Faux, *Roe v. Wade* (New York: Macmillan, 1988), 188; Andrew H. Merton, *Enemies of Choice* (Boston: Beacon Press, 1981), 36.

8. Katha Pollitt, "Abortion in American History," *Atlantic*, May 1997, http://www.theatlantic.com/magazine/toc/1997/05/.

9. In 1965, the US Supreme Court ruled in *Griswold v. Connecticut* that the Constitution implies a right of marital privacy, establishing the legal right of married couples to use birth control. In 1972, the court issued a ruling in *Eisenstadt v. Baird* that established the legal right of unmarried people to obtain contraception on the same basis as married people.

10. Betty Friedan, *The Feminine Mystique* (New York: Dell, 1963), 204.

11. Theodore Caplow, *Recent Social Trends in the United States, 1960–1990* (Montreal, Quebec: McGill-Queen's University Press, 1994), 124.

12. Ibid., 174.

13. John H. Bishop, "The Explosion of Female College Attendance," Cornell University, November 1, 1990, Center for Advanced Human Resource Studies (CAHRS), http://digitalcommons.ilr.cornell.edu/cgi/viewcontent.cgi?article=1389&context=cahrswp.

14. Coontz, *A Strange Stirring*, 10; US Census Bureau, "Women in the Workforce," http://www.census.gov/newsroom/pdf.

15. American Medical Association, "Women in Medicine: An AMA Timeline," http://www.ama-assn.org/resources/doc/wpc/wimtimeline.pdf; Coontz, *Strange Stirring*, 173.

16. "Sources of Inequality in Earnings," *Monthly Labor Review* (April 1989), 6, http://www.bls.gov/mlr/1989/04/art1full.pdf; Coontz, *Strange Stirring*, 121.

17. Coontz, *Strange Stirring*, 121.

18. Ibid., 124.

19. "The Negro Family: The Case for National Action," Office of Planning and Research, United States Department of Labor, March 1965, http://www.dol.gov/dol/aboutdol/history/webid-meynihan.htm.

20. Ibid.

21. Report of the National Advisory Commission on Civil Disorders (New York: Bantam Books), 1968, 1–29, http://www.eisenhowerfoundation.org/docs/kerner.pdf.

22. Ibid.

23. Ibid.

24. Patricia Hill Collins, *Black Feminist Thought: Knowledge, Consciousness, and the Politics of Empowerment* (London: Routledge, 2002), 23.

25. Ibid.

26. Linda Nicholson, *Gender and History: The Limits of Social Theory in the Age of the Family* (New York: Columbia University Press, 1986), https://www.marxists.org/reference/subject/philosophy/works/us/nichols2.htm.

27. Jo Freeman, "No More Miss America! 1968–69," JoFreeman.com, http://www.jofreeman.com/photos/MissAm1969.html.

28. Alice Echols, *Daring to Be Bad: Radical Feminism in America, 1967–1975* (Minneapolis: University of Minnesota Press, 1989), 92–94.

29. Ibid., 141–42.

30. Ibid., 142.

31. Katha Pollitt, "Abortion History 101," *Nation*, April 13, 2000, http://www.thenation.com/article/abortion-history-101.

32. Minda Bickman, "The Ladies' Invasion of Man's Home Journal," *Village Voice*, March 26, 1970, http://blogs.villagevoice.com/runninscared/2010/09/womens_lib_inva.php.

33. Susan Brownmiller, *In Our Time: Memoir of a Revolution* (New York: Dial Press, 1999), 84.

34. Ibid., 85–86.

35. "The 1972 Virginia Slims American Women's Opinion Poll," study conducted by Louis Harris and Associates, http://www.icpsr.umich.edu/icpsrweb/ICPSR/studies/7326.

36. "Women of the Year: Great Changes, New Chances, Tough Choices," *Time*, January 5, 1976.

37. Harriet A. Washington, *Medical Apartheid: The Dark History of Medical Experimentation on Black Americans from Colonial Times to the Present* (New York: Random House, 2006), 200.

38. Kimberly Springer, *Living for the Revolution: Black Feminist Organizations, 1968–1980* (Durham, NC: Duke University Press, 2005), 48.

39. Ibid., 49.

40. Alma M. García, *Chicana Feminist Thought: The Basic Historical Writings* (New York: Routledge, 1997), 159–60.

41. Ibid., 21–22.

42. bell hooks, *Aint't I a Woman? Black Women and Feminism* (Boston: South End Press, 1981), 5.

43. Jennifer Nelson, *Women of Color and the Reproductive Rights Movement* (New York: NYU Press, 2003), 109.

44. Ibid., 114.

45. Jael Silliman, Marlene Gerber Fried, et al., *Undivided Rights: Women of Color Organize for Reproductive Justice* (Cambridge, MA: South End Press, 2004), 111.

46. Ibid., 127.

47. Moraga and Anzaldúa, *This Bridge Called*.

48. Ibid., xliii.

49. Ibid., 98.

50. Ibid., 71–72.

51. hooks, *Aint't I a Woman?*, 8.

52. Quoted in Moraga and Anzaldúa, *This Bridge Called*, 61.

Chapter Four

1. Naomi Wolf, *Fire with Fire: The New Female Power and How It Will Change the 21st Century* (London: Chatto & Windus, 1993), 221.

2. Stephanie Coontz, *A Strange Stirring: The Feminine Mystique and American Women at the Dawn of the 1960s* (New York: Basic Books, 2011), 140.

3. Ibid., 126.

4. Ibid., 114.
5. Nancy MacLean, "Rethinking the Second Wave," *Nation*, September 25, 2002, http://www.thenation.com/article/rethinking-second-wave#, 31.
6. Betty Friedan, *The Feminine Mystique* (New York: Dell Publishing Company, 1963), 22.
7. Ibid., 362.
8. Coontz, *A Strange Stirring*, 101; MacLean, "Rethinking the Second Wave."
9. Evelyn Reed, "A Study of the Feminine Mystique," *International Socialist Review* (Winter 1964): 24–27, http://www.marxists.org/archive/reed-evelyn/1964/friedan-review.htm.
10. Ibid.
11. Friedan, *The Feminine Mystique*, 263–64.
12. Katha Pollitt, "Betty Friedan, 1921–2006," *Nation*, February 27, 2006, http://www.thenation.com/article/betty-friedan-1921-2006.
13. National Organization for Women, "Bill of Rights, 1968," http://coursesa.matrix.msu.edu/~hst306/documents/nowrights.html.
14. Gilbert Y. Steiner, *Constitutional Inequality* (Washington, DC: Brookings Institution, 1985), 43.
15. Janet A. Flammang, *Women's Political Voice: How Women Are Transforming the Practice and Study of Politics* (Philadelphia: Temple University Press, 1997), 305.
16. Marilyn Danton, "Protective Legislation and the ERA," *Workers Power*, October 9–22, 1970, 3–4.
17. Ibid.
18. Steven M. Buechler, *Women's Movements in the United States: Woman Suffrage, Equal Rights, and Beyond* (New Brunswick, NJ: Rutgers University Press, 1990), 157; Rickie Solinger, ed., *Abortion Wars: A Half Century of Struggle, 1950–2000* (Berkeley and Los Angeles: University of California Press, 1998), 192; Shirelle Phelps, ed., *Contemporary Black Biography: Profiles from the International Black Community*, vol. 13 (Farmington Hills, MI: Cengage Gale, 1996), 87.
19. Ibid., 25.
20. National Organization for Women, "NOW Leading the Fight: Timeline of NOW's Work on Lesbian Rights," http://www.now.org/issues/lgbi/timeline.html.
21. Marcia M. Gallo, *Different Daughters: A History of the Daughters of Bilitis and the Rise of the Lesbian Rights Movement* (New York: Seal Press, 2007), 173.
22. Patricia Cronin Marcello, *Gloria Steinem: A Biography* (Westport, CT: Greenwood Biographies, 2004), 111.
23. Jane J. Mansbridge, *Why We Lost the ERA* (Chicago: University of Chicago Press, 1986), 130–31.
24. "About; Mission," Feminist Majority, http://feministmajority.org/about.
25. Susan Spalter Berman, "*California Federal Savings & Loan Association v. Guerra*: The State of California Has Determined that Pregnancy May Be Hazardous to Your Job," *Golden Gate University Law Review* 16 (1986). http://digitalcommons.law.ggu.edu/ggulrev/vol16/iss3/4.
26. William Saletan, *Bearing Right: How Conservatives Won the Abortion War* (Berkeley and Los Angeles: University of California Press, 2003), 72–73.
27. "A Step Backward for Abortion Rights," *International Socialist Review* 1 (Summer 1997): http://isreview.org/issues/01/notes01.shtml.
28. Ibid.
29. Jane Roh, "Stakes High for Dean," Fox News, February 12, 2005.

30. Patrick D. Healy, "Clinton Seeking Shared Ground over Abortions," *New York Times*, January 25, 2005, http://www.nytimes.com/2005/01/25/nyregion/25clinton.html.

31. Roh, "Stakes High for Dean."

32. Kate Michelman, letter to the editor, *New York Times*, January 27, 2005.

33. Barack Obama, "Executive Order 13535—Patient Protection and Affordable Care Act's Consistency with Longstanding Restrictions on the Use of Federal Funds for Abortion," The White House, March 24, 2010, https://www.whitehouse.gov/the -press-office/executive-order-patient-protection-and-affordable-care-acts-consistency -with-longst.

34. "National Organization for Women PAC Endorses Obama-Biden for Re-election: Statement of NOW/PAC Chair Terry O'Neill," press release, July 11, 2012. http://now.org/media-center/press-release/national-organization-for-women-pac -endorses-obama-biden-for-re-election.

35. Tina Daunt, "Jay Leno and Mavis Leno Turn Serious about the Plight of Afghan Women," *Los Angeles Times*, April 3, 2009, http://articles.latimes.com/2009/apr /03/entertainment/et-cause3; Janelle Brown, "Terror's First Victims: When Fanatics Like the Taliban Seize Control of Islamic Countries, Women Are the First to Suffer," *Salon*, September 24, 2001, http://www.salon.com/2001/09/24/taliban_women.

36. Brown, "Terror's First Victims."

37. Ibid.

38. Mariam Rawi, "Betrayal," *New Internationalist* 364, January–February 2004, http://www.newint.org.

39. Mariam Rawi, "Rule of the Rapists: Britain and the US Said War on Afghanistan Would Liberate Women. We Are Still Waiting," *Guardian*, February 12, 2004, http://www.theguardian.com/world/2004/feb/12/afghanistan.gender.

40. Ibid.; Meena Nanji, "Afghanistan's Women After 'Liberation,'" *ZNet*, December 29, 2003, http://www.zmag.org.

41. Saleha Soadat, "42,450 Cases of Violence Against Women in Nine Months: AIHRC," *RAWA News*, February 16, 2015, http://www.rawa.org/temp/runews/2015/02/16 /4250-cases-of-violence-against-women-in-nine-months-aihrc.html#ixzz3TMH9vlGp.

42. Wolf, *Fire with Fire*, xvi.

43. Ibid., 263.

44. Ibid., 318.

45. Ibid., 57.

46. Ibid., 58.

47. Ibid., 42.

48. Ibid., 57.

49. Ibid., 51.

50. Ibid., 222.

51. Ibid., 256–57.

52. Ibid., 142.

53. Naomi Wolf, "Pro-Choice and Pro-Life," *New York Times*, April 3, 1997.

54. Jodi Kantor, "Naomi Wolf: Al Gore's Alpha Female," *Slate*, November 5, 1999, http://www.slate.com/articles/news_and_politics/assessment/1999/11/naomi_wolf.html.

55. Naomi Wolf, "Female Trouble," *New York*, May 21, 2005, http://nymag.com /nymetro/news/columns/thesexes/9911/.

56. Ibid.

57. Naomi Wolf, "Tea Time in America," *Project Syndicate*, February 26, 2010, http://www.project-syndicate.org/commentary/tea-time-in-america.

58. Ibid.

59. Feminist Majority Foundation, "Feminist Majority Hosts Women, Money, Power Summit Tomorrow," press release, October 2013. https://feminist.org/blog/index .php/2013/10/07/feminist-majority-hosts-women-money-power-summit-tomorrow.

Chapter Five

1. bell hooks, *Feminist Theory: From Margin to Center* (London: Pluto Press, 2000), 72.

2. "Port Huron Statement of the Students for a Democratic Society, 1962," http://coursesa .matrix.msu.edu/~hst306/documents/huron.html.

3. Judith Hole and Ellen Levine, *The Rebirth of Feminism* (Chicago: Quadrangle Books, 1971), 110.

4. Ibid., 112.

5. Robin Morgan, *Sisterhood Is Powerful: Writings from the Women's Liberation Movement* (New York: Vintage, 1970), xxi.

6. Hole and Levine, *Rebirth of Feminism*, 113–14.

7. Sara Davidson, *Loose Change: Three Women of the Sixties* (Berkeley and Los Angeles: University of California Press, 1997), 180.

8. Kirkpatrick Sale, *SDS: The Rise and Development of the Students for a Democratic Society* (New York: Random House, 1973), 508, 526.

9. Echols, *Daring to Be Bad*, 120.

10. Ruth Rosen, *The World Split Open: How the Modern Women's Movement Changed America* (New York: Viking, 2000).

11. Echols, *Daring to Be Bad*, 117.

12. Rosen, *World Split Open*, 135.

13. Ibid.

14. Michael Friedman, ed., *The New Left of the Sixties* (Berkeley, CA: Independent Socialist Press, 1972), 194.

15. Ibid., 195.

16. Ibid., 182.

17. Max Elbaum, "Maoism in the United States," *Encyclopedia of the American Left*, 2nd ed., 1998, https://www.marxists.org/history/erol/ncm-1/maoism-us.htm.

18. Echols, *Daring to Be Bad*, 121.

19. Ibid., 60.

20. Edith Hoshino Altbach, *From Feminism to Liberation* (New Brunswick, NJ: Transaction Publishers, 2007), 77–78.

21. Linda Nicholson, *Gender and History: The Limits of Social Theory in the Age of the Family* (New York: Columbia University Press, 1986), https://www.marxists.org/reference /subject/philosophy/works/us/nichols2.htm.

22. Echols, *Daring to Be Bad*, 63.

23. Ibid., 60.

24. Sara Evans, *Personal Politics: The Roots of Women's Liberation in the Civil Rights Movement and the New Left* (New York: Vintage Books, 1979), 190.

25. See Shulamith Firestone, "The Jeanette Rankin Brigade: Woman Power?" (1968), Chicago

Women's Liberation Union (CWLU) Herstory Website Archive, https://www.uic.edu/orgs/cwluherstory/CWLUArchive/rankin1.html.

26. Harold Jacobs, ed., *Weatherman* (Berkeley, CA: Ramparts Press, 1970), 53.

27. Ibid., 185.

28. Sale, SDS, 526.

29. Echols, *Daring to Be Bad*, 62.

30. Nicholson, *Gender and History*.

31. "CLUW Mission Statement," Coalition of Labor Union Women, http://www.cluw.org/?zone=/unionactive/view_article.cfm&HomeID=252411&page=About20CLUW.

32. "A DARE Analysis of the Coalition of Labor Union Women (CLUW)," CWLU Herstory Website Archive (1974), https://www.uic.edu/orgs/cwluherstory/CWLUArchive/cluw.html.

33. Jennifer Nelson, *Women of Color and the Reproductive Rights Movement* (New York: NYU Press, 2003), 47.

34. Nicholson, *Gender and History*.

35. Susan Brownmiller, *Against Our Will: Men, Women, and Rape* (New York: Fawcett Columbine, 1975), 11.

36. Frederick Engels, *The Origin of the Family, Private Property and the State* (New York: International Publishers, 1972), 120–22.

37. Martha Gimenez, *Science & Society* 69, no. 1 (January 2005): 12.

38. "Organizing Principles of the New York Radical Feminists," quoted in Hole and Levine, *Rebirth of Feminism*, 153–54.

39. Kate Millett, *Sexual Politics* (Chicago: University of Illinois Press, 1970), 33.

40. Shulamith Firestone, *The Dialectic of Sex: The Case for Feminist Revolution* (New York: Bantam Books, 1971), 12.

41. Brownmiller, *Against Our Will*, 14.

42. Ibid., 15.

43. Ibid., 17–18.

44. Firestone, *Dialectic of Sex*, 108.

45. Angela Y. Davis, *Women, Race & Class* (New York: Vintage Books, 1981), 178.

46. Brownmiller, *Against Our Will*, 272.

47. Ibid., 247.

48. Alice Walker, letter to the editor, *New York Times Book Review*, November 30, 1975, 65–66. Quoted in *Gwendolyn Brooks: Poetry and the Heroic Voice*, D. H. Melhem (Lexington: University Press of Kentucky, 1988), 249.

49. Davis, *Women, Race & Class*, 188–89.

50. Ibid., 178.

51. Judy Klemesrud, "Joining Hands in the Fight Against Pronorgraphy [sic]," *New York Times*, August 26, 1985, http://www.nytimes.com/1985/08/26/style/joining-hands-in-the-fight-against-pronorgraphy.html.

52. Nadine Strossen, *Defending Pornography: Free Speech, Sex, and the Fight for Women's Rights* (New York: NYU Press, 2000), 231–39.

53. Ibid., 238–39.

54. Ibid., 237.

55. Ibid., 238.

56. Mickey Kovisto, "The Customs Game," *Northern Woman Journal*, 15, nos. 2 and 3, Special Issue (March 1994): 8–11, http://northernwomansbookstore.ca/resources/NWJ

/1994%20Vol%2015%20No.%202&3%20Special%20Issue.CV01.pdf.

57. Marcus McCann, "Little Sister's Declares Defeat in the Wake of 7–2 Supreme Court Ruling," *Daily Xtra*, January 19, 2007, http://dailyxtra.com/canada/news/little-sisters-declares-defeat-in-the-wake-7-2-supreme-court-ruling-53695.

58. Echols, *Daring to Be Bad*, 198.

59. Hole and Levine, *Rebirth of Feminism*, 140–41.

60. Ibid., 160–61.

61. Combahee River Collective, "The Combahee River Collective Statement," April 1977, http://circuitous.org/scraps/combahee.html.

62. hooks, *Feminist Theory*, 78.

63. Ibid., 71.

64. Ibid., 72.

65. Carol Hanich, Kathy Scarbrough, et al., "Forbidden Discourse: The Silencing of Feminist Criticism of 'Gender,' an Open Statement from 37 Radical Feminists from Five Countries," August 12, 2013, https://feministuk.wordpress.com/2013/08/19/forbidden-discourse-the-silencing-of-feminist-criticism-of-gender/.

66. bell hooks, *The Will to Change: Men, Masculinity, and Love* (New York: Simon and Schuster, 2004), 17.

67. Ibid., 18.

68. Ibid., 17.

69. Zillah R. Eisenstein, *Capitalist Patriarchy and the Case for Socialist Feminism* (New York: Monthly Review Press, 1979), 5.

70. Heidi Hartmann, "The Unhappy Marriage of Marxism and Feminism: Towards a More Progressive Union," in Lydia Sargent, ed., *Women and Revolution: A Discussion of the Unhappy Marriage of Marxism and Feminism* (South End Press, 1981), 2.

71. Ibid., 9.

72. Karl Marx and Frederick Engels, *The German Ideology*, in *Collected Works*, vol. 5 (New York: International Publishers, 1976), 53.

73. Ibid., 14–16.

74. Ibid., 2.

75. Ibid., 5.

76. Elizabeth Cady Stanton, "Solitude of Self," address before the US Senate Committee on Woman Suffrage, February 20, 1892, http://www.sscnet.ucla.edu/history/dubois/classes/995/98F/doc43.html.

77. Lise Vogel, *Marxism and the Oppression of Women*, 38.

78. Martha Gimenez, "Capitalism and the Oppression of Women: Marx Revisited," *Science & Society* 69, no. 1 (January 2005), 15.

79. Nancy Holmstrom, *Socialist Feminist Project: A Contemporary Reader in Theory and Politics* (New York: Monthly Review Press, 2002), 7.

80. Gimenez, "Capitalism and the Oppression of Women," 12.

81. Vogel, *Marxism and Women's Oppression*, 29.

82. Holmstrom, *Socialist Feminist Project*, 6.

83. Hartmann, "Unhappy Marriage," in Sargent, *Women and Revolution*, 92.

84. Ibid., 94.

85. Holmstrom, *Socialist Feminist Project*, 6.

86. Lise Vogel, "Historical Critical Dictionary of Marxism: Domestic Labor Debate," *Historical Materialism* 16 (2008): 241.

Chapter Six

1. Lise Vogel, "Domestic Labor Revisited," *Science & Society* 64, no. 2 (Summer 2000): 151.
2. Karl Marx, *Capital*, vol. 1, in Karl Marx and Frederick Engels, *Collected Works*, vol. 35 (New York: International Publishers, 1996), 572.
3. Stephanie Coontz, "Taking Marriage Private," *New York Times*, November 26, 2007, http://www.nytimes.com/2007/11/26/opinion/26coontz.html.
4. Quoted in Garry Wills, "The Myth about Marriage," *Roving Thoughts and Provocations* (*New York Review of Books* blog), May 9, 2012, http://www.nybooks.com/blogs/nyrblog/2012/may/09/marriage-myth/.
5. Joan Smith, "Women and the Family, Part 1," *International Socialism* (1st series) 100 (July 1977), https://www.marxists.org/history/etol/newspape/isj/1977/no100/smith.htm.
6. Jill Shenker, "A Selective History of Marriage in the United States," *Against the Current* 112 (September–October 2004), http://solidarity-us.org/site/node/370.
7. Coontz, "Taking Marriage Private."
8. Dorothy A. Mays, *Women in Early America: Struggle, Survival, and Freedom in a New World* (Santa Barbara, CA: ABC-CLIO), 111–13.
9. Coontz, "Taking Marriage Private."
10. Shenker, "Selective History of Marriage."
11. *Andersen v. King County*, 75934-1 (consol. w/79596-1) (2006).
12. The court issued its ruling on June 26, 2013. See John Schwartz, "Between the Lines of the Defense of Marriage Act," *New York Times*, June 26, 2013, http://www.nytimes.com/interactive/2013/06/26/us/annotated-supreme-court-decision-on-doma.html.
13. Marx quotes a report by the Medical Officer for Health in 1875, and references the "Opening Address to the Sanitary Conference, Birmingham, January 15, 1875, by J. Chamberlain, Mayor of the town, now (1883) President of the Board of Trade," (in Marx, *Capital*, vol. 1, 636).
14. Ibid., 651.
15. Frederick Engels, *The Condition of the Working Class in England* in Marx and Engels, *Collected Works*, vol. 4 (New York: International Publishers, 1975), 438.
16. Ibid., 439.
17. Marx, *Capital*, vol. 1, 536.
18. Frederick Engels, *The Origin of the Family, Private Property and the State* (New York: International Publishers, 1972), 43.
19. Smith, "Women and the Family, Part 1."
20. Ibid.
21. Lise Vogel, *Marxism and the Oppression of Women: Toward a Unitary Theory* (Chicago: Haymarket Books, 2014), 150.
22. Johanna Brenner, *Women and the Politics of Class* (New York: Monthly Review Press, 2000), 44.
23. Vogel, *Marxism and the Oppression of Women*, 21.
24. Writing in *New Left Review*, Maxine Molyneux estimated that more than fifty articles on this subject appeared in US and British journals alone. Maxine Molyneux, "Beyond the Domestic Labor Debate," *New Left Review* 1, no. 116 (July–August 1979).
25. Margaret Benston, "The Political Economy of Women's Liberation," *Monthly Review* 21 (1969).

26. Ibid.
27. Karl Marx, *A Contribution to the Critique of Political Economy*, in Marx and Engels, *Collected Works*, vol. 29 (New York: International Publishers, 1987), 269.
28. Ibid.
29. Benston, "Political Economy of Women's Liberation."
30. Ibid.
31. Ibid.
32. Ibid.
33. Ibid.
34. Ibid.
35. Quoted in Vogel, *Marxism and the Oppression of Women*, 18.
36. Quoted in Pat Armstrong and Hugh Armstrong, "Beyond Sexless Class and Classless Sex: Towards Feminist Marxism," *Studies in Political Economy* 10 (Winter 1983), 18.
37. Ibid.
38. Ibid., 19.
39. Vogel, *Marxism and the Oppression of Women*, 19.
40. Vogel, *Historical Materialism*, 239.
41. Vogel, *Marxism and the Oppression of Women*, 142.
42. Mariarosa Dalla Costa and Selma James, *The Power of Women and the Subversion of the Community*, 2nd ed. (Bristol, UK: Falling Wall Press, 1973).
43. Ibid., 31–32.
44. Frederick Engels, "Appendix [to the American Edition of The Conditions of The Working Class in England]," Marx and Engels, *Collected Works*, vol. 26 (New York: International Publishers, 1990), 401.
45. Karl Marx, *Capital*, vol. 1, 178.
46. Armstrong and Armstrong, "Beyond Sexless Class," 20.
47. Ibid., 21.
48. Ibid., 20.
49. Dalla Costa and Selma James, *The Power of Women*, 18–19.
50. Ibid., 53.
51. Ibid., 25–26.
52. Ibid., 32.
53. Armstrong and Armstrong, "Beyond Sexless Class," 21.
54. Wally Seccombe, "Domestic Labor—Reply to Critics," *New Left Review* 1, no. 94 (November–December 1975): 88.
55. Armstrong and Armstrong, "Beyond Sexless Class," 25.
56. Smith, "Women and the Family, Part 1."
57. Vogel, "Domestic Labor Revisited," 161.
58. Like most writers of his time, Marx used gendered language and typically referred to all workers as male.
59. Marx, *Capital*, vol. 1, 571.
60. Ibid., 182.
61. Marx, *Capital*, vol. 1, 577.
62. Marx, *Capital*, vol. 2, in Marx and Engels, *Collected Works*, vol. 36 (New York: International Publishers, 1997), 209.
63. Ibid., 391.
64. Vogel, "Domestic Labor Revisited," 156.

65. Marx, *Capital*, vol. 1, 539.
66. Marx, *Capital*, vol. 1, 50. For a useful analysis of these concepts, see Phil Gasper, "Review: *Capital*, Volume 1," *International Socialist Review* 49 (September–October 2006).
67. Vogel, *Marxism and the Oppression of Women*, 158–59.
68. Vogel, "Domestic Labor Revisited," 161.
69. Ibid., 162.
70. Ibid.
71. Sue Ferguson and David McNally, "Introduction," in Vogel, *Marxism and the Oppression of Women*, xxxiii–xxxiv.
72. Vogel, "Domestic Labor Revisited," 162, note 13.
73. Smith, "Women and the Family, Part 1." Smith uses the term "mode of reproduction" not as a system that is parallel (and autonomous) from the mode of production but as part of the superstructure that supports the economic base, or social relations of production, at any given stage of historical development.
74. Marx, *Capital*, vol. 3, in Marx and Engels, *Collected Works*, vol. 37 (New York: International Publishers, 1998), 626.
75. Smith, "Women and the Family, Part 1."
76. Vogel, "Domestic Labor Revisited," 160.
77. Vogel, *Marxism and the Oppression of Women*, 71.
78. Smith, "Women and the Family, Part 1."
79. Marx, *Capital*, vol. 1, 398–99.
80. Vogel, *Marxism and the Oppression of Women*, 70.
81. Marx, *Capital*, vol. 1, 638.
82. Vogel, "Domestic Labor Revisited." 163.
83. Smith, "Women and the Family, Part 1."
84. Vogel, "Domestic Labor Revisited," 157.
85. Ibid., 157.
86. Ibid., 161–62.
87. Ibid., 157.
88. Vogel, *Marxism and the Oppression of Women*, 150.
89. Vogel, "Domestic Labor Revisited," 158.
90. Ibid., 159.
91. Vogel, *Marxism and the Oppression of Women*, 189.
92. Vogel, "Domestic Labor Revisited," 159.
93. Vogel, *Marxism and the Oppression of Women*, 194–95.
94. Vogel, "Domestic Labor Revisited," 165.
95. Lenin's full quote appears in chapter 1.
96. Martha Gimenez, "Capitalism and the Oppression of Women: Marx Revisited*," *Science & Society* 69, no. 1 (January 2005): 27.
97. Ibid., 27–28.
98. Smith, "Women and the Family, Part 1."
99. Joan Smith, "Women and the Family, Part 2," *International Socialism* (January 4, 1978): 13.
100. Martha Gimenez, "Marxism and Feminism," *Frontier: A Journal of Women's Studies* 1, no. 1 (Fall 1975), http://www.colorado.edu/Sociology/gimenez/work/marx.html.
101. Vogel, "Domestic Labor Revisited," 164.
102. Ibid., 165.
103. Vogel, *Marxism and the Oppression of Women*, 178.

104. Ibid., 179.
105. Ibid.
106. Ibid., 181.

Chapter Seven

1. Combahee River Collective, April 1977. Quoted in Beverly Guy-Sheftall, ed., *Words of Fire: An Anthology of African-American Feminist Thought* (New York: New Press, 1995), 235. The statement is also available online at http://circuitous.org/scraps/combahee.html.
2. Barbara Smith, ed., *Home Girls: A Black Feminist Anthology* (New Brunswick, NJ: Rutgers University Press, 2000), xxxiv.
3. Kimberlé Crenshaw, "Demarginalizing the Intersection of Race and Sex: A Black Feminist Critique of Antidiscrimination Doctrine, Feminist Theory, and Antiracist Politics," University of Chicago Legal Forum, 1989, 139–67.
4. Ibid., 149.
5. Crenshaw, "Demarginalizing the Intersection," 142.
6. Ibid., 143.
7. Ibid.
8. See, for example, Guy-Sheftall, *Words of Fire*.
9. Sojourner Truth, "Ain't I a Woman?," Women's Convention, Akron, Ohio, May 28–29, 1851. Quoted in Crenshaw, "Demarginalizing the Intersection," 153.
10. Ibid.
11. Ibid., 140.
12. Patricia Hill Collins, *Black Feminist Thought: Knowledge, Consciousness, and the Politics of Empowerment*, 2nd ed. (New York: Routledge, 2001), 11–12.
13. Ibid., 18.
14. Guy-Sheftall, *Words of Fire*, 345.
15. Ibid., 146–55.
16. Ibid., 146.
17. Ibid., 147–48.
18. Ibid., 153.
19. Ibid., 149.
20. Ibid., 151.
21. Davis was a longstanding member of the Communist Party USA (CPUSA) who went on to help found the Committees of Correspondence for Democracy and Socialism in 2000.
22. Angela Y. Davis, *Women, Race and Class* (New York: Vintage Books, 1981), 213–15.
23. Solinger, *Abortion Wars*, 132.
24. Committee for Abortion Rights and Against Sterilization Abuse (CARASA) and Susan E. Davis, eds., *Women Under Attack* (Boston: South End Press, 1988), 28; A. Davis, *Women, Race and Class*, 219.
25. Quoted in Meg Devlin O'Sullivan, *'We Worry About Survival': American Indian Women, Sovereignty, and the Right to Bear and Raise Children in the 1970s* (PhD diss., University of North Carolina at Chapel Hill, 2007), 35.
26. A. Davis, *Women, Race and Class*, 204.
27. Jael Silliman, Marlene Gerber Fried, et al., eds., *Undivided Rights: Women of Color Organize for Reproductive Justice* (Cambridge, MA: South End Press, 2004), 10.

28. A. Davis, *Women, Race and Class*, 204.
29. Ibid., 215.
30. Ibid., 175.
31. Ibid., 24.
32. Ibid., 176.
33. A. Davis, *Women, Race and Class*, 182.
34. Quoted in ibid., 174.
35. Ibid., 173.
36. Danielle L. McGuire, *At the Dark End of the Street: Black Women, Rape, and Resistance—a New History of the Civil Rights Movement from Rosa Parks to the Rise of Black Power* (New York: Random House, 2010), xix–xx.
37. Ibid., 253.
38. McGuire, *Dark End of the Street*, 249.
39. Ibid.
40. Ibid., 261.
41. Ibid., 262.
42. Ibid., 266.
43. Ibid., 274–75.
44. Combahee River Collective, "Statement."
45. Ibid., 267.
46. Barbara Smith, "Introduction," in Smith, ed., *Home Girls*, xxxi.
47. Cherrie Moraga and Gloria Anzaldúa, eds. *This Bridge Called My Back: Writings by Radical Women of Color* (Kitchen Table, Women of Color Press, 1983), 146.
48. Ibid., 126–27.
49. Smith, "Introduction," *Home Girls*, xxxi.
50. "Combahee River Collective Statement," *Home Girls*, 267–68.
51. Martha Gimenez, "Marxism and Class, Gender and Race: Rethinking the Trilogy," *Race, Gender & Class* 8, no. 2 (2001): 22–33, http://www.colorado.edu/Sociology/gimenez/work/cgr.html.
52. Martha Gimenez, "Marxism and Feminism," *Frontier: A Journal of Women's Studies* 1, no. 1 (Fall 1975), http://www.colorado.edu/Sociology/gimenez/work/marx.html.
53. Ibid.
54. Ibid.
55. Leila Ahmed, *Women and Gender in Islam* (New Haven, CT: Yale University Press, 1992), 153.
56. Ibid.
57. Gimenez, "Marxism and Feminism."
58. Ibid.
59. Chandra Talpade Mohanty, *Feminism without Borders: Decolonizing Theory, Practicing Solidarity* (Durham, NC: Duke University Press, 2003), 40–41.
60. Ibid., 41.
61. Gimenez, "Marxism and Feminism."
62. Ibid.
63. Mohanty, *Feminism without Borders*, 243.
64. Ibid., 242.

Chapter Eight

1. Patricia Hill Collins, *Fighting Words: Black Women and the Search for Justice* (Minneapolis: University of Minnesota Press, 1998), 127.

2. Barry T. Hirsch and David A. Macpherson, "Union Membership and Coverage Database from the Current Population Survey (CPS)," January 24, 2015, http://www.unionstats.com; Emmanuel Saez, "Striking It Richer: The Evolution of Top Incomes in the United States," updated September 3, 2013, http://eml.berkeley.edu/~saez/saez-UStopincomes-2012.pdf.

3. Susan Faludi, *Backlash: The Undeclared War Against American Women* (New York: Crown Publishers, 1991).

4. Ibid., 99–100.

5. Katie Roiphe, *The Morning After: Sex, Fear and Feminism on Campus* (Boston: Little, Brown, 1993).

6. Mary Matalin, "Stop Whining," *Newsweek* (October 25, 1993).

7. Kathleen Parker, "Due Process Restored on Sex Charges," *Tribune Media Services*, May 12, 2002.

8. Robin Warshaw, *I Never Called It Rape: The Ms. Report on Recognizing, Fighting, and Surviving Date and Acquaintance Rape* (New York: Harper & Row, 1988), 11.

9. American Academy of Pediatrics, Committee on Adolescence, "Sexual Assault and the Adolescent," *Pediatrics* 94, vol. 5 (November 1, 1994): 761–65.

10. Mary Eberstadt, *Home-Alone America: The Hidden Toll of Day Care, Behavioral Drugs, and Other Parent Substitutes* (New York: Sentinel HC, 2004).

11. Quoted in Edward Wyatt, "New Salvo Is Fired in Mommy Wars," *New York Times*, November 2, 2004.

12. Lisa Belkin, "The Opt-Out Revolution," *New York Times Magazine*, October 26, 2003.

13. Ibid.

14. Judith Warner, "The Opt-Out Generation Wants Back In," *New York Times Magazine*, August 7, 2013. http://www.nytimes.com/2013/08/11/magazine/the-opt-out-generation-wants-back-in.html.

15. Ibid.

16. Bureau of Labor Statistics, US Department of Labor, "Happy Mother's Day from BLS: Working Mothers in 2012," *Economics Daily*, May 10, 2013, http://www.bls.gov/opub/ted/2013/ted_20130510.htm.

17. Vogel, "Domestic Labor Revisited," 166.

18. Helene A. Shugart, Catherine Egley Waggoner, and D. Lynn O'Brien Hallstein, "Mediating Third-Wave Feminism: Appropriation as Postmodern Media Practice," *Critical Studies in Media Communication* 18, no. 2 (June 2001): 196.

19. Terry Eagleton, *The Illusions of Postmodernism* (Oxford: Blackwell Publishing, 1996), 22.

20. The definition of "third-wave feminism" is unclear. Many regard it as a generational conflict based upon age, identifying third-wave feminists as "Generation Xers" who rebelled against their second-wave predecessors. But Susan Archer Mann makes a political distinction, identifying the third wave as those influenced by poststructuralism. See Susan Archer Mann, "Third Wave Feminism's Unhappy Marriage of Poststructuralism and Intersectionality Theory," *Journal of Feminist Scholarship* 4 (Spring 2013), http://www.jfsonline.org/issue4/pdfs/mann.pdf.

21. Teresa L. Ebert, "Rematerializing Feminism," *Science & Society* 69, no. 1 (January

2005): 33.

22.   Ernesto Laclau and Chantal Mouffe, *Hegemony and Socialist Strategy: Towards a Radical Democratic Politics* (London: Verso, 1985). There are two useful Marxist critiques of *Hegemony and Socialist Strategy* that help provide clarity to Laclau and Mouffe's arguments. One appears in Ellen Meiksins Wood's *The Retreat from Class: A New 'True' Socialism* (London: Verso, 1986). The other is the chapter entitled "Post-Marxism?" in Norman Géras's *Discourses of Extremity: Radical Ethics and Post-Marxist Extravaganzas* (London: Verso, 1990).

23.   Laclau and Mouffe, *Hegemony and Socialist Strategy*, 178.

24.   Ibid.

25.   Ibid., 164.

26.   Jeffrey Escoffier, "Sexual Revolution and the Politics of Gay Identity," in *Socialist Review* (US), 1985, 149.

27.   Jeffrey Escoffier, "Socialism as Ethics," *Socialist Review Collectives*, eds, *Unfinished Business: Twenty Years of Socialist Review* (London and New York: Verso, 1991), 319.

28.   Joan W. Scott, "Deconstructing Equality Versus Difference: Or, the Uses of Poststructuralist Theory for Feminism," in *Conflicts in Feminism*, Marianne Hirsch and Evelyn Fox Keller, eds. (London: Routledge, 1990), 135.

29.   Eagleton, *Illusions of Postmodernism*, 25–26.

30.   Teresa Ebert, "(Untimely) Critiques for a Red Feminism," in Mas'ud Zavarzadeh, Teresa Ebert, and Donald Morton, eds., *Post-Ality: Marxism and Postmodernism* (College Park, MD: Maisonneuve Press, 1995), http://www.marxists.org/reference/subject/philosophy/works/us/ebert.htm.

31.   Kimberlé Williams Crenshaw, "Mapping the Margins: Intersectionality, Identity Politics, and Violence Against Women of Color," *Stanford Law Review* 43, no. 6 (July 1991): 1296.

32.   Ibid.

33.   Ibid., 1297.

34.   Patricia Hill Collins, *Black Feminist Thought: Knowledge, Consciousness, and the Politics of Empowerment*, 2nd ed. (New York: Routledge, 2001), 297.

35.   Collins, *Fighting Words*, 127.

36.   Archer Mann, "Third Wave Feminism's Unhappy Marriage."

37.   Leslie Heywood and Jennifer Drake, eds., *Third Wave Agenda: Being Feminist, Doing Feminism* (Minneapolis: University of Minnesota Press, 1997), 208.

38.   Rebecca Walker, "Becoming the Third Wave," *Ms.*, September–October 1992.

39.   Rebecca Walker, *To Be Real: Telling the Truth and Changing the Face of Feminism* (New York: Anchor, 1995), xxxiii.

40.   Stacy Gillis, Gillian Howie, and Rebecca Munford, *Third Wave Feminism: A Critical Exploration*, (Basingstoke, UK: Palgrave Macmillan, 2004), 70–71.

41.   Ibid., 52–53.

42.   Rebecca Walker, "Becoming the Third Wave."

43.   Jennifer Baumgardner and Amy Richards, *Manifesta: Young Women, Feminism and the Future* (New York: Macmillan, 2000).

44.   Third Wave Foundation, "Third Wave Is Founded," http://www.thirdwavefoundation.org/third-wave-is-founded/#more-320.

45.   Tamara Straus, "A Manifesto for Third Wave Feminism," *AlterNet*, October 24, 2000, http://www.alternet.org/story/9986/a_manifesto_for_third_wave_feminism.

46. Baumgardner and Richards, *Manifesta*, 136.

47. Stacy Gillis and Rebecca Munford, "Genealogies and Generations: The Politics and Praxis of Third Wave Feminism," *Women's History Review* 13, no. 2 (2004): 169.

48. Heywood and Drake, *Third Wave Agenda*, 208.

49. Gillis and Munford, "Genealogies and Generations," 171.

50. Lisa Jervis, "Premiere," *Bitch* 1 (Winter 1996), http://bitchmagazine.org/article /introduction.

51. Straus, "Manifesto."

52. Marcelle Karp and Debbie Stoller, eds., *The Bust Guide to the New Girl Order* (New York: Penguin, 1999), 82–83.

53. Susan Ferguson, "Building on the Strengths of the Socialist Feminist Tradition," *New Politics* 7, no. 2 (new series) (Winter 1999), http://nova.wpunj.edu/newpolitics /issue26/fergus26.htm.

54. Ibid.

55. Michelle Alexander, *The New Jim Crow: Mass Incarceration in the Age of Colorblindness* (New York: New Press, 2010).

56. Erik Wemple, "Rush Limbaugh's 'Personal Attack' on Sandra Fluke? More Like 20 Attacks," *Washington Post*, March 5, 2012, http://www.washingtonpost.com/blogs /erik-wemple/post/rush-limbaughs-personal-attack-on-sandra-fluke-more-like-20 -attacks/2012/03/04/gIQA1OkHtR_blog.html.

57. Amy Siskind, "Why Bill Maher Should Be Taken Off the Air," *Daily Caller*, March 29, 2011.

58. Hunter Walker, "Romney Vows to 'Get Rid of' Planned Parenthood," *New York Observer*, March 13, 2012, http://observer.com/2012/03/romney-vows-to-get-rid-of -planned-parenthood/.

59. Jaeah Lee, "Charts: This Is What Happens When You Defund Planned Parenthood," *Mother Jones*, March 14, 2013, http://www.motherjones.com/politics/2013/03/what -happens-when-you-defund-planned-parenthood.

60. Ed Pilkington, "SlutWalking Gets Rolling After Cop's Loose Talk about Provocative Clothing," *Guardian*, May 6, 2011, http://www.theguardian.com/world/2011 /may/06/slutwalking-policeman-talk-clothing/print.

61. Ibid.

62. Aman Batheja, "After a Senate Filibuster, All Over but the Shouting," *New York Times*, June 27, 2013. http://www.nytimes.com/2013/06/28/us/after-a-senate-filibuster-all -over-but-the-shouting.html.

63. Teresa Ebert, "(Untimely) Critiques for a Red Feminism," http://www.marxists .org/reference/subject/philosophy/works/us/ebert.htm.

64. Martha E. Gimenez, "Capitalism and the Oppression of Women: Marx Revisited," *Science & Society* 69, no. 1 (January 2005): 11–32.

65. Ibid.

66. Saez, "Striking It Richer."

67. Connie Stewart, "Income Gap between Rich and Poor Is Biggest in a Century," *Los Angeles Times*, September 11, 2013, http://articles.latimes.com/2013/sep/11/nation /la-na-nn-income-inequality-20130910.

68. Bureau of Labor Statistics, US Department of Labor, "Work Stoppages Summary," February 11, 2015, press release, http://www.bls.gov/news.release/wkstp.t01.htm.

69. Bureau of Labor Statistics, US Department of Labor, "Union Membership Rate in Pri-

vate Industry Was 6.6 Percent in 2014; Public Sector 35.7 Percent," *Economics Daily*, http://www.bls.gov/opub/ted/2015/union-membership-rate-in-private-industry -and-public-sector-in-2014.htm.

70. Rebecca Vevea, "Starting Early to Create City Teachers," *New York Times*, October 6, 2011, http://www.nytimes.com/2011/10/07/us/chicago-program-aims-to-create-more -black-and-hispanic-teachers.html.

71. Eric (Rico) Gutstein and Pauline Lipman, "The Rebirth of the Chicago Teachers Union and Possibilities for a Counter-Hegemonic Education Movement," *Monthly Review* 65, no. 2 (June 2013), http://monthlyreview.org/2013/06/01/the-rebirth-of-the -chicago-teachers-union-and-possibilities-for-a-counter-hegemonic-education-movement.

72. Robert Barlett, "Creating a New Model of a Social Union: CORE and the Chicago Teachers Union," *Monthly Review* 65, no. 2 (June 2013), http://monthlyreview .org/2013/06/01/creating-a-new-model-of-a-social-union.

73. Cynthia Dizikes and John Byrne, "She Will Not Cower: Union President Karen Lewis Forged Her Confrontational Style in the Classroom," *Chicago Tribune*, September 11, 2012, http://articles.chicagotribune.com/2012-09-11/news/ct-met-teachers-strike -karen-lewis-20120911_1_chicago-teachers-union-union-president-chemistry-teacher.

74. Chicago Teachers Union, *The Schools Chicago's Children Deserve* (Chicago: CTU, 2012), http://www.ctunet.com/blog/text/SCSD_Report-02-16-2012-1.pdf.

75. Lee Sustar, "Toward a Renewal of the Labor Movement: US Labor after the Chicago Teachers' Strike," *International Socialist Review* 89 (May 2013), http://isreview.org /issue/89/toward-renewal-labor-movement.

76. Lee Sustar, "What the Chicago Teachers Accomplished," *International Socialist Review* 86, November 2012.

Chapter Nine

1.   Alexandra Kollontai, "Make Way for Winged Eros," in *Bolshevik Visions: First Phase of the Cultural Revolution in Soviet Russia*, ed. William G. Rosenberg (Ann Arbor: University of Michigan Press, 1990), 92.

2.   See Tony Cliff, *Revolution Besieged, 1917–1923* (Chicago: Haymarket Books, 2012).

3.   Leon Trotsky, *History of the Russian Revolution* (Chicago: Haymarket Books, 2008), 649.

4.   Tom Lewis, "Marxism and Nationalism: Part One," *International Socialist Review* 13 (August–September 2000).

5.   Tom Lewis, "Marxism and Nationalism: Part Two," *International Socialist Review* 14 (October–November 2000).

6.   Ibid.

7.   Richard Stites, *The Women's Liberation Movement in Russia: Feminism, Nihilism and Bolshevism 1860–1930* (Princeton, NJ: Princeton University Press, 1978), 287; Trotsky, *History of the Russian Revolution*, chapter 38, "The Problem of Nationalities."

8.   V. I. Lenin, "The Attitude of the Workers' Party Toward Religion," *Collected Works*, vol. 9 (Moscow: Progress Publishers, 1977), 403.

9.   V. I. Lenin, "Socialism and Religion," in *Collected Works*, vol. 10 (Moscow: Progress Publishers, 1978), 83.

10. Ibid., 84.

11. Ibid., 87.
12. "Theses on the National and Colonial Question," in John Riddell, ed., *The Communist International in Lenin's Time: Workers of the World* and *Oppressed People's, Unite! Proceedings and Documents of the Second Congress, 1920*, vol. 1 (New York: Pathfinder Press, 1991), 288.
13. Lenin, "The Question of Nationalities or Autonomization," in *Collected Works*, vol. 36 (Moscow: Progress Publishers, 1977), 608.
14. Trotsky, *History of the Russian Revolution*, 648–49.
15. Richard Pipes, *The Formation of the Soviet Union: Communism and Nationalism 1917–1923* (Cambridge, MA: Harvard University Press, 1997), 73, 77, 84.
16. V. I. Lenin, *On the Emancipation of Women* (Moscow: Progress Publishers, 1972), 69.
17. C. E. Hayden, "The Zhenotdel and the Bolshevik Party," in *Russian History* 3, part 2: 160, 162.
18. Richard Stites, "Women's Liberation Movements in Russia, 1900–1930," *Canadian American Slavic Studies* 7, no. 4 (Winter 1987): 472.
19. Hayden, "Zhenotdel and the Bolshevik Party," 160, 162.
20. Alexandra Kollontai, *Selected Writings of Alexandra Kollontai*, ed. Alix Holt (Westport, CT: Lawrence Hill & Co., 1977), http://www.marxists.org/archive/kollonta/1920/communism-family.htm.
21. Leon Trotsky, "From the Old Family to the New," in *Problems of Everyday Life* (New York: Pathfinder Press, 1973), 42.
22. Ibid., 43.
23. Holt, Selected *Writings of Alexandra Kollontai*, 262–65.
24. Leon Trotsky, *The Revolution Betrayed* (New York: Pathfinder Press, 1972), 145.
25. Adrienne Lynn Edgar, "Emancipation of the Unveiled: Turkmen Women Under Soviet Rule, 1924–29," *Russian Review* 62 (January 2003): 132.
26. Stites, "Women's Liberation Movements," 339.
27. Trotsky, *History of the Russian Revolution*, 649.
28. "Theses on the National and Colonial Question," in Riddell, *Proceedings and Documents of the Second Congress*, 285.
29. Trotsky, *History of the Russian Revolution*, 655.
30. V. I. Lenin, "What Is to Be Done?," in *Collected Works*, vol. 5 (Moscow: Progress Publishers, 1973), 423.
31. September 7, 1920, Seventh Session, Baku Congress of the Peoples of the East, https://www.marxists.org/history/international/comintern/baku/.
32. Stites, "Women's Liberation Movements," 340.
33. Holt, *Selected Writings of Alexandra Kollontai*, 258–59.
34. Kollontai, "Make Way for Winged Eros," 84–94.
35. Ibid., 92.
36. Ibid., 91.
37. Ibid., 90.
38. Ibid., 94.

Index